START YOUR OWN BUSINESS 2009
The Ultimate Step-By-Step Guide

EDITED BY IAN WHITELING

crimson

This edition first published in Great Britain 2009 by
Crimson Publishing, a division of Crimson Business Ltd
Westminster House
Kew Road
Richmond
Surrey
TW9 2ND

A catalogue record for this book is available from the British Library.

ISBN 978 1 85458 448 9

Printed and bound by MPG Books Ltd, Bodmin

CONTENTS AT A GLANCE

CONTENTS

FOREWORD

As I write the UK and indeed the world is in probably its most severe period of economic uncertainty for several decades. Can it possibly make sense to start a business in such a time? I believe it can.

I started my first business at the start of the recession of the early 1990s. And while it was definitely tough, the economic ills of the nation led directly to making it easier and cheaper for me to set up my business. The same could well be true for you today.

Tough times can create opportunities. That might be a redundancy cheque providing you the cash you need, or your ideal premises finally becoming available, or simply reduced competition as companies pull out of peripheral activities to concentrate on their core. And the digital world is creating new opportunities every day while at the same time reducing the cost to set up and expanding your potential markets. There are fabulous opportunities for new businesses today.

Having said that, there will be some businesses which will be better to start now than others. Think about the market you want to enter, and how the tough economy will affect it. Will your target customers still have enough money to spend on your products or service? Will you be able to find enough money to see your business through to profitability?

Those of you who start and survive will surely go on to real success. The discipline of managing when times are tough will serve you well when good times return. Those who don't make it will find a tougher landing than in better times. They say that fortune favours the brave, and that a fool and his money are soon parted. I say that if you believe in your business, if you're sure that there will still be customers for you over the next year or two, then embrace this opportunity to start, work damned hard, brace yourself for some very tough situations, but go for it. If running your own business is right for you, you'll find a way to make it work, and never look back.

David Lester
Founder, Startups.co.uk
November 2008

SEND US YOUR FEEDBACK

At Crimson Publishing we pride ourselves on the quality and usefulness of our books. *Start Your Own Business 2009* is an annual publication that we are constantly seeking to improve, to make sure we deliver all the resources that budding entrepreneurs need. We'd love to hear your comments and suggestions for our next edition.

Email info@crimsonpublishing.co.uk to give us your thoughts.

ABOUT STARTUPS.CO.UK

Startups.co.uk is the UK's most popular website for small businesses. Started by a successful entrepreneur, it has been helping people start their own business since 2000, and now helps over 300,000 people every year.

Small business owners and new businesses consistently rate startups.co.uk as the leading source of information for UK entrepreneurs.

ABOUT THE EDITOR

Ian Whiteling has written extensively about marketing, and worked on a number of business and financial guides and magazines. An accomplished video journalist, he has personal experience in starting a business, having successfully launched virtual design and communications agency D&PC, while playing a pivotal role in the creation of innovative video-led web channels EVENTS:review and MEETINGS:review, of which he is currently editor in chief.

INTRODUCTION

What are the elements of a successful business? In this chapter we profile four successful, inspiring businesses, learning what drove them to start up, the challenges they faced along the way and the key lessons they learnt.

There's never been a better time to start up...

If you have picked up this guide and are reading this page, the chances are that you are thinking about starting your own business. And, despite whatever the prevailing economic wind is blowing in your face, it's actually easier than ever. Also, you're not alone. More and more people are feeling the entrepreneurial urge. Small and medium-sized businesses are a key driver of the UK economy. They account for 59.2% of private sector employment and 51.5% of private sector turnover. What's more, business startups are now fundamental to the economy. The days of thousands of large companies employing millions of staff are no more. The number of aspiring entrepreneurs starting small businesses has surged in recent years, and their companies now make up 99.9% of the total businesses in the UK, and are responsible for almost half of the UK's workforce.

Technology has advanced to such a stage it's now possible to start a global business from a laptop, forcing the entrepreneurial doors wide open to teenagers, the retired, single parents or those who quite sensibly want to dip their toes in the water (or at least on eBay) before taking the plunge. There's also more access to finance to help make your entrepreneurial dreams a reality than ever before. Despite the recent tightening of banking belts in the face of a global recession, if your idea is good enough – and presented in the right way – people will want to invest in you. It might seem that you only ever hear bad news about the condition of the economy, but in fact there has never been a better time to start a business. For one thing, never before has there been so much help and information from business startup services available to people wanting to go it alone as there is today. Also, there has never been more funding available for new companies, and the government

> **Over 180,000 businesses are registered on the VAT books in 2006, the government reported in November 2007 – up 0.5% on 2005 and 16,000 more than a decade before in 1996**

has never been so geared to encourage enterprise. In fact, if you can gain investment in tougher economic times, it's tantamount to a rubber stamp of success.

Prime time television shows such as *Dragons' Den*, *The Apprentice*, *Tycoon* and *Risking It All* have pushed the very idea of running your own business to the forefront of the national psyche – no longer is it exclusive to the daring or the pinstriped, it's for everyone. Celebrity entrepreneurs are the new celebrity chefs and, believe it or not, business is the new rock 'n' roll.

Of course, startups.co.uk has been championing business pioneers and helping those inspired to follow in their footsteps for some time now, through its website, awards and other events. As such, startups.co.uk has been more aware than many of the rise in interest in entrepreneurialism. But even we were surprised when our first book *How They Started*, telling the startup stories behind some of the UK's best-loved brands, from Innocent Drinks to PizzaExpress, hit Amazon's Top 20 on its release in 2007, and garnered considerable media coverage. Such is the current buzz around business.

The startups.co.uk website has become a font of knowledge and debate on starting your own business, and this book draws all this fabulous information together in a definitive guide to starting your own company. The great news is that it's presented in the readable, sharp, jargon-free style that characterises startups.co.uk, with key tips, action points and engaging case studies to help you on your way.

So whether you have designs on becoming the next Richard Branson or simply want to strike out alone and be your own boss, you have come to the right place. The following pages will guide you through choosing the right business to run and deciding whether you are up to the job of launching your own company, to drawing up your business plan and everything else involved in preparing you for take off.

So fasten your seatbelt and get ready for the ride of your life…

How they started

For some people, the word entrepreneur automatically brings to mind Peter Jones and his ilk – those high flyers who set up and run more successful businesses than most of us could manage in several lifetimes. But actually an entrepreneur is anyone who chooses to go it alone and make the most of a business opportunity for themselves, no matter how big or small.

Nowadays, being an entrepreneur is becoming a legitimate career choice for more and more people. Gone are the days when you had to have years of business experience under your belt before you might even consider taking the plunge with a startup of your own. Before getting down to the nuts and bolts of how to start a business, here's a brief insight into why a selection of successful entrepreneurs decided to start their own business.

People choose to become entrepreneurs for a variety of reasons. For some it's an opportunity to escape their mundane nine-to-five existence and to commit their working life to something that is a lot closer to their heart. For the 'lifestyle' entrepreneurs, the important part of the deal is not how much their business grows, but the effect it has on their life.

David Creswell, the 27-year-old founder of the comics website ComicDomain.co.uk falls into this category. 'I don't care if I'm a comic geek, it's my hobby and I've turned that into a small business,' he says. 'I'm proud of the service we provide and our customers are also happy.' For others, the motivation for starting up will come from spotting a gap in a market they know well. Self-confessed 'ski bums' **Tim Slade** and **Jules Leaver** spotted an opportunity for 'been there done that' T-shirts to sell to skiing holidaymakers. Their high-street chain Fat Face has gone on to become a rip-roaring success.

And for **Dee Edwards**, 29, the same sort of insight helped her to launch internet company Habbo. 'I really believed internet business could be made successful by using technology to run a company effectively, and leveraging the different way people were changing their communication,' she says. Whether it's T-shirts or technology, the world is

> **Gone are the days when you had to have years of business experience under your belt before you might even consider taking the plunge with a startup of your own**

littered with those who've been able to see a business opportunity others simply can't. In fact, a lack of business experience could well give you the kind of perspective those with a blue-chip curriculum vitae would struggle to attain. Nowhere is this better illustrated than by **Lena Bjorck**. Arriving in the UK from Sweden with no qualifications she landed a job as a kitchen porter, but quickly realised the country's service industry was just not up to scratch. So without a pound in her pocket or even the most basic equipment, she quit. She now runs one of the country's most successful catering companies, Inn or Out.

To help inspire you to greatness, here are profiles of four companies, started by entrepreneurs with quite different backgrounds and ideas, who took the decision to launch a business, without having any previous experience of doing so.

Innocent Drinks

Although it may seem hard to believe, until the turn of the new millennium, 'smoothie' was more a term used to describe a somewhat sleazy or sycophantic individual rather than a healthy fruit drink. That was, of course, until three friends Richard Reed, Adam Balon and Jon Wright decided to launch Innocent Drinks, which now turns over more than £75 million a year.

The trio had flirted with the odd venture together at university, but left to pursue separate careers in advertising and management consulting. Although they had often dreamed about starting their own company, the right idea never came along.

However, they all kept in touch, and, during the late 1990s when they were each 26 years old, they suddenly became inspired by the concept of healthier eating, which was starting to gain ground in the UK. All three were aware of how hard they were working and how it was important to eat well to stay fit. Juice bars, serving drinks of blended fruit, yoghurt and ice, had begun to open, and the trio thought it would be a great idea if you could simply buy them off the shelf instead of having to queue while one was made.

Although it was the last kind of business they would have expected to launch, they decided that there could be some mileage in the concept of making bottled smoothies – as these drinks became known – and so set up work creating their own versions at home. Their first attempt blended strawberries with bananas, a variety that still sells well today, but at the time they had no real experience making fruit juices or in the soft drinks market. So they had no idea if the product would sell.

Like every would-be entrepreneur, before they could hope to gain any financial backing for their idea they had to assess its real potential for success, so some serious market research was needed. This came in the form of a smoothie stall at the Jazz on the Green festival in West London, which Balon and Reed had been running for a few years. They came up with a fun concept of asking the festival goers to taste their smoothies and vote on whether they should give up their day jobs by placing the empty bottles in the appropriately labelled bin. The crowd overwhelmingly voted for them to start up a smoothie business, and rather rashly and prematurely, all three immediately quit their jobs. After all, not only had they not gained any financial investment, but they also had no business plan and didn't even have a name for their company.

'We were hopelessly naive' recalls Reed. 'We stopped working with just a month's pay to keep us going, but it was nine months before we were up and running.'

They went into overdrive to find a name for their venture. 'We ploughed through thousands,' says Reed. 'It was a case of getting the thesaurus out until we came up with innocent.' Then they commissioned a design agency to come up with the logo, which is still used today.

Although they found it hard to decide on a name, it was nothing compared to the difficulty they encountered securing the funds they needed to buy fruit and bottles. Investors were put off by Reed, Balon and Wright's lack of experience in the drinks sector, as well by the product's fresh ingredients, which gave it a short shelf life, and meant if it was not sold quickly it would go off, making it very high risk. What's more, in the late 1990s, the investment world was caught up in the dotcom boom, and far less interested in ventures that weren't online.

Reduced to having to get their friends to buy them the odd pint and living off eating cereal three times a day, desperation struck, and Reed

> **Reduced to having to get their friends to buy them the odd pint and living off eating cereal three times a day, desperation struck**

sent out an email entitled 'Does anybody know someone rich?', in a final push to get investment. By a stroke of luck, it eventually reached wealthy American Maurice Pinto, who had a lot of experience in financing new companies and helping them grow – the kind of investor known as a business angel.

To Reed, Balon and Wright's relief, Pinto signalled his interest and the three flew out to meet him in person. Pinto liked their business plan, aware that there was a huge demand for smoothies in the USA, which he believed would soon be reflected in the UK, making it the ideal time to launch Innocent. But as with many angel investors, and investors in general, it wasn't just the concept that Pinto liked. He was also keen to buy into the trio and their highly original unconventional approach to business. Reed, Balon and Wright had high ideals about how they should treat employees and suppliers well and with respect, while protecting the environment. Pinto was also impressed by their democratic approach of never rushing into decisions, but always debating issues thoroughly before reaching a conclusion. Their answer to Pinto's initial question of 'Who's in charge?', was: 'We all are.'

This stance was unlikely to endear them to more conventional investors, but luckily in the maverick Pinto they had found a soul mate, who promptly decided to invest £250,000 for a 20% stake in the business. The three were delighted, and more than a little relieved, that they could now get Innocent Drinks up and running. However, one problem was holding them back: finding a manufacturer to make Innocent smoothies. Throughout the fundraising stage they had been trying to find the right company, only for their advances to be rejected. The problem was that Reed, Balon and Wright were adamant that Innocent smoothies would contain fresh fruit and nothing else.

'We went round virtually every drinks manufacturer,' says Reed, 'and they were all saying that we needed to make our smoothies with concentrate. However, we responded by saying that we had tested this and consumers don't want drinks made from concentrate, but something natural.'

With no one prepared to manufacture their drinks, it looked like the business was a non-starter, until eventually they came across a small family business that agreed to make smoothies in the way they wanted, as long as Innocent supplied them with the machinery to do it.

Having jumped a number of hurdles in the quest to launch Innocent, Balon, Reed and Wright, faced the final one: convincing retailers, and supermarkets in particular, to stock their smoothies. But with Pinto's money materialising in early 1999 and the manufacture of three flavours (strawberries and bananas, cranberry and raspberries, and oranges, bananas and pineapples) ready to go, finding a way to get them in front of the general public was imperative.

High-end retailers, such as Harvey Nichols and Harrods, took the bait first, along with what was then a small coffee chain called Caffè Nero. Supermarkets were an altogether harder nut to crack.

"They don't even return your calls at first," recalls Reed. 'Then they say: "No," and then if you're persistent you get a chance.'

Waitrose was the first to see the light. 'When we managed to get in front of Waitrose, they could appreciate the drink was just right for their audience,' say Reed. Sainsbury's followed and shortly after that all the big retailers climbed aboard.

From April 1999 to the end of the year, Innocent generated sales of around £400,000 and Balon, Reed and Wright knew they were onto something big. However, they never forgot their principals, and it has been these values that have helped guide the company to its current lofty position. The founders were determined to set strong foundations for growth, establishing strong relationships with suppliers, which they viewed as vital to their success, and carefully planning ahead to get a firm idea of where the business would be a year down the line. Soon they were taking on more and more staff, and Innocent gained a reputation for being a great place to work.

Second-year turnover hit £1.6 million, then £4.2 million, £6 million, £10.6 million, £17 million, £37 million, and by 2007 it had reached an incredible £100 million. Not bad for three guys who had not made a smoothie between them before 1998. And even now they're sticking to their vision and values of making great-tasting smoothies from fresh fruit, while treating staff and suppliers with the respect they deserve.

Bravissimo

Like many great business ideas, Sarah Tremellen's Bravissimo began life as a solution to a problem. She become pregnant in 1993, and became frustrated at not being able to find any attractive lingerie to fit her. Her bust size had grown to a D-cup, which it seemed was the point when underwear ceased to be remotely stylish or sexy. Had she discovered a golden niche in the highly competitive retail sector?

Chatting with a friend who was encountering the same problem, Tremellen soon realised she was not alone and that this was a common issue on the high street. What's more, those outlets that stocked a large range of lingerie that stretched to the larger sizes had very few styles on offer, with those available often not on display, meaning women would be forced into the awkward situation of having to ask for a D-cup or higher, making the buying process embarrassing and demoralising.

Angry at the way high-street retailers were treating pregnant and larger women, Tremellen made it her mission to create a pleasant environment where women had a great selection of lingerie to choose from, whatever their size. Her goal was to set up a lingerie mail-order business specialising in larger bust sizes, where 'everything was provided under one roof', while creating a forum where big-breasted women would not only feel comfortable, but could also actually celebrate their size.

Mail order appealed to Tremellen, as opening a shop would require significant investment, and she would also be able to launch the business from home, which would prove ideal when she became a new mum. What's more, having budgeted with her partner at the start of her pregnancy for one income to allow her the option to become a full-time mother, Tremellen had the time to investigate her business idea, without the pressure to earn a living.

Her background in marketing also came in handy at this stage, as she launched herself into research, contacting high-street stores, writing to fashion magazines and reading market reports in libraries. However, Tremellen had no experience in actually starting or running a business, but a government scheme offering a £60 weekly allowance to people starting up their own business in exchange for compulsory attendance on an eight-week evening course seemed like the perfect opportunity to get some invaluable help.

Signing up immediately, she began learning all about registering for VAT, self-employed income tax and how to deal with lots of other typical startup issues. The course culminated in all students presenting a business plan to an expert panel. Tremellen used this as a way of practising for producing a real one for her lingerie business idea, and worked really hard on her presentation. She soon found that putting in the effort had been worthwhile when a bank manager who happened to be on the panel was really impressed by her idea and offered her a £10,000 loan if Tremellen and her friend – who had now become her business partner – would invest £3,000 each. They accepted.

With the business having been given the green light, Tremellen's husband wisely pointed out that the first thing a mail-order company needed was a database of relevant people to contact, and he offered to start building one for her. This was no mean feat, and the first version took him three months, with the experience he had gained in his job as planning manager for Tetley Tea coming in useful. A more complete version followed a few months later, which was tailor-made to suit Bravissimo's needs and it was used for the next seven years. Buying in a database like this would have proved very expensive, but then starting up your own business is all about drawing on every resource you have to hand.

> **Starting up your own business is all about drawing on every resource you have to hand**

Just when things started to fall into place, Tremellen suddenly hit a brick wall. Having worked hard locating a network of suitable manufacturers of lingerie, one by one they began to contact her to say they'd decided against doing business with her, and this was no coincidence. The reason for the suppliers' change of heart was that another mail-order company based just four miles from Bravissimo – and which was already trading – was sourcing lingerie from the same manufacturers. The owner of the business was furious that Tremellen had set up her business close by to theirs, and persuaded the manufacturers that supplying such a competitor would damage their established business relationship. Suddenly, supplying Bravissimo was too great a risk for them to take.

Now this was a major setback, but in true entrepreneurial fashion, rather than giving up, Tremellen became even more determined that her business would succeed. However, she still faced the dilemma of how to convince the manufacturers to supply her. Her first strategy she describes as 'begging and pleading', but once this failed she remembered an article she had read at her university's career centre. It said people who phone companies asking for a job were usually rebuffed, whereas those that asked for advice were often seen and stood more chance of eventually being taken on. As a result, Tremellen approached manufacturers simply to 'talk' to them about the market, and this helped her to maintain contact while she considered further options.

She resolved to compile a marketing document that would be so strong it would convince the suppliers of the great opportunity they'd be missing if they refused to work with her. Preparing the document helped her think about what her business was really about. During this process she came up with an idea for a magazine, rather than a catalogue, featuring not only her range of bras, but also articles and letters from and about large-busted women. Once again using resources close at hand, she asked a friend who was starting up herself to design it, securing a special rate. Then, delving deeper into her contacts, she asked a friend of a friend, actress Honour Blackman, to feature in the magazine, which she was 'only too happy to do', says Tremellen.

This magazine-cum-catalogue proved to be a masterstroke. Its mix of celebrity, articles, features and photos set Bravissimo apart as a brand. What's more, the manufacturers loved it and all three that had turned Tremellen down signed up to supply her company. They also agreed to provide promotional pictures of their lingerie for the first published magazine, saving Bravissimo production costs. The struggle had been worth it, and Tremellen's dream was finally coming to life.

She overcame the competitor problem by creating the perception that her company was actually based in Oxford, by establishing a 'virtual office' at her parent's home, setting up an Oxford PO Box and phone number, which was on permanent divert to London. This meant driving up to her parents' twice a week to pick up items, but Tremellen says it was worth it as it allowed her to focus on Bravissimo as a positive brand rather than a victim of its competitor's negative campaign. By the time the competitor finally realised Tremellen was still based close by, it was too late as she had built strong relationships with her suppliers and Bravissimo was an established company in its own right.

The experience has influenced Tremellen's business practise, as she states: 'I want people to shop with us, whatever the competition, because they want to shop with us, not because we stop them shopping elsewhere.'

Brandishing support from three manufacturers and armed with a finished magazine, Tremellen finally officially launched Bravissimo in January 1995. Three days after sending out her first catalogue, Bravissimo made its first sale. Although it was from her business partner's mother-in-law, it was just the start, and 150 people registered on the Bravissimo mailing list over the next three weeks, with around 30 bras sold.

Sending copies of the magazine out to the media, Tremellen struck a chord, generating an explosion of interest. The surge continued and by the end of Bravissimo's first year 11,000 women had registered on the database and sales had hit £134,000. By the second year, this had risen to £400,000. Today the company turns over in excess of £37 million and has opened 20 high-street stores to date, finally truly fulfilling Tremellen's aim of offering choice and a great shopping experience to her customers.

> **Tremellen struck a chord, generating an explosion of interest**

Black Circles

Those wishing to debate whether entrepreneurial talent is born or manufactured may wish to examine the breakneck speed of 30-year-old Michael Welch's ascent. It's clear that just being another employee was never an option for the Black Circles founder, even at an early age.

'I was the kid in school who would buy a compilation CD and copy it onto blank tapes and sell them,' he says. 'I was a trader – there was no motivation to do it, I just did it for the money and the buzz of the sell.'

Welch decided to leave school at 16. After scouring the papers for a job, an apprentice tyre fitter's vacancy caught his eye. He went for an interview and was taken on, and almost immediately his entrepreneurial instincts kicked in.

> **I was a trader – there was no motivation to do it, I just did it for the money and the buzz of the sell**

'I had a minor responsibility within the company, but it was obvious that these guys were buying for x price and selling for y, and the bit in the middle was quite substantial,' Welch explains. 'More importantly, the customers didn't quibble. There was no negotiation over price, so it was obvious there was money in it.'

So Welch decided he would have a go himself. The bigger the tyres, the more margin there was to be made, so he thought it would be logical to start a mail-order, high-performance specialist tyre business, which is exactly what he did.

Welch, who was only just 18, got a £500 grant from the Prince's Trust and started selling tyres via motoring magazines, such as Max Power and Redline. However, he admits that he knew nothing about running a business at the time and needed help with basics, such as finance management.

After taking a college course to plug his knowledge gaps, Welch worked for a year under Sir Tom Farmer, founder of tyre giants Kwik-Fit, gaining invaluable experience. He credits this time for setting the foundations for Black Circles.

'Kwik-Fit are the biggest tyre retailers in the world, they are market leaders,' Welch says. 'It was my chance to see not what they do right, but what they do wrong, where their weak spots are and how their business model and proposition could be improved'.

It became clear very quickly to Welch that the market leaders, such as Kwik-Fit, weren't doing the best job possible.

'I wanted to be the chief executive of Kwik-Fit,' says Welch, 'but I was 20, so there was no way that was ever going to happen. So I built my own Kwik-Fit.'

Black Circles is the result. The company allows customers to order tyres on the internet and get them fitted within a day at one of its affiliated garages. The low-cost, speedy service has proved a stunning success for Welch, with sales ballooning from £50,000 in the first year to £10 million by 2007.

However, these rewards have only come with painstaking work and sometimes painful boardroom clashes. The introduction of a 'challenging' shareholder to Welch's then-fledgling business nearly

> **It became clear very quickly to Welch that the market leaders, such as Kwik-Fit, weren't doing the best job possible**

sunk the enterprise before it got off the ground. He admits that naivety nearly cost him.

'It turned into a nightmare,' he says. 'My company was being wrestled away from me. For the first year, I spent my time building the business and fighting the shareholder. It was dirty play. And it became a priority to buy him out and replace him with a team of investors, which I did.'

Learning from his bitter experience, Liverpudlian Welch assembled a team that complimented his skills and compensated for his lack of legal and accountancy knowledge.

'It was a challenge,' he admits. 'When I left Kwik-Fit, I had a month's wages, which got me trading. I was well supported by the local enterprise council, who gave me a short-term free period within the lease of the office and some basic funding.

'Myself and an investor started in an office, with me in the corner on an old desk that we picked up by the bin outside. Slowly but surely, we started to build the network and get the sales through the door. We took on our first member of staff within six months and then it was pretty rapid growth from then on. But it was a very lonely period.'

Welch has certainly crammed a substantial entrepreneurial career into a short time frame. Despite his obvious determination, he realises that his lack of years is seen as a disadvantage by some.

'People seem to relate age to experience, which is quite a misconception,' he says. 'If you have the will and put the work in, you are inevitably going to get much further much younger'.

> **If you have the will and put the work in, you are inevitably going to get much further much younger**

'Bank managers, lawyers and accountants aren't qualified to judge purely on age, but unfortunately they do. I mention those three professions in particular because they are the ones you come up against. It's a problem in other people's eyes, not mine.'

In order to provide quick tyre fitting – Black Circles aims to give wheels a new coating in eight hours, compared to the industry-standard 48 – Welch needed to sign up reliable garages. He undertook the meticulous task of approaching and checking fitters across the country. He now has a network of more than 900 bolt-on franchisees.

'We knew how to target,' he says. 'Within the first year, we had 60 or 70 stores recruited. In the second year, we needed profit coverage and vetting, so we bought in some networking people to populate the UK in a formulaic manner, according to demographics. We'd already done the data and knew where the core penetration would be'.

'We concentrated on those areas first and then painstakingly recruited the garages, and made sure they kept up their service level.'

Black Circle's call centre contacts every single customer, seeking scores for the job and the experience. Welch can then can see who is or isn't performing and act accordingly, with area representatives discussing problems with garages or handing out rewards. It's a costly and painstaking process, but the upside is the retention of Black Circle's existing customers and the attraction of new ones.

'We've now got a very stable ship, we've spent time on the basics,' says Welch. 'We look at making sure the customers are getting the right service, even if it's to the detriment of the speed of business growth.'

'I would question how many people spend enough time making sure their core proposition is right, rather than getting distracted by growing the business quickly. It's not all about that.'

Welch clearly has lofty ambitions for Black Circles. In 2006 a franchise model was launched, giving independent garages access to Black Circles' systems and stock, and 300 franchisees are already on board. Asked if he wishes to rival Kwik-Fit, he almost bristles at the suggestion that he wouldn't want to do so.

> **I'm not here to run a small to medium-sized business, I'm here to create the next big thing in the industry**

'I wouldn't be doing this unless I thought we could,' he insists. 'I'm not here to run a small to medium-sized business, I'm here to create the next big thing in the industry. The UK tyre industry is worth £1 billion – we're going to concentrate on increasing our market share and maybe taking the business into Europe.'

Welch is keen to point out the role of Scottish Enterprise (Black Circles is based in Peebles, in the Borders) in helping him to start up, comparing the government agency favourably with its English counterpart. He feels it's important that entrepreneurs seek as much advice as possible.

'The younger you are, the less of a risk there is, so if you're going to do it, do it as young as possible,' he advises. 'But if you are dealing with venture capitalists, investors or banks, make sure you seek the right advice from government agencies. Get a good accountant and lawyer around you and consume as much information as quickly as possible.'

Coffee Republic

For a nation of tea lovers, the British drink a lot of coffee. Whether it's the growing influence of continental Europe or just a simple change in tastes, research shows that coffee has actually replaced the traditional cup of tea as the nation's favourite drink. And as ever, where social trends develop, business follows closely behind. To supply the growing demand for quality fresh coffee, a burgeoning sector of coffee bars has emerged – and established itself to the extent that there is now a Starbucks or a Costa Coffee in almost every high street, train station and shopping centre the UK.

Coffee Republic was one of the coffee bar chains to pioneer the market in the mid-1990s. It was co-founded by Bobby Haschemi, a man who, like all true entrepreneurs, is constantly on the look out for new business ideas. The concept for Coffee Republic was sparked by an idle chat with his sister who had just returned home from a holiday.

'The idea came from the USA where my sister was travelling as a tourist in New York,' he explains. 'She discovered that there were coffee shops everywhere, a Starbucks on every corner, and while she was there she got hooked on the tall slim cappuccinos they served. When she came back, she told me how much she had liked these places, and commented that there were not any in this country – and a lightbulb went on inside my head.'

The pair did some research and discovered that people actually drink more coffee than tea in the UK, but that there were no outlets serving this market. They had found a niche. As any businessperson will tell you, the secret to a successful enterprise is to find a gap in the market. Haschemi was quick to focus in on where exactly this gap was, and how he was going to fill it.

'What was available in the UK basically wasn't up to standard,' he says. 'To have a good coffee, you had to go to a restaurant, sit down and wait for a waiter to serve you. Alternatively you could go to a sandwich bar where the coffee was invariably poor quality. We, therefore, found a gap for a 10-minute gourmet coffee experience at an affordable price.'

Encouraged by the discovery, Haschemi and his sister founded Coffee Republic and opened their first store in Mayfair, London in November 1995. However, it wasn't long before he realised that his business would not remain a single shop operation. Expansion quickly became a core strategy for the business.

'The first store in Mayfair took off pretty quickly and within six months I realised the business was going to work,' he recalls. 'So we went to the business angel market and raised £600,000 to fund the opening of five more stores.'

It is notoriously hard to convince private investors, or business angels, to part with their cash. Haschemi is proof, however, that if your business plan is solid enough, they can be a very good source of funding. 'It's supposed to be difficult raising funds from business angels, but I didn't find it so,' he says. 'It was a good idea and, in the end, I received offers for double the amount I requested.'

So what part of the business plan did Coffee Republic's investors find most appealing?

'The product is good quality, convenient and at an affordable price,' says Haschemi. 'Our customers are pretty broadly spread depending on the location of the store. We attract the suits in the City, and shoppers in the stores situated in shopping centres. Up north, our customers tend to be older'. 'There isn't really a specific target segment that one can outline. The wide appeal is what made the idea so attractive.'

This also meant that Haschemi wasn't concerned about the threat posed by large multinational competitors, such as the US chain Starbucks or Costa Coffee.

'The market is big enough for the top three players,' he says. 'That is ourselves, Costa and Starbucks. We actually choose locations where there is already a Starbucks, for the same reason that Indian and Chinese restaurants locate close together – it attracts a larger catchment area.'

With the business angel money in the bank, Haschemi set about expanding the business. Conscious of the danger of over-stretching his

> "
> **It's supposed to be difficult raising funds from business angels, but I didn't find it so** "

company's resources, expansion was limited to the London area to begin with.

However, the outlets continued to thrive and the chain quickly expanded beyond the capital until, before long, a Coffee Republic outlet could be found in nearly every major town in Britain. Only six years after the first store was opened, there are now almost 193 outlets throughout the country. But how did Haschemi ensure that such a rapid expansion programme could proceed as smoothly as possible?

'There are always problems related to expansion, always challenges,' he says. 'The key is having the infrastructure in place ahead of growth, and hiring ahead of growth. If you don't, you find you're chasing your own tail.'

For Haschemi, getting the right staff was a high priority. He has a strong human resources department and a pipeline of people coming through that. Also word of mouth plays a large part – young people who work for Coffee Republic recommend their friends, for example.

Having successfully built a business with almost total coverage in the UK, you would be forgiven for thinking that Haschemi might like to sit back for a while to enjoy what he has achieved. Far from it. Showing the ambition and drive of a born entrepreneur, he continues to push for even higher standards.

'The company's mission is to become the main competitor to Starbucks not just in the UK, but also internationally,' he says, 'and we believe we're well positioned to achieve this.'

> **The key is having the infrastructure in place ahead of growth, and hiring ahead of growth**

Can you do it too?

These case studies also highlight the qualities you need to have if you are going to become an entrepreneur – of which one of the most important is passion. No matter how much potential your business might have for making money, unless you believe in it, how can you expect anyone else to? A bit of self-belief can go a long way. Hand in hand with passion comes commitment to the cause. From day one you'll need to work hard, often forgoing friends and family to get your venture off the ground. Ask yourself whether you're prepared to make that kind of sacrifice and whether you can keep yourself motivated to put in those long, long hours. If you're the sort of person whose new year resolution lasts until 2 January you might want to think again whether you've got what it takes, particularly when things might not be going your way.

Also, as you've probably realised, the chances are you'll be going through all of this on your own. While escaping the office might seem like paradise now, you could soon be longing for a bit of gossip and backchat. You'll need to dig deep to find the kind of emotional resilience to keep you from losing the plot when there's no one around to lend a helping hand. So while you don't need qualifications on paper, not just anyone can become an entrepreneur. But if you think you've got what it takes then it could be one of the best decisions you ever make.

EXPERT OPINION

STAY AHEAD OF THE GAME

There was a time when budding entrepreneurs and marketeers just had to come up with a catchy, quirky name and image to launch their business and capture the attention of customers. Using a clever play on words or a fashionable buzzword, a business could be launched into the marketplace with the hope of capturing the public imagination.

However in today's competitive environment this is not enough. With an overcrowded and sometimes saturated market, many other factors have to be addressed.

Importance of online presence

It wasn't so long ago when we were all being told to 'go online' and 'get a website'. Many were suspicious of the e-commerce revolution, but here we are in 2009 and in a business sense, if you're not online, you're not alive. Unfortunately it is no longer a straight choice of 'Do I get a .com or a .co.uk?' There are so many gtld's (domain suffixes) to choose from, including .eu, .tv to .mobi and the list will only get bigger and bigger! Then there are the numerous website design options to be considered 'Do I want flash? Do I need a shopping basket? How much web space do I need?' The list goes on and on…

Once you are finally up and running online, you are competing with literally millions of websites to be seen and this is where search engine optimisation comes in. It is no longer enough to just 'have a website', you have to make sure it can be found through the many online search engines. So you have to consider metatags, pay per click and sponsored listings amongst other options.

Of course all of these preferences can be expensive, coupled with sorting out branding and trade marks, business names and company names. You will need to find out if your chosen business name, company name, domain name and trade mark is not already in use in relation to your chosen nature of business and intended market area. You then need to consider registration to protect your corporate identity.

Time management

When setting up a business, you will have to juggle these and many other responsibilities and ensure adequate time is set aside.

Time is one commodity that is very precious in today's commercial arena and is usually in very short supply. Owner managers just want to run and manage their business within their area of expertise and not get bogged down with additional responsibilities.

Staying ahead of your competitors

All of these responsibilities are not just prevalent when starting your business, but just as important is to ensure that you are one step ahead of your competitors and constantly monitoring and evolving where required. This can involve repeatedly checking to see if your current trading style is being copied and updating your corporate image periodically, making sure it does not become tired or outdated.

The modern business environment is changing and if you're not moving forward you can be sure that your rivals will be.

Keeping up with business news

It is essential that owners of businesses, whether sole traders, partnerships or limited companies keep up to date with the latest business news, changes in legislation and financial updates. Whether business is good or bad, the economic climate is optimistic or pessimistic it is important to keep informed and aware, and to not be slow in seeking the advice and guidance of experts in the areas that owners may not have the time or knowledge to fully embrace.

Use the free tools available on the internet and take the experts' advice and opinions wherever possible, because you know your competitors will…

If you need more information on business names, trademarks or company formation the National Business Register can help you and your business. Contact tel 0870 700 8787.

10 reasons to start a business

1. **You can be your own boss**

   If you have your own business, the only person you have to answer to is yourself. Being your own boss gives you the freedom to do things your way and implement your own plans. Of course, you live or die by your decisions, but that's what's good about it, isn't it?

2. **You get to do what you love – or at least have a keen interest in**

   The good thing about being an entrepreneur is that you can choose what kind of firm you start up, and where. So, provided that you've done your research properly and there is a gap in the market, you can turn a hobby or interest into a profitable enterprise.

3. **You can play by your own rules**

   Start your own firm and you get to set and meet your own deadlines. Of course, you won't be able to just lie in bed until 2pm – you will need self-discipline. But meeting your own targets can be a huge motivation to work hard and drive the business forward.

4. **You have the freedom to express yourself**

   If you have considered going it alone, you will have thought out how you would do things your way. You will have the freedom to express yourself and develop your concept in any way you choose. Of course, there may be financial constraints, but you will have the opportunity to be as creative as you like.

5. **You will need to work hard**

   The news is full of stories about the amount of red tape and taxes that small firms have to face on a daily basis. However, over the past few years, several measures have been introduced that should make it easier to go it alone. From the Small Firms Loan Guarantee to various inner-city projects, the government certainly can't be accused of doing absolutely nothing for budding entrepreneurs. With the Prince's Trust, Shell LiveWIRE and other support organisations also up and running, you should be able to secure the help and funding needed to get you started.

6. **You can make your fortune – or at least enough to live**

   There are countless stories of entrepreneurs hitting on a great idea, exploiting it successfully and being well on their way to their first million by the end of the year. Although the startup process can be tough, with long hours and little money not uncommon, if you run your business well, the rewards can be huge. And, from a purely selfish point of view, you will get most of the profits yourself.

7. You will have a variety of things to do

Dealing with spreadsheets one minute, suppliers the next and then having a look around your new office – an entrepreneur's work is not just busy, it is also extremely varied. If you want a career where every day is different, going it alone could be for you.

8. You can have a second career

Of course, if you don't want to give up a regular income, you can always get the best of both worlds and remain as an employee while running your own firm. Although juggling the two can be tricky, having a successful sideline should be a profitable option. Do something that you are interested in and go for it.

9. You can cut the commuting by setting up close to home

Although most small firms operate from offices, many entrepreneurs find that operating from home reduces costs dramatically in the early stages. As well as having familiar, comfortable surroundings to work in, you don't have to endure the daily tangle with public transport or clogged up roads.

10. Your big dream really can become reality

You may feel that starting up a small firm won't lead to anything more than having your own desk and taking on a few extra staff. However, it's possible to make it really big – just think of the late Anita Roddick, who became a Dame thanks to her entrepreneurial achievements. She started a small shop in Brighton on a shoestring in the 1970s. Before long, she had a chain of Body Shop stores across the UK and was launching her concept in the USA. So, don't dismiss your dreams as a mere fantasy – it really could happen. What are you waiting for?

EXPERT OPINION

GETTING ADVICE

Communication technology specialists BT offer tips on how to find the right help.

The world of British business is changing, with hundreds of thousands of new businesses starting every year. But going it alone is as much about finding the right help as it is about relying on your own knowledge. It's important that small and medium enterprises (SMEs) get the right support from the outset. The good news is, there is a range of expert support and information out there to ensure businesses get off on the right foot.

BT Business Insight (www.bt.com/insight) is one such place where startup businesses can get advice. The website is a unique resource providing UK small businesses with information and advice about how technology and services can help them succeed. BT Business Insight includes advice, guides, case studies and articles, helping UK SMEs at all stages of their business development.

1.0

IDEAS

WHAT'S IN THIS CHAPTER

- Not everyone starts a business following a 'eureka!' moment – in fact few people actually do. Some simply want to work for themselves. But, of course, to do this you need to find the right business for you, and hopefully one that has a good chance of success. Starting up is likely to take quite a bit of your time, energy and money, so it pays to think carefully about the kind of business to launch. This chapter should provide some inspiration…

What kind of business?

Although thousands of people dream of escaping the nine-to-five grind and becoming their own boss, many are unsure of what sort of business they want to start up and how they can ensure their new venture is a success. Ultimately, this is your choice, but it can help if you initially think about what you want from your business. Before **Kirsty McGregor** launched her web-based company Entertainthekids.com, which provides inspiration for parents looking for ways to keep their children entertained, she laid down her vision of 'business utopia', as she puts it.

'I had quite a strict list of what I wanted any business to be for me, in my circumstances,' she says. 'These were my requirements:

- The business shouldn't be reliant upon my input as the limiting factor in the growth of the business. This is a personal thing, as I wanted to start and grow the business and then be able to get "time freedom" as quickly as possible. It's the whole point of being able to run my own

" I drew up a strict list of what I wanted any business to be for me "

" The risks can be enormous, but so can the rewards "

! TIPS

CHOOSING THE RIGHT BUSINESS

- ! Base it on a key skill or interest
- ! Draw up a list of what you're looking for from your ideal business
- ! Search out the most successful businesses nationally and locally
- ! Find a gap in your local market
- ! Canvas opinion from friends and family about your idea
- ! Consult business contacts about your idea, such as your accountant
- ! Check out local competition and decide if you can do it better
- ! Look into the level of finance you'll need and whether you'll be able to secure it
- ! Find out if anyone likes your idea enough to go into business with you

business – flexibility for the family while being financially comfortable and secure.

- It either had to provide a product or service that was niche and high value, or have mass-market appeal with a low price.
- The business needed to be scaleable, without any major scarce resource, such as fixed employee or machinery hours, etc.
- Overheads/fixed costs had to be as low as possible, so that I could break even on a fairly low turnover.
- The product should preferably not be a fashionable item or have laws or regulations that will change quickly.
- The business should not have to deal with any stock issues, such as storage, delivery and suppliers – it had to be a service!
- It had to have low startup costs (unfortunately that also means low barriers to entry for competitors).'

PJH5

To find out how McGregor went on, look out for the 'Kirsty's Story' boxes throughout this guide. Of course, your vision could be completely different from hers, but getting it down on paper can give you key pointers about the kind of business you would like to launch. To give you some food for thought, this chapter gives you 20 business ideas. Some have popped up recently due to certain trends, while others have been around for some time, but all are either very popular now or growing rapidly in popularity. If none of them appeals to you, then at least you know what you don't want to do – and they might inspire you to find the business that's right for you.

A big problem for many people who want to start a business is being able to afford to do it. But don't let a lack of financial resources put you off. Starting a business on a shoestring seems like an impossible task, conjuring up visions of compromises and cutting corners that will ultimately undermine your best efforts. But it doesn't have to be that way as many industries are well suited to budget beginnings. This is not a case of restricting yourself to mean margins. There are simply a number of steps you can take to keep overheads down:

> " **Many industries are well suited to budget beginnings** "

- The most obvious costs in the early days are premises and staffing. If you start working from home then your office space or workshop budget can go elsewhere. Obviously, this is easier if you are in a desk-bound profession. If it doesn't matter where you are based, rents on out-of-town premises or those in unfashionable areas will keep costs down. And if you don't have the money for staff immediately, don't forget friends and family. Provided that you don't abuse their goodwill, most will be prepared to help you out on the odd occasion.

- It's inevitable that you will have to put 120% into the business at first, so try to become competent in as many tasks as possible. It will save you money if you can do things such as basic desktop publishing and accounting yourself. You will also gain a better understanding of the day-to-day running of the business.

- Where possible, lease rather than buy and purchase second-hand. Tools, machinery and ovens, for example, are widely available to lease if you can provide assurance that payments will be made. You can also make great savings if you opt for used desks, chairs and filing cabinets. Search on the internet or in the *Yellow Pages* for outlets and warehouses. Most large offices refurbish reasonably regularly, so the market is generally well stocked.

Half of the business ideas that follow are relatively inexpensive to launch, while the other 10 require more capital input, but no matter how much money you have, the points above are worth bearing in mind, because during the startup phase of a business, every penny counts.

Shoestring startups

AN EBAY BUSINESS

Setting up a company on eBay is an increasingly popular choice among would-be entrepreneurs. With millions of potential customers just a couple of clicks away from your products, setting up an eBay store is a cheap and easy way to do business online.

Once you've created a business account you can set up an online shop for just £6. It then costs between 15p and £2 to list an item on eBay, depending on the opening value or reserve price of the item. eBay takes a slice of the selling fee once an item is sold, depending on how

> **The most important thing is to find a niche that few other people are competing in**

much the item is worth. For items under £30, eBay takes a 5.25% share. For items between £30 and £599.99, eBay's share is 3.25% for the part of the bid above £30, and for items over £600, eBay takes 1.75%. Making and receiving payments through Paypal, eBay's online payment system of choice, also incurs a small transaction charge.

Julie King, from Newcastle, gave up her job as an IT consultant after she found she could buy and sell designer shoes and handbags on eBay for a profit. Her eBay business, **Killer Heels**, now makes more than £6,000 a month buying shoes and bags from wholesalers and selling them on eBay. Meanwhile, **Wilmamae Ward** set up a vintage clothing business, **The Gathering Goddess**. 'The most important thing is to find a niche that few other people are competing in,' she says. 'Start with selling something that you know about and/or love doing. Then research the eBay market in your particular sector, as well as on the internet in general, to see what the competition is doing and what is being offered. This will mean you can find a point of difference that will set you apart from your competitors.'

'It's also important to build up your positive feedback, as this is the bedrock of eBay and is what sets you apart as a good seller,' she continues. 'Excellent customer service equals great positive feedback, so never slack on processing orders.'

CONSULTANCY

> **Ideally you want the skills you're offering to match a growing area of demand**

Helping other people run their business may seem daunting at first, but many budding entrepreneurs have the skills and experience to become first-class consultants. If you think you have key skills you can pass on to others, this could be a cheap and easy way to strike out on your own. To find out, first you need to audit your knowledge, skills, experience and expertise. Do you have a wealth of knowledge that you could pass on to others? Ideally you want the skills you're offering to match a growing area of demand, where they will be in short supply, so initial research is vital. You will also need self-motivation, good inter-personal skills and plenty of confidence, as you will be working alone initially.

One of the most important aspects of establishing and marketing yourself as a consultant is developing a 'product' set. Clients have problems

CASE STUDY
THE GATHERING GODDESS
AND THE EBAY ADVENTURE

Having used the online trading website eBay for years to satisfy her personal passion for vintage clothing, **Wilmamae Ward** decided to set up an eBay business selling them, called The Gathering Goddess.

'I was amazed at the prices achieved, so I began to sell more and more and it just snowballed. eBay allowed me reach many customers,' says Wilmamae. 'I soon decided this was a business I would love doing, as I was able to indulge my fashion obsession and make a great living at the same time. It also enabled me to work from home and make my own hours… In addition, unlike a bricks and mortar shop which has to rely on passing trade and extensive marketing, eBay provide, all of this on a global basis without the overheads. I'd be mad to open up my own shop. It makes complete sense to me to have my business on eBay.

'Starting an eBay business was quite easy, I think the most important thing is to find a niche that few other people are competing in, if you can do this then this is probably the best way to start'.

buying advice and expertise in the abstract form; they're much happier buying something specific. You want to be seen as specialist, expert and knowledgeable. So package your expertise into 'products' that clients can understand and recognise.

Your main area of expense will be marketing. There are no short cuts here, although a successful marketing campaign needn't cost the earth, particularly if you make the most of your personal skills and network a lot. The main investment will be in good corporate design and branding to help you stand out and exude professionalism. This should include a well-thought-out website.

ACTION POINT
LAUNCH AN EBAY BUSINESS

START WITH SELLING SOMETHING THAT YOU KNOW ABOUT AND/OR LOVE DOING: This will help to drive your motivation and will be vital in maintaining your work levels, which will be heavy initially.

RESEARCH THE EBAY MARKET: In particular do this in your sector, as well as on the internet, to see what the competition is doing and what is being offered. Find a point of difference that will set you apart from your competitors.

BE COMMITTED TO IT: It isn't easy, but it can be extremely rewarding.

BUILD UP YOUR POSITIVE FEEDBACK: This is the bedrock of eBay and what sets you apart as a good seller. Excellent customer service equals great positive feedback. Never slack on good customer service.

ALWAYS KEEP TRACK OF YOUR COMPETITION: Don't just research them once or occasionally. Remember they are looking at you and as your business steams ahead, they are plotting and planning to take over. Half of Wilmamae's eBay time is spent researching competitors and new marketing techniques.

BE AS TRANSPARENT AS YOU CAN WITH YOUR POTENTIAL CUSTOMERS: Don't hide costs and describe your items clearly and honestly. Building trust builds business on eBay.

DON'T SPEND HUGE AMOUNTS OF MONEY ON STOCK AND SETTING UP: Start small and grow it slowly. The world of eBay can be complex and the best way of discovering this world is by experiencing it. If you plow in with a huge store full of lots of stock and you don't know the ins and outs then you risk falling quickly on your face.

PERSONAL TRAINER

Britain's gyms have experienced a 58% increase in membership over the past six years, so could you see yourself capitalising on this by giving customers some one-on-one workouts? For this you will first need to decide which area you want to specialise in, for example helping people to lose weight by combining fitness and nutrition, working with pregnant women or training elite athletes. Next, find a suitable and respected course that will give you the training and qualifications you need. While there is no singular qualification that allows you to be a fitness instructor, some courses are better respected than others, so it is worthwhile weighing up the alternatives.

Other than the cost of training, which can range from £300 to £5,000 depending on your speciality and prior knowledge, other overheads are limited. Public liability insurance is a must, and will often be in the region of £100 a year, and transport is also vital, but other costs depend on you. Most personal fitness trainers work from their clients' homes, so investment in the necessary equipment, such as free weights or a blood pressure machine, for example, is usually an early outgoing.

Linda Grave, a personal fitness trainer based in Suffolk, says, 'Most of my clients know each other because friends have recommended me to them.' How much you make depends on several factors, not least how hard you want to work, but the low overheads associated with the profession does mean that it can prove quite profitable. **Steven Jones**, sales manager at Premier Fitness, says the average hourly rate charged by fitness trainers is between £20 and £50. 'It depends on several factors, such as how well known you are, your location, your specialist skills, etc,' he explains. 'I know one guy in London who charges £100 an hour.'

> " The low overheads associated with the profession does mean that it can prove quite profitable "

DATING AGENCY

Soaring divorce rates and the scarce social time enjoyed by hard-working employees have resulted in a large rise in the number of single people in the UK looking for partners. You could play cupid while making money at the same time by starting a dating agency. To run one, you need to be the kind of person who can deal well with other people's emotions, and be both diplomatic and supportive.

> " Introductions can be made at organised social events such as dinners or drinks, or in lunch appointments as opposed to evening dates "

Introductions can be made at organised social events such as dinners or drinks, or in lunch appointments as opposed to evening dates. They can also be made to give people the chance to meet those in the same situation as them, for example, single, widowed or divorced parents. An agency could offer any combination of these services, but you would do better to specialise in order to offer a good service, particularly if you are starting very small. Organised dinners, for instance, can be a good way of starting to build up a database of people. Each guest will have a friend to recommend you to, who will recommend you in turn and so on. To help decide which area to specialise in, check out the local competition for a gap in the market. Bringing people together in the more traditional 'one-to-one' basis can be achieved in one or a combination of three ways:

- Personal introductions, where all clients are personally interviewed.
- Computer comparison, where software compares submitted client details for suitability.
- Lists method, where the clients receive a list of selected members.

This obviously makes for an agency with a local focus. To start small, but have a national clientele would mean running a largely computer and internet-based agency. So, you need to decide this from the start as the routes are very different.

Costs will revolve around setting up a website with a payment processing facility, and initial marketing. An agency might charge £50 for computer matching up to £2,000 plus for executive or hand-picked selection.

CATERING

Whether it's a major sporting event or a low-key wedding, the need for food and drink at gatherings doesn't go out of fashion. In fact, with a growing population of foodies and people becoming more nutritionally aware, it has become a key part of any event. So if you've got a passion for food and are creative with it, perhaps a catering company is for you. The key to success is excellent quality food and service, along with exploiting any gap in the catering marketing that may exist in your area.

> **It won't be until you have a large operation that you start bringing in good money, so it could be worthwhile to start up part time**

As an independent there are two main sectors you can target – private and corporate events. The former category will consist of family occasions such as weddings, birthday parties, dinner parties and funerals. In serving the corporate world, you are more likely to provide food for business breakfasts, business lunches, board meetings and evening receptions. Some caterers specialise in one or the other, while others try to cover both.

Taking into account the professional equipment you'll need, you are looking at between £20,000 and £50,000 to start up, depending on the size of business and whether you are starting up at home or moving into premises. It won't be until you have a large operation that you start bringing in good money, so it could be worthwhile to start up part time. **Sue Roberts** did this and has grown Bristol-based Topline Catering gradually over 20 years, moving from sandwich delivery to business lunches, and finally to corporate and private events for anything up to 1,000 guests. From first-day takings of £13, the business now turns over £300,000 a year. It obviously takes several years to build up to this size, but a small yet successful business could nevertheless turn over £100,000 and earn a net profit of £40,000.

COURIER

With many businesses needing a fast, efficient delivery service, why not get on your bike and start a courier company? The courier industry is easy to get into. In effect, all you need is an office, a telephone and a set of wheels – two or four. As a result there are many new businesses starting up each year. But, inevitably, there is a lot more to making a success of it. Even a smallish motorbike or cycle company requires considerable effort and knowledge. Usually, you would have people working with you on a self-employed basis. They would have their own bikes and equipment and would be responsible for storing and maintaining this themselves. Cycle couriers are also a greener option with so many city centres plagued by traffic gridlock and plans for no-car zones.

This is an industry where you're not buying in stock or making big wage payouts. Riders should get their percentage of the client's bill on a weekly basis whereas you will most likely invoice clients each month. As such it is

> Cycle couriers are a greener option with so many city centres plagued by traffic gridlock and plans for no-car zones

not the size of outgoings that matter but the regularity. It's important that you keep cash flow steady even when business isn't. 'There are weekly and seasonal booms in the courier industry,' says **Phillip Stone** of the Despatch Association. 'Fridays are busy as people send things before the weekend and Mondays and Tuesdays are generally slow. Then July and August might be quiet with the run up to Christmas much busier.' Therefore, you need to make sure you have the cash to keep the business going in the leaner times.

In this business, image is key, so striking branding enables your couriers to stand out and carry your message with them. It also pays to treat your staff well and make sure they are personable as your reputation stands or falls on their attitude and ability.

DRIVING SCHOOL

"

You can choose to start out on your own or train with and sign up to an established franchise "

With approximately 1.6 million learner tests conducted annually the demand for new instructors is there so if you have the time, patience, skill, concentration and are more than competent enough to teach other people to learn to drive, then perhaps you should consider this as a career. You'll also need a healthy sense of humour and bags of patience. First, you have to pass a three-stage exam to become an approved driving instructor (ADI). Then you can choose to start out on your own or train with and sign up to a pre-established franchise that already has a list of pupils, contacts and trainers. In both cases you are self-employed but with varying degrees of individuality and support.

If you have your own car, costs are fairly minimal. If not, you will have to either invest in one with dual controls, which will be a major expense, or be supplied with one by the franchise you work under. You will spend a large amount on fuel each week so it may be worth holding an account with a petrol station. However, the major cost lie in training (up to £2,500 plus training licence, £100; ADI licence, £200; literature, £50), the three-part exam (under £200) as well as the on-going franchise fee (£40–£300), which, with a larger brand name, may be a high percentage of the work they supply you with. Against these costs, **Nick Zapettis** of A2Z Motoring gives a rough indication of what you can expect to earn. 'If you charge around £15 to £16 an hour, which is the going rate, take between 30 and 50 lessons a week, including weekends and evenings, and take into account the franchise fee, then you could be earning a net salary of roughly between £15,000 and £22,000 per year,' he explains.

This can be more if you go it alone, and of course the idea is that ultimately you'll have your own school and franchisees.

TUTORING

If you are a good communicator and enjoy passing on your skills, then you may find tutoring attractive. Essentially, you'll be offering extra tuition that provides children and young people (from primary to A-level) with one-to-one or few-to-few attention they can't get in school or college. This is a profession that is ideal for people who need to be at home for certain times of the day, for example those with children. It can be operated from home, although by travelling to your clients you can increase your appeal and income. You must have a comprehensive knowledge across the complete range of your subject, being at least one level in advance of the level you are tutoring. It isn't essential to be a qualified teacher, but having some teaching experience can reassure parents.

Cost-wise you'll need access to the correct year's syllabus (around £2), sample exam papers (50p–£1) and a range of up-to-date relevant textbooks (£10 upwards). Lessons are generally charged by the hour and fees vary across the country and for different levels, but you might charge between £15 and £20 at home, plus a few extra pounds for travel. This isn't a big money business, but it can easily be built up into much more than a part-time one if you are prepared to work at weekends and longer evenings.

To make tutoring a success, it's vital to keep up to date with the curriculum, and as word of mouth is so important, make sure you get on with your pupils and that they get better grades than predicted.

INTERIOR DESIGN

Although home makeover television shows appear to have run their course, there is still a huge interest in interior design. So if you can marry creativity with practicality, this low-cost startup option could be for you. Initially you might start small with furnishings and curtains. But this can grow into a complete interior design service through visiting people in

> " By travelling to your clients you can increase your appeal and income "

> " Any design experience or training is helpful, but if you intend to start with a small business, it may be enough to have an eye for colour "

their home for a consultation, to making up and fitting anything from carpets and curtains to furnishings and lighting.

Every job is obviously different, and meeting people to talk through and combine their and your ideas can be challenging. Any design experience or training is helpful, but if you intend to start with a small business, it may be enough to have an eye for colour. You will certainly need practical cutting and sewing skills. You can get a good industrial sewing machine second-hand for between £400 and £1,200, depending on sophistication, and you'll also need pattern books from material manufacturers, which cost £20–£80 each. Furthermore, as you'll be visiting people's homes, public liability insurance is a must.

Remuneration varies according to the size of windows or room, to the cost of fabric. But for a width of hand-sewn curtain, for example, you might charge anything from £20 through to £40 or £60. And a small two-seater sofa could be anything from £300 upwards plus fabric (at around £18 plus a metre). There is always a demand for this kind of work, as people are constantly on the move, and within an area you can quickly build up word-of-mouth recommendations. The key is to be genuine with your customers. If they choose a fabric that won't work, tell them in a friendly way and suggest alternatives.

PUBLIC RELATIONS

> **You will need to understand the objectives of the client and identify a strategy for achieving them**

A public relations and communications agency promotes and represents businesses in the general marketplace, in their specialist field and within the media. It's concerned with creating a name for the client and helping it succeed, and gives you the chance to work closely with a variety of companies, identifying their needs, while focusing on an area of personal interest and increasing relevance to each client's core business. You will need to understand the objectives of the client and identify a strategy for achieving them through increasingly diverse communication channels. Then you have to sell that story effectively to a chosen audience.

The bare essentials would be rented office premises (£650 a week), computers (£2,000), printer (£300), desks and furniture (£700), telephones (£200), print costs (£1,000) and legal expenses (£120). But initially you could run it from home. A sample hourly rate for executive time is £70 and you should focus on securing retained clients on a regular monthly income. In theory, therefore, two executives should be able to generate an annual income of around £150,000.

It is essential that you identify a market area to focus on that is not only new, but also experiencing growth, as this indicates that there is a proven market and also competition, so that companies will need help to stand out. For example, **Tim Lewis** and **Greg Moore** of Synapse Communications specialise in corporate social responsibility (CSR), working with companies that promote responsible practices to benefit business and society. Remember that this is a people business, so there's no point in going into it if you don't like talking, and you will need to be both friendly and persuasive. It is also important that you employ people who are aware of this. Keep focused and don't forget to market your own the company, even when busy.

Other popular options

INTERNET CAFÉ

Although the number of households with a broadband connection is soaring, internet cafés are still proving to be highly popular among people who need to get online while on the move. This business could see you log on to a tidy profit. And although wifi is on the increase, those with laptops still need somewhere comfortable to base themselves between appointments or simply to while away a few hours.

'Many of our users have a PC at home and work and yet still use us or other cafés, simply because they are so used to it,' says **Jason Deane** of Quarks (www.quarks.co.uk), a chain of internet cafés in and around London. 'Once you have chosen a suitable space for your café, you will need to set a budget for all the equipment and add-ons you plan to provide customers.'

'Our own branches have cost between £17,000 and £150,000 to start, so the amount is hugely varied,' he continues. On top of this, you're also likely to have to pay out for internet access (£4,000 a year), PCs (£400 a year), networks (up to £1,000 a year), timing systems to ensure customers

> Any kind of specialisation is beneficial

> Many of our users have a PC at home and work and yet still use us ... simply because they are so used to using it

do not go over their time limit (£500 a year), a website and hosting (£1,000 a year), plus equipment such as printers, fax, scanners and CD burner (around £1,000 depending on requirements). These costs are just a guide as internet cafés vary in size and what they provide. To make money with an internet café, you must plan carefully and meet public demand for additional services. Research the businesses that will surround your café – do they offer the services that you could offer, such as gaming, printing, scanning and, most importantly, web surfing? If no companies in your area offer these things, you should consider incorporating them into your internet café. 'This market is very competitive and internet access is a commodity, nothing more,' says Deane. 'Therefore your service has to be different and priced accordingly.'

CLOTHES SHOP

If you get it right, you can do really well

With such a wide range of clothes shops out there, you have several options when trying to tap into this huge market. Although this is a highly competitive environment, if you find the right niche in the right area and make sure you have a strong online presence – in fact this is where you could start out – there are opportunities. This may centre on the style of clothing you sell or on the type of customer you want to attract. For example, you may stock only suits or second-hand clothes. Alternatively, you may look to sell clothes to a particular group, such as schoolchildren or extra-large men. Whatever type of shop you eventually decide to open, one thing is certain, you will have to put a lot of effort and money into making it work.

The set-up costs depend greatly on how large your shop is and where you locate, since rental costs will be a major expense. For example, around 800sq ft on the high street will cost about £22,000 a year to rent in Chester, but can top £100,000 in Manchester. Then there's the cost of refitting. 'Renovating my shop cost £15,000, although it was done expensively and involved a new floor and all new fixtures and fittings,' says **Liz Urwin**, who runs Bottega, a ladies' fashion boutique in Cheshire. 'But the clothes are upmarket, so need to be displayed in a nice environment.' Finally, you will need to purchase the stock. Initially this could be expensive since, as a new business, suppliers may refuse to give you credit. 'If you get it right, you can do really well,' says **Michael Goodmaker** of the Institute of Business Advisers. 'The risks can be enormous, but so can the rewards.'

FLORISTS

Opening a florists may be the result of a gardening hobby, but even if you are new to the sector you can start up and make a success of this business. Of all retail businesses, this is one that could probably be almost recession-proof, as people always want to send, and love getting, flowers, whether the occasion is happy or sad. But an online presence is also a must these days.

The good news is that the flower market itself has also been on the increase since the early 1990s with UK fresh flowers and indoor plants representing £1.5 billion at retail level. Before setting up, you will need to carry out some thorough market research of the area you want to cover, the type of people who live and work there and the existing competition. 'Any kind of specialisation is beneficial. Florists should also emphasise the additional design input and technical skill that goes into their work,' says **Andrea Caldecourt** of the Flowers and Plants Association. 'This often has a personal touch – just as artists and clothes designers are recognisable by their work.'

Of the 6,700 businesses, around 80% of these belong to a relay organisation such as InterFlora, Teleflower or Flowergram, which allow people in one part of the country to 'send' flowers to a someone in another part through a network of florists. The benefit of this membership is that by providing support in marketing and sales, and product and design, and as a result of the organisations' international links, they allow the business to compete with multi-national firms, and respond to a changing market. Floristry has the classic retail cost base of premises and stock, so the initial outlay can be significant. As with clothing retail, risks are high, but get it right and the rewards can be substantial.

WINE BAR

With the popularity of wine rising sharply in recent years, if you have a thirst for profits as well as red or white, a wine bar could be the venture

> **Floristry has the classic retail cost base of premises and stock, so the initial outlay can be significant**

> **Wine consumption in the UK has risen by 60% in the past 10 years**

for you. And there's also the potential to branch out into a gourmet eatery. According to Vinexpo, the world's largest wine trade fair, wine consumption in the UK has risen by 60% in the past 10 years. A wine bar can capitalise on this and the growing appreciation of fine food, while being more upmarket than a pub, means profits can be higher if your customer base is big enough. As with any startup, the right location is key, so you'll need to know the local market and what it wants, as well as competitor activity. This will determine everything from the size of the operation to what you sell. Sometimes small and intimate is better that big and crowded, or ambience takes precedence over wine selection. That's why thorough research is essential.

Some wine bars are bought outright, some are managed or franchised under a brand name while others are leased from private companies and brewers. Many are also run by private bar owners and simply rented by a private landlord. So, the capital you put in could range from £20,000 to £200,000 plus. Then there are fixtures and fittings (£3,000–£30,000), stock (up to £9,000), glassware and crockery (up to £1,200), tills (three for around £1,000) and insurance (around £500). **Michael Davis** of Virtualpubs.com, which helps people buy and sell licensed properties in the UK and Spain, suggests that you can make up to 60% gross profit from running your own wine bar, but that after costs and wages, for example, are taken out, the turnover figure is more likely resemble around 10%. So it's vital to get your business plan down to a tee and give your venture a huge amount of thought before you toast to your own success.

GIFT SHOP

Boosted by the tourist trade and increasing public interest in quirky arts, crafts and nick-nacks, gift shops are a very popular business. According to the Giftware Association, the national trade body for the UK gift industry, the sector is worth an estimated £10 billion per year. The gift market is large and there is potential for considerable profit. It's impossible to quote an exact figure for startup costs since they will depend greatly on your location, the size of your shop, the products you sell and whether you rent your premises or buy a freehold. The cost of buying freehold premises varies in much the same way as house prices vary throughout

> "There are certain techniques that can help you boost your gift shop profits"

the country. Once you have the premises you will need to fit out the shop, and then there's the payment transaction equipment and stock, all of which will cost you a minimum of £50,000.

Feedback from one owner suggested a market town gift shop, for example, should be turning over £200,000–£250,000 a year, from which you would get a gross profit margin of around £100,000, with rent, rates, staff costs and other overheads still to pay. Therefore, an owner-manager with a reasonably sized gift shop in a market town should be able to take £50,000–£60,000 a year out of the business, assuming it's doing well. There are certain techniques that can help you boost your gift shop profits, ranging from accepting credit cards and developing a strong online presence to specialising in more exclusive gifts – but this depends on how receptive your customer base is to such products.

HOTEL

Whether you just offer a simple bed and shared bathroom or full en suite luxury, somewhere for the weary traveller to stay for the night is always in demand. Obviously, location is the key to success, but the rise of boutique establishments means that many people are increasingly going for style and ambience over five-star blandness.

The first thing to consider is what type of hotel you want to run. Is it going to be a small, cosy affair catering for couples seeking a romantic weekend break, or a larger, metropolitan establishment servicing the corporate market? Some hotels pitch for both business and private clients. The types of client you attract depend, to a large extent, on the hotel's location. The size of the hotel, its location and the clientele you are aiming to attract will all determine costs. It is possible to rent, but buying means you keep more of the profits.

> **The size of the hotel, its location and the clientele you are aiming to attract will all determine costs**

As an example, **Stephen Hipwell** bought a 20-year lease on the Granville Hotel in Brighton for £350,000, with the total expenditure, excluding VAT, expected to be £280,000 a year. There are basically two schools of thought when it comes to turnover. The first is to keep earnings below the VAT threshold, which is £54,000, which at a usual 40% profit margin you're looking at clearing £20,000. The alternative is to go all out to earn as much as possible. To make it worthwhile you need to earn considerably more than the VAT threshold, which means taking £100,000 plus. Hipwell is forecasting turnover of £400,000 this year.

ANTIQUES

Although Lovejoy and his wild mullet added a bit of glamour to the antiques world, most people regard the sector as the preserve of fusty shops with pensionable owners. However, the antiques business, although time consuming, can prove to be a very rewarding way to capitalise on a private passion. The prime antique collectors seem to be the more affluent population born in the 1950s and 1960s. Since the number of people in their 30s and 40s is the fastest growing segment of the population, it would seem that the sales of antique objects will continue to be strong over the long term. If you can find a niche, such as coins, early 20th-century furniture, art deco, art nouveau or Second World War memorabilia, then you already have an edge, but be aware that what you make up for in lack of competition you lose in possible buyers as the smaller the niche the smaller the available clientele. 'Remember that it's a luxury market whether it's a £50 porcelain jar or a £600,000 painting,' says antique dealer **Ingrid Nilson**. 'Food, rent and clothes come first. If the economic climate is good then trade is good.' But the market is quite constant. 'There are now fairs throughout the whole year, even July and August, and they can work as well in September as October,' says Nilson.

Typical running costs for an antique dealer will be rental, be it a shop or stall, antique fair stand costs, insurance, car upkeep costs, petrol costs plus phone and mailing charges. Then there's initial stock which you should expect to cost £25,000–£35,000 and should represent around 65% of your overall startup costs. With costs of this calibre and stiff competition in the marketplace, you'll need to know your stuff and regularly network with auction house experts to get your prices right and pick up bargains.

HAIRDRESSERS

Now if there was a service that you couldn't ever imagine there not being demand for, this could be it. Sure, competition is fierce, you do need to

> **Remember that it's a luxury market whether it's a £50 porcelain jar or a £600,000 painting**

> **Getting paid for something you love doing and working with friends in a nice atmosphere can't be beaten**

train hard to gain the necessary qualifications and it involves long hours. But find the right location and you will certainly make money. With the variety of customers, from kids to adults, it pays to be a people person, and unless you open your own chain of shops, it's unlikely to make you a millionaire. But as **Linda Heald** from Keeping Up Appearances in Chichester, West Sussex, says: 'Getting paid for something you love doing and working with friends in a nice atmosphere can't be beaten.'

A number of hairdressing companies currently for sale over the internet indicate that purchasing a business can cost anywhere between £5,000 and £59,000. This will generally include fixtures and fittings. If you're starting from scratch, there'll be the usual outlay for either renting or buying premises, plus fixtures, fittings and equipment. Keeping it basic, Heald spent £1,000 on basic salon fittings and a further £3,000 on chairs and dryers. Having sat down and costed all the equipment she had to buy to fully kit out her salon, she found out that it set her back £1,800. But this could be a lot more expensive depending on the level of ostentation. 'You could stagger these costs though and just get essentials and then buy extras as you begin to make a profit. Also, you must remember to set aside money for the taxman right from day one,' she says. On a good week, Heald can earn around £1,300. But when you take away costs, she will be left with a figure more likely to be between £300 and £400. So if you're in business purely for the money, then hairdressing is probably not the way to go, unless you have ambitions to be the next Toni & Guy.

DAY NURSERY

Day nurseries are vital to the many families that can't afford to give up a regular income to stay at home. Clearly, you need a love of the little darlings, but this is a growing area and one that appears to be increasingly in demand. It is a business that tends to attract working parents – either because they think they could do a better job than the nurseries already on offer or they discover that there is nothing available in the area at all.

Finding suitable premises is a must

Running a nursery is certainly not a 'get-rich-quick' plan. But, if you want a job – and a business – that offers hourly challenges and a lot of rewards then this could be just right for you. Finding suitable premises is a must. The regulations set out how much space you will need per child, so once you have worked out how many children you want to have you will know the minimum space required. You can either rent, buy or build from scratch, but this can be very expensive. However, some local authorities allow modular nurseries, which are much cheaper to build and can be up and running quickly – for 25–30 children they cost around £80,000.

Freya Derrick set up her Hopscotch Day Nursery for £600,000 and is now turning over £50,000 per month with 82 children currently attending the nursery. 'You've got to decide right from the beginning if you want to run the business as a lifestyle choice, or as a profit-making thing, and that will determine the size of the operation,' she says. 'I wanted to have the freedom to spend time with my children, but I also wanted to run a successful business.'

RESTAURANT

Eating out is big business with a huge variety of restaurants now inhabiting British high streets. The bad news is that many don't survive for long due to the sheer amount of competition. The good news is that if you think strategically and find the right niche for your location, the rewards can be great in terms of both job satisfaction and money. For his restaurant, which seats 40 people, **Stephane Luiggi**, owner of the French Living restaurant in Nottingham, spent £5,000 on kitchen equipment, some of which was second-hand, and £5,000 on tables and chairs. Then there's the premises. 'You need to have quite a lot of money, particularly in central London, where an 80-seater restaurant, would cost you about £1 million,' explains restaurant consultant **Torquil Macleod**. However, if you are going for something slightly more modest, a restaurant on a suburban high street for example, then you should have between £70,000 and £150,000 in your pockets, explains **Mike Rogers**, director of startups and small businesses at Barclays.

Aside from the equipment, staff are one of your biggest fixed costs. If you are open seven days a week, you will need more than one chef. Head chefs can these days command salaries of between £30,000 and £40,000 – and getting a good one is critical to your business. To avoid

> **"If you are open seven days a week, you will need more than one chef"**

being just another restaurant casualty, be prepared to run a business rather than merely indulge a hobby. Market research is essential. 'You need to check out the location and the competition,' says Rogers. 'What's your catchment area? What's more, you can't charge a premium when you first open. You need to know what will make people want to come and spend their money with you. With local research you can see what is popular whether it be Mexican, Thai, Japanese, whatever.' There are also all the hygiene and health and safety regulations to negotiate, and initially long hours to cope with, but think strategically and implement carefully, and there is money to be made.

KIRSTY'S STORY
MY LIGHTBULB MOMENTS

The website Entertainthekids.com was recently set up by **Kirsty McGregor** and her brother Gregg. It provide a one-stop shop for parents and carers looking for some inspiration when it comes to the difficult job of keeping kids entertained, and is proving highly successful. Throughout this guide she'll be giving you an insight into setting up her business and some of the problems she has faced. Here she describes the moment she came up with the idea, and how beforehand she had listed the criteria her business had to meet:

'My lightbulb moments came in early January 2005, both of them borne out of sheer frustration at trying to entertain my own baby, then only 12 months old. After the initial idea popped into my head, I started researching the market (namely, the internet) and found that what I wanted to do appeared to be fairly unique. Most of the "competition" was more general sites, offering a whole range of things for parents, but no site appeared to specialise in just providing activity ideas… We have amended the product slightly since those early days. For example, we thought about recommending books and toys, but then decided that we were straying away from our core focus area, and to provide personal opinions could alienate some members who didn't agree with our tastes.

'We also considered a chat room or message board, but again decided that it wasn't for us. There are plenty of great "community" sites that do this really well, and we didn't want to compete with them. We knew what we wanted, and we just had to see if it was viable! As well as provide parents and carers with inspirational activities for children, we also wanted the site to be:

- Quick to load and easy to use
- Clean, uncluttered (the company's strapline is "…and now you can relax!")
- No banner advertising or pop-ups, instead the business model is based on members paying a subscription
- Original content, not just a myriad of links to other sites
- Focused on traditional entertainment activities for children aged 0–11, not straying into other areas, such as advice, health or education.'

Look out for more from Kirsty throughout this guide.

EXPERT OPINION

INTELLECTUAL PROPERTY

The UK IP office provides key detail on protecting your idea:

What does Intellectual Property (IP) have to do with 'Ideas'?

Virtually every product or service that we use in our daily lives is the result of a long chain of big or small innovations that make a product look or function the way it does today. Take for example the mobile telephone, the technology can be traced back to an idea pioneered by the Hollywood actress Hedy Lamarr back in the 1940s which was seen as a breakthrough in the area of communication. Since then, many others have improved the design and function of such products, and legally protected their improvements through IP rights.

'What is worth copying is worth protecting,' so spoke the judge in a copyright dispute in 1916, and his words are just as valid today. It is a plain fact of modern business life that if your intellectual property gets you market share, then your competitors are going to want to copy it.

Surely this is only relevant to big business?

Regardless of what product your business makes or what service it provides, it is likely that you are using and creating IP. Almost every business will have a trade name or a trademark and should consider protecting them. Many will have valuable confidential business information that they may wish to protect. Others may have developed creative original designs or invented a new process. Enforcing IP rights is often the only way to ensure that your creativity is not exploited by someone else.

Why should you use IP?

IP may assist you in almost every aspect of your business planning and competitive strategy, from product development to marketing. It may also play an important role when considering exporting or expanding your business abroad.

- **Trade marks:** These are in many ways the face of your business; they allow your customers to distinguish your products and services from your competitors. They are often the single most valuable marketing tool a company will have whatever its size. Registration of the mark gives an immediate right to stop someone else using the same, or similar, mark on the same or similar goods and services.

- **Designs:** The outward shape and appearance of products of all kinds are protectable by either a registered design or design right. The appearance of this outward aspect may be crucial for the market success or failure of a product, whatever its other attributes. Design right is an automatic right without the need for registration however a registered design right will offer stronger protection.

- **Patents:** When it comes to novel products and processes, patent protection is what is required. You could rely on keeping the information confidential to protect your product but without a patent you would lack the right to stop others from making, selling or importing the product or process you have developed. Patents cover such diverse subjects as agriculture, medicines, games, paints, electronics, and photography: anything in fact from a small detail in an electric switch, to a

new form of transport like the first hovercraft. A patent owner may license their rights in exchange for royalties.

- **Copyright:** This, in some form, is owned by most businesses. Although they may not be directly involved in making money from their copyright, businesses print brochures, publish advertisements and own websites that contain copyright-protected materials. There is no registration system for copyright in the UK; it comes into operation automatically.

In all cases, IP gives legal recognition to the ownership of new ideas or new brands and gives proprietors the right to stop other people exploiting their property.

How can the UK-Intellectual Property Office (UK-IPO) help?

The UK-IPO is the government agency responsible for granting patents, registered designs and registered trade marks within the UK and a wealth of free advice can be obtained by telephoning the Enquiry Unit on 08459 500 505 or through the UK-IPO website (www.ipo. gov.uk).

DECISION TIME

WHAT'S IN THIS CHAPTER

- Having formulated your idea, or even if you're still trying to choose the right kind of business for you, you may feel ready to start taking the first steps to starting up on your own. But before you do so you need to make sure you know what it takes to be an entrepreneur. This chapter will help you find out about the commitment it involves and the kind of person you need to be to succeed, and when to take the plunge and quit your present job. By the time you reach the end of this chapter, you should know for certain whether you are cut out for entrepreneurialism, so read on...

Have you got what it takes?

So you are thinking of launching your own business. Maybe you haven't decided exactly what as yet, but you are certain you do want to start out on your own. Whatever it is, once that first entrepreneurial seed has been sown, the chances are that before long you will be starting up on your own. However, if you have any doubts about your entrepreneurial abilities now is the time to think about them:

- Are you sure you really want to start your own business?
- Are you really cut out for it?
- And even if you are, is it too great a risk to give up a secure income?

> **Many successful entrepreneurs have no business qualifications or experience prior to starting up**

Starting up your own business will change your life. It will change the way you think, the way you work, the way you spend money and the way you socialise. It's one of the most demanding challenges you will ever take on. You will most likely need to work every hour possible to get your business off the ground, then even longer to keep it afloat during the early days. You probably won't have another holiday for a couple of years and virtually your entire life will become focused on making your business venture succeed. If you are in a relationship, it will undoubtedly feel the strain, and if you've got a family, prepare to be repeatedly torn between them and 'the business'.

This is the harsh truth of starting your own business. If you thought you would be reducing your hours rather than increasing them, that it wouldn't disrupt your family life and that, frankly, it all seems a bit too much trouble, then you should think of a different way to improve your everyday life. However, if what you have just read hasn't curbed your desire, keep reading – you are now showing the attributes an entrepreneur needs when starting up in business. Sure, you will still have plenty of anxieties and unanswered questions, but like every successful entrepreneur starting a small business, the thought of a challenge excites and enthuses you.

If you're going to succeed, you will most likely need to concentrate all your energy into the new business because it will be 'your baby' and you and your family will be the ones reaping the rewards – instead of some fat cat purring contentedly at the helm of a multinational on 10 times your salary thanks in part to all your hard work. You will also have the enthusiasm and ideas to find solutions to the obstacles in your path. And remember, you won't be the first one to have anxieties or to face obstacles as you're starting your own business. Every successful entrepreneur has overcome many barriers and continues to do so every week with whatever new business he or she is bringing to market.

> **People with the passion, drive and courage to start up their own business are seen as role models**

What's more, many successful entrepreneurs have no business qualifications or experience prior to starting up. Many spent months, even years, formulating their idea into a viable business proposition, and every single one will have made mistakes, accepted help and learnt lessons as they've gone along. The reason they've succeeded is because they have remained determined, focused, worked extremely hard and had the clarity of thought to realise they couldn't do it all on their own. If you share these attributes, you're half way there.

The average entrepreneur

> **Men are twice as likely to start a business as women – but the gap is rapidly narrowing**

So in the UK, what type of person is likely to start a business today? The last available government statistics on business startups revealed that the average entrepreneur is white, male, aged 36, lives in the south-east, is involved in the construction industry, and educated to degree level with previous work experience in the same sector as their business. However, the above facts aren't necessarily a true reflection of entrepreneurial trends in the UK. For example, although men are still twice as likely to start a business as women, the gap is rapidly narrowing. For a better indication of the types of people who are starting up businesses, this section looks at the statistics and trends for each characteristic of the entrepreneurial make-up.

Age

The average age might be 36, but one in six new businesses started in the UK are by those over the age of 50. Indeed, 23% of entrepreneurs are aged between 45 and 54. According to research by Barclays Bank, new businesses run by the over-50s are growing in number and this trend looks set to continue in line with the UK's ageing population.

Starting a business is being promoted as a viable career option for young people more than ever before, with the number of young business owners under 25 years of age in 2007 reaching 20,700. However, statistically, while this sector is likely to grow in the future, young people are more likely to consider starting on their own as a sideline venture or as something to do later in life.

> **Starting a business is being promoted as a viable career option for young people more than ever before**

Gender

As mentioned above, men are twice as likely to start a business as women – but female numbers are quickly catching up. In 2004 the number of businesses founded by women was 155,000, while businesses founded by men numbered 297,400. Four years later, it is now estimated that there are 602,000 female-owned businesses in the UK, accounting for 14% of total business. This figure is still low compared with the USA, where female business accounts for 30% of the total. With the government keen to continue to encourage more women to go into business, there's every indication the trend will continue. But for now on the global level, the UK remains near the bottom of the rankings when it comes to the ratio of male versus female startups. When compared with 29 other developed countries, the UK currently ranks a lowly 26th. In the past 20 years there has been a 46% rise in the number of self-employed women with this figure now accounting for 7.6% of the total number of women in employment. You can read more about the challenges facing female entrepreneurs later in this chapter.

> **Men are twice as likely to start a business as women – but female numbers are quickly catching up**

Education and career history

Educational background clearly has a large impact on entrepreneurship and rising levels of education can be associated with higher relative rates of enterprise activity. However, a significant minority – almost one in five – has no educational qualifications whatsoever, with 19% having left school at 15 or 16. In fact just over a quarter of self-employed people have been educated to GCSE level or equivalent while just 7% have a university degree. Half of active entrepreneurs have previously worked in the sector they start a business in, with over 90% of entrepreneurs having owned more than one business.

Ethnicity

> **Ethnic groups are more likely to be thinking about starting a business than the country as a whole**

According to the Small Business Service, every ethnic minority group is less likely to start a business in the UK than the white population. In 2006 the Department for Business Enterprise and Regulatory Reform (BERR) found that only around one in 10 small businesses (9.8%) in England had owners with ethnic minority backgrounds, with 66,000 in London alone. However, ethnic minority groups have a self-employment rate equal to British and other white groups – around 8% of their population. The BERR report found there are 275,000 ethnic minority small and medium-sized enterprises (SMEs), accounting for around 6% of all SMEs in the UK.

Ethnic groups, especially the black population, are more likely to be *thinking* about starting a business than the country as a whole. Sadly, the reason many people from ethnic minority groups are only considering going it alone, rather then actually doing it could be because of discrimination. On average, ethnic minority-owned businesses pay higher bank loan charges than white-owned businesses and black African and black Caribbean-owned businesses are significantly more likely to feel discouraged from applying for finance than Indian, Pakistani and white-owned businesses. However, with the launch of the Ethnic Minority Business Task Force in 2007 by the BERR hopefully this situation will be rectified in the near future.

Location

On average, London boasts the largest number of new businesses, followed closely by south-east England. In fact, these two regions account for around 40% of startup businesses, with London claiming 35%. But while the north/south divide still exists, it's not widening. Government initiatives to decentralise enterprise funding means there should be greater support for entrepreneurs outside the south-east in the coming years, with startup activity increasing in all but one of the English regions, with some of the biggest increases found in the north-east.

Attitude

Unsurprisingly, the differing attitudes of entrepreneurs aren't recorded – but perhaps they should be. Regardless of your age, background, sex or ethnicity, your success as an entrepreneur is likely to be down to your attitude to business. Following this, it has been found that successful entrepreneurs are more likely to take risks, with 60% of those with over £1 million claiming that a willingness to take risks had a huge impact on their career. If you're determined, prepared to make personal sacrifices, have the ability to plan ahead and take on board advice while remaining focused on your goal and also, of course, have a decent business idea, you will have every chance of success wherever you're from and whatever age or gender you are.

The entrepreneurial personality

You need to ensure that not only can you draw up a viable business plan, but you also possess the essential skills and personal traits required to make that plan work. To help you decide, read about the core skills you need to have or develop to make your business a success in the sections below, from commitment to self-motivation. But remember that although starting up does demand an array of talents, the trade off is the freedom and flexibility of running your own show.

Commitment

Can you work incredibly hard, all day, every day? Before you answer 'Yes of course!', just think about the implications for a moment, bearing in mind the words of **Bob Pierce**, joint managing director of online style emporium Pupsnuts.com: 'There will be more work and it will be more difficult than you can possibly imagine. And it will be around you all the time.'

So, it isn't about putting in a couple of late nights, or making an extra effort for a one-off project. By launching your first business, you could find yourself on the wrong end of a potentially gruelling timetable that could go on for weeks and weeks, even months and months. Or, in the case of **Dylan Wilk**, a whole year. When Wilk was setting up Gameplay.com during the 1990s, he claims he was permanently 'doing 24/7... I was working every single second of every single minute,' he says. 'Sure I had to give up a few things, like sleeping and eating, but I was willing to do that.' Are you prepared to make the same commitment?

> **Sure I had to give up a few things, like sleeping and eating, but I was willing to do that**

Motivation

Linked to your level of commitment is your ability to be motivated, and most crucially, self-motivated. This is not the same as being pushed to do something because someone else tells you to or because someone else demands you do it. This motivation has to come from within you. It has to come from your energy, your discipline, your focus. This is difficult enough when things are going well, but what about when things are going badly?

'It's really tough', admits Wilk, who recalls just a few things that went wrong in the early days. 'We were burgled around eight times; we had tens of thousands of pounds in stock stolen; we had someone register our name and then try to slap a writ on us – that was pretty hairy; we had moments where it looked like the business was going to go under. And, at times, I didn't really know what to do.' So even the most determined of entrepreneurs have moments when they are not sure what direction to take. Even if they do know, some have simply had enough and can no longer be bothered taking it.

'This can affect all of us', admits **Alan Denbigh**, executive director of the Teleworkers Association. 'To succeed in self-employment you have really got to be a self-starter.' Wilk couldn't agree more, adding: 'You have to really believe in yourself and decide that, no matter what, you will not be beaten.'

Emotional resilience

Belief in yourself is not enough though. You must also have a capacity to work for yourself, often by yourself. At first this might sound like bliss, with no more irritating workplace politics and tiresome gossip. But what about the banter and the social life? More seriously, what about the brainstorming of solutions and the bouncing around of ideas? Won't you miss all this? If you are like most solo entrepreneurs, then you most certainly will. 'The simple fact is that it can be very lonely', says **Andrew Ferguson,** founder of the Breakthru Centre, which counsels people on new ways to work. 'You can feel, professionally at least, very isolated at times.'

You can feel, professionally at least, very isolated at times

Gwen Rhys, founder and director of a networking organisation called EW agrees. 'But there is a solution', she says. 'You need to build up a virtual team. You need to develop a circle of colleagues that you communicate with in much the same way you did in the office, except now it may be over the phone, via email, or face to face, but once a month rather than

CASE STUDY
AMBITION 24HOURS AND THE FLYING PIGS

When you list the qualities needed to become a successful entrepreneur, determination and self-motivation would come pretty high up on the list. If you looked around for someone who embodies such virtues, you would be hard-pressed to find anyone to top **Penny Streeter**, founder of Ambition 24Hours, an employment agency for medical staff that she launched in 1996.

Defying the odds, South African-born Streeter, a single mother, has overcome a lack of finance and negative attitudes to build up a company that, in less than 10 years, has an annual turnover of £60 million.

Having your bank manager write the words 'Pigs will fly' on your business plan or experiencing clients looking over your shoulder as you enter a meeting, looking for a more senior male to talk to, would crush lesser people. But for Streeter, the adversity she faced did not dent her belief that she could start up on her own and develop her idea into a world-class, multi-million-pound business.

With successive bank managers looking down their noses at her business plan, Streeter had to build up her firm without any funding at all. To make ends meet, she worked weekends as a children's entertainer. 'It was essential for our funding,' she says. 'We've never had any outside investment or loans for the business – initially because no one was interested in financing us!'

Looking back at her early struggles, it seems slightly astonishing that Streeter has built up Ambition 24Hours into a business with such a big annual turnover, around 13,500 healthcare staff on its books and 19 branch offices.

'We relied very much on our own resources, with no outside help, so we made mistakes, but we never made the same ones twice,' she says. 'Ultimately, you have to rely on yourself and be prepared to make the big decisions, although now we have an excellent management team.'

EXPERT OPINION

WHAT MAKES AN ENTREPRENEUR?

Shell Live Wire runs through the big attributes. How do you compare?

The problem

Entrepreneurship is something that seems to be on television screens constantly, and more people are becoming interested in the benefits of starting their own business, be it to try to make their fortune – or more often these days, to fit into their lifestyle. The word 'entrepreneur' seems to be bounded around everywhere! But, starting a new business is unlike any other job – it's an enterprise, it's an adventure, it's a once in a lifetime decision. You will be in many new and often difficult situations which you need to be able to overcome. Your future will be in your own hands – you are well and truly in control!

- Can you trust yourself with this responsibility?
- Will you give yourself the job?

The answer: thorough self-evaluation

You will have your own view of who you are. But what about how others see you? Your parents, your friends, your colleagues, your work mates, your boss may all have a different image of you, and there may be elements of truth in what they think. One great trait of entrepreneurs is to be reflective on themselves. There's no single stereotype, but experience has shown that there are some things that successful self-employed people often have in common. Think for a moment what qualities might be important; then compare your list with this one.

- Persistent, enduring, have loads of stamina
- Aware
- Positive, optimistic, enthusiastic
- Tenacious
- Logical, perceptive, organised, realistic, responsible – good at getting things done
- Patient
- Have a sense of humour
- Willing
- Creative, imaginative – always coming up with new ideas
- Assertive
- Out-going, confident, cocky
- Flexible, adaptable
- Open-minded – able to take advice
- Forgiving
- Sociable, approachable, good leader – can win people over instead of getting their backs up
- Single-minded, decisive, independent
- Communicator – able to get a point across
- Opportunist, risk taker, ambitious

- Hard working, committed, determined, 'get up and go' type
- Self-motivated
- Self-belief, individual – not afraid to stand out from a crowd, or of what others think ·
- Recognise importance of quality

How do you compare? How many of those qualities do you possess? You don't need all of them. You may discover that you do possess many of them but have never had to demonstrate it before. It's not easy to get a true picture of yourself. You have to work at it. You need to do the following:

Be honest – You are not selling yourself to an employer. There's no point in conning yourself. Face up to what you really are, not what you wish you were. If you don't feel ready for self-employment now, perhaps you will in a few years time, with more experience and qualifications. Remember you need to do what the customer wants not what you think they want!

Get an opinion – Different people have different views of you. Talk to someone who you know well, and trust. Get a good range of views. Try to sort out when they have a point (even if it makes you feel uncomfortable) and when they are just trying to make you fit in with an image that happens to suit them. Often, it's a mixture of both.

Prove it – Wherever possible, look for an example of the qualities that you have identified. If you think you are an organiser, what have you organised? Remember to look at all aspects of your life, not just work experience and qualifications.

Keep notes – Everyone, young or old should have a file on themselves. It's useful for planning, as well as applying for jobs. The great thing about enterprise is that it helps you to grow and develop as a person. You need to keep tabs on yourself – what are your strengths and weaknesses? What do you need to learn?

The future for entrepreneurs in the UK is somewhere that will be immensely exciting, where more and more people make a specific choice on leaving education to start their own enterprise and create their own futures. New technology will allow relatively small businesses to flourish further, and because of their size they will be able to react to changes in the market and compete with larger established corporations, challenging them at every level. The small firm will dominate as time goes on flourishing in a knowledge-based economy – not only in the UK but all over the globe. Most importantly we will see entrepreneurs who care about their surroundings and environment, entrepreneurs who have a social conscience and a drive to make the world a better place. Have you got what it takes?

every day. You also need to make sure that you do get out there and mix with people. It is worth joining a professional group you connect with, even if it is only to learn that there are others who have been through what you're going through and identify with how you're feeling. In itself this can be a great source of support.' So this shouldn't put you off altogether. But you need to be aware that there will be some lonely times.

Optimism and opportunism

All this talk about what can go wrong may sound daunting. Facing this kind of onslaught, the last thing you will probably expect to be feeling is optimistic. However, Gameplay's Wilk says that this is exactly what you have to be. 'There is no point doing something if you think it will not work,' he says. 'But sometimes you just have to think of ways of making it work better.'

Ferguson of the Breakthru Centre is equally encouraging. 'It's an opportunity to do something you've always wanted to do but never quite found anyone to pay you to do it. It's your big chance to do something that makes you happy.'

How and when to quit your job

Like many entrepreneurs, you have probably come up with the idea to launch your own business while still in employment. As mentioned above, many people actually launch businesses into a similar market to that which they were previously working as an employee. Of course, starting up by yourself will have serious ramifications on your existing job, and you have probably decided to quit it. But what is the best time to hand in your notice, and what exactly do you say to your boss?

A lot of research and planning will need to be put into your business before you can even think about giving up the nine-to-five routine, and more importantly, a monthly salary. Continuing to earn while you're

> " Continuing to earn while you're planning the business will allow you to save up some cash to act as a buffer "

planning the business will allow you to save up some cash to act as a buffer. That way you will be able to focus your attention on the business rather than worrying about next month's gas bill.

Tina Jesson put away half her salary for two years before quitting her job to set up property development company Home Stages, so she had personal income to cushion her through the first year of the business. She spent two years researching and planning, so her move from employee to business owner was a gradual one. 'I was spending about 30 hours a week on the business. I told my company that I either wanted to go part-time or leave, and I guess they thought that by allowing me to work part-time they could keep my skills for a while,' she explains.

Before you make the leap to self-employment, get as much done as you possibly can. You may have been using your spare room to sell a couple of items a week through your website while you were working, but if you're going to make a living out of it, perhaps you need to think about commercial premises. You might also want to use this period to prove the business model, through an eBay shop, or some other form of e-commerce selling and marketing. Potential investors will have far more confidence in an idea that has been tested.

Ask yourself if your revenue predictions are accurate, too. If you've budgeted for selling more than is realistic, you could find yourself in a

! TIPS
LEAVING YOUR JOB

! Don't do it immediately after your 'eureka!' moment
! Get as much preparation done as possible first
! Consider going part time for a period
! Make sure you have at least some customers before ditching your income stream
! Keep your venture quiet before you leave if it's in a similar market
! Check your contract for possible legal issues relating to your startup
! Talk to your boss about your idea if he could be a possible customer
! Leave on a positive note – thank your boss for their support, etc

tight spot when your last pay cheque gets used up. 'You should have some idea of at least two or three potential customers who can provide the beginnings of an income stream,' says **John Lees**, author of *How to Get a Job You'll Love* (McGraw-Hill, 2006). 'Only when you get customers saying "yes" to your offer should you really consider making the leap.'

Jeremy Martin, co-founder of men's health drinks brand For Goodness Shakes, says he and his business partner **Stuart Jeffreys** did as much work as possible while still in full-time employment. But eventually you need to make the move. 'It was definitely the right thing to do,' argues Martin, adding that cutting the cord 'commits you 100%. When you make the leap, it's surprising how fear gets you working harder and makes you more committed than ever before.'

If your business is going to compete with the company you work for, then it's probably not a good idea to mention it until you've handed in your notice, if at all. 'It's best to say as little as possible if you're becoming a competitor,' recommends Lees. In addition, if you are likely to compete with the company you work for, you need to check your employment contract carefully for competition clauses, notice periods or anything else that could cause legal problems if you decide to start your own business. If there's nothing threatening in your contract, though, and your employer's biggest worry is losing your skills, it may help to talk about your idea. 'Thank your boss for his or her support,' says Lees. 'Make it clear that you are leaving for entirely positive reasons. Your previous employer could be in a position to refer you new business, so if you can, be as clear as possible about what you plan to do.'

When **Liz Jackson** left to set up Great Guns Marketing, her employers actually provided her with a few days worth of work a week, which gave her crucial income while she was trying to win new clients. The lesson here is don't burn your bridges. There are just as many risks as rewards when setting up your own business, but if you plan your exit carefully, you may just manage to tip the balance in your favour.

Women entrepreneurs

> **The important thing is to not focus on obstacles but on goals**

As a woman interested in starting your own business, you will be faced with a number of stiffer challenges that men, mainly due to your gender. So to help you make sure you're ready for the experience, this section is specially for you.

The 2006 Global Entrepreneurship Monitor (GEM) Report on women and entrepreneurship revealed some interesting characteristics of women's route to self-employment:

- Female entrepreneurs worldwide, for example, are much more likely than men to start their businesses when still employed. This may not only have benefits in terms of resources and social capital, but also act as a safety net, as women typically express less self-confidence in their entrepreneurial ventures than men (although perhaps men are simply far less willing to admit their fears).

> **More than a third of people involved in entrepreneurial activity are women**

- Early-stage entrepreneurship in women continues to grow globally, although startup rates among men are still higher. More than a third of people involved in entrepreneurial activity are women. However, in high-income countries, men are almost twice as likely to be early-stage or established business owners than women.
- Female entrepreneurship is an increasingly important part of the economic profile of any country. But the male/female gap is still significant, especially in high-income countries and technology-intense sectors.
- In addition, the 2004 GEM Monitor showed that independent startup activity among women is 3.1% of the adult female population, but 6% among men. Russia is the only country where the rate of female early-stage entrepreneurship is significantly higher than the male rate.

Regionally, the highest number of female startups is based in London, where 8.4% of the female workforce is self-employed, and female entrepreneurs are least active in the north-east, according to the Labour Force Survey 2003. And finally, a recent White Paper, entitled *The Observed*

Characteristics of Outstanding Women in Business, found that while businesses run by women contribute £70 billion to the UK economy and employ more than a million, there would be 750,000 more female-led startups if rates matched those in the USA.

Finding funding

Access to investment is unfortunately one of the biggest barriers facing female entrepreneurs. Recent eye-opening research from the Women's Enterprise Task Force showed the scale of the problem. The task force found that when starting up, businesses owned by women access an average of only £10,000 worth of funding, compared to £15,000 for men. The task force believes that this disparity is likely to 'constrain business performance'. Furthermore, it has been found that women tend to be charged higher rates of interest when taking out loans – an average of 2.9%, substantially more than the 1.9% average charged to men. **Pam Alexander**, co-chair of the task force, says: 'The undercapitalisation of women-owned businesses results in under performance and slower growth'. For this reason, the task force has said that its key priority will be creating better access to funding and appropriate investment for women.

'We need to work with business support providers and banks to encourage women to be ambitious in their business plans and investment ready', says Alexander. But this isn't to say that women aren't finding funding opportunities. Female entrepreneurs generally make better use of alternative sources of funding, with the British Chambers of Commerce (BCC) finding that although women put in less of their own money than men in the startup stage (£10,106 compared with £13,500), 27% of women will obtain further funding from family, compared with just 17% of men. What's more, 33% of women-owned businesses, compared to 20% of men-owned firms, had used government programmes to fund their business startup.

For both men and women, however, the bank is still the main provider of startup finance, funding 46% and 43% of new businesses, respectively. The BCC found there is no statistically significant difference between men and women with regard to usage of bank finance. It makes sense then that there is evidence that banks are waking up to the growth of female entrepreneurship and making more effort to attract female clients.

> **"**
> Women tend to be charged higher rates of interest when taking out loans — an average of 2.9%, substantially more than the 1.9% average charged to men **"**

Prejudice

The world of business is changing. But there's still a lingering attitude that assumes that a successful business is owned by a man. Women, especially young women, often report coming away from meetings or pitches feeling patronised or not taken seriously. As an entrepreneur though, a thick skin is something of a necessity.

Claire Nicholson, co-founder of marketing agency More2, finds her job surprises people even in a social environment. 'When I meet new people socially they often assume you are at home bringing up the children and not running a business,' she says. It's not just Nicholson's gender, but also her age that surprises people, with the combination of the two causing looks of disbelief. 'We set up More2 when I was just 28 and so many people don't expect you to have your own business at that age,' she adds.

Despite these challenges, many female entrepreneurs never experience any form of prejudice or negative reaction on account of their gender. 'I do feel that male/female prejudice is a bit of a red herring – the main problem with startups is access to good advice and supportive subsidised incubators, as well as government bureaucracy, anti-competitive practices from large incumbents,' says **Katie Allcott** of FRANK Water. 'I am aware of a few situations where it has taken longer for me to gain respect, but I think this is not just because I am a woman, but also because I am considered to be young and that I run a very ethical, values-driven company.' It's important to remember that every entrepreneur faces specific problems, and whatever you battle through will leave you even more determined to succeed. As Allcott articulates: 'Varying problems exist for tall people, short people, thin people, fat people, men, women, young people, old people – if you look for them. But the important thing is to not focus on obstacles but on goals.'

Self-confidence

Findings do show that women are more put off by the fear of failure when it comes to starting a business. Women are less positive about their skills, according to **Prowess**, and perceive fewer opportunities than men. However, this may just demonstrate that women are more honest or realistic than their male counterparts! Entrepreneurs are by their nature confident people who like taking risks, and anyone with these qualities won't be held back long by a fear of failure. 'I think that as long as women have plenty of support around them they can be very successful,' says Allcott. 'That's support from friends and family as well as colleagues, support agencies, bank managers, suppliers and customers. Whether a man or woman, you do need a reasonable amount of self-confidence, even more so, total confidence and passion for the business or idea itself... then with good support networks you have a great start.'

Bring it on! Women entrepreneurs have their say

CLAIRE YARWOOD-WHITE

Yarwood-White

'When I was younger, "entrepreneur" was a scary word! In my 20s, I thought business was a secret that no one had let me in on, and running a business was best left to the big boys. As I worked my way through various companies and bosses as an employee, I realised that much of the secret was common sense, making good decisions at the right time and that confidence played a huge part in success. As my own confidence grew, I began to think: "I could do that."'

GEMMA STONE

Rock and Ruby

'I am probably part of the smallest statistic of entrepreneurs — under 30, female, mother of two, without a degree. But I work hard, enjoy what I do and am motivated to be a loving and giving mother and a successful businesswoman. If there are barriers in my path then I say: "Bring it on!"'

CLAIRE NICHOLSON

More2 (integrated marketing agency)

'Within a few months of starting up the agency, I discovered I was expecting my first child. My husband was studying full time, so money was extremely tight and life was very stressful. At the beginning, to succeed you have to work every spare hour and with a small team you have to be prepared to do everything. Even now that the agency is five years old I wrestle with how little I see my two daughters. My top tip is work on the train. I save work to do on my journey home so that when I step in the door I can be a mum. Once they are in bed I can open up my laptop and get back to work.'

SARAH TREMELLEN

Bravissimo

'I never saw a ceiling for it, I just thought it would be fun, setting up from scratch and making something from nothing.'

ANITA RODDICK

The Body Shop

'No one talks of entrepreneurship as survival, but that's exactly what it is.'

RACHEL ELNAUGH

Red Letter Days

'Key is understanding what type of entrepreneur you are, and then doing business in a way that is true to yourself, and above all, one that brings you personal happiness and fulfilment.'

KATIE ALLCOTT

FRANK Water

'Varying problems exist for tall people, short people, thin people, fat people, men, women, young people, old people — if you look for them... But the important thing is to not focus on obstacles but on goals.'

CASE STUDY
BABYLICIOUS AND
THE LAW OF HARD KNOCKS

Many prominent entrepreneurs have suffered setbacks on the path to success. Some have had to overcome a severe lack of funds, others have had to battle against negative attitudes. But few business owners have had to deal with as much adversity as **Sally Preston**, founder of Babylicious – www.babylicious.co.uk

Having endured an acrimonious divorce, she was diagnosed with skin cancer. She chose this turbulent period in her life to launch Babylicious, a frozen baby food business. But the knocks kept coming for Preston – someone deliberately tried to steal her business' name and a hoax caller untruthfully told her retailer customers that the company was under investigation by the Advertising Standards Authority.

Preston remains tight-lipped about the identity of the malicious character who plagued her business, but admits it was a dispiriting time.

'It was the ongoing knock-backs – you can take one and you can take two, but they keep coming at you and it's very wearing after a while and it begins to wear you down,' she says. 'I think you have to be like one of those Weeble things, you get pushed over and you constantly keep picking yourself back up again.'

To her credit, Sally has made a stunning success of Babylicious since the launch of the company in September 2001. The business has picked up a host of awards and expanded overseas. The various setbacks have certainly not defeated the ambitious and refreshingly honest Sally, who is planning further expansion over the coming year.

So you've made your decision...

You started reading this chapter with an idea that you think you can turn into your own business, or because you simply want to be your own boss. If you now think that the trials and tribulations of entrepreneurialism are not for you, then simply close the book and walk away, safe in the knowledge that you've at least carefully considered setting up on your own. However, if the last few pages have made you even more determined to launch your own company, then it's fair to say that you have decided to join the ranks of entrepreneurialism, and there's no better time to start planning your next move than the present.

So where should you start? The next step is easy – simply keep on reading and you will be guided through the key steps of starting your own business, from researching your idea to writing a business plan and raising finance and how to deal with the upheaval. Work–life balance is an over-used term you will hear from every business coach and all the business startup services you're ever likely to encounter. But if you've worked 20 hours a day for two months in a row you will be physically and mentally drained and appreciate the need for striking that balance.

In the next chapter you will be taken through the research stage, which will help you to test drive your idea to see if it's commercially viable and if there's the market demand for it. Then you will learn how to make cost and revenue forecasts and to present your idea in the form of a business plan that you can then take to prospective business investors and partners. Further chapters deal with naming your venture and how to register that name, as well as the format your business should take, from a limited company or partnership to a sole trader. On top of this, there's advice on developing the key skills you will need when starting up. For instance, there's a guide on safely negotiating the minefield that is tax and the practices, products and systems that will help you organise your accounts efficiently. If you're raising finance, there are plenty of sources from which to choose. There's a rundown of the advantages and disadvantages of using different financiers, from high-street banks to venture capitalists and business angels – and how best to impress them while still getting a good deal. There's also guidance on whether to work from home or seek premises, along with the right space for your business and how to get the best from your chosen location.

You will also find advice on how to get the most from your working day and ways that you can ensure your time is put to good use, such as the best way to take calls when you are in a meeting with clients. Do you need to use a virtual secretary, and would it be cost effective? There are tips on tracking down reliable and affordable suppliers, which can be one of the hardest tasks for new business owners, as well as talking to other entrepreneurs. Networking is a word that often strikes fear into the hearts of new business owners. Walking into a room of people who've been in business for decades can be quite daunting. But select the right networking groups and a format that you're comfortable with, and it will help you build a valuable source of contacts that can help to drive your business forward.

Word of mouth may not be enough to get your business working to its full capacity and it's likely that you will need at least some marketing and public relations (PR). There are clear explanations of all the options available to you, what is most likely to prompt the best response rates and advice on how to handle PR companies. You will also gain an insight into the type of marketing and PR that you can do for yourself for very little money.

If you are launching an internet business, website design, marketing and internet connectivity will be important issues from day one. Even if you're not starting an internet business, you might want a website or even to sell online too. You will find guidance on the process of getting a website designed from one of the millions of companies now specialising in the service. There's help on deciding the level of complexity your website needs, along with advice on how to drive traffic to it.

If you will need to take on one or two people straightaway, do you think you are experienced enough at recruiting? You might know a friend of a friend who can help out, but you need to make sure that you can entrust this person with your business' future. So read on and you will be taken through all the issues involved in recruiting and employing staff, along with health and safety issues, employer liability insurance, virus protection and general employment legislation. Red tape is the bugbear of every business owner, but the weight of the problem is significantly lessened if you're organised and know what's expected of you.

ACTION POINT
THE MAIN HURDLES TO OVERCOME WHEN STARTING UP

When you're considering starting your own company, you're bound to fret over lots of things – from what you will call it and where to base it to how to prepare the best business plan. Once you've launched your company, all these concerns will be replaced by a number of others that you may not have considered previously – and certainly not if you used to hold a permanent position. And they all revolve around finance. Here, **Simon Smith**, general manager of MYOB UK Business Division, the accounting software supplier, highlights the six main concerns facing those starting out in business today. And if you still want to go it alone after reading through these fears, you really are ready to become an entrepreneur.

'We recently asked our customer base to tell us about the major hurdles they faced when starting out and found some common concerns emerged,' says Smith:

A LACK OF ACCOUNTING KNOWLEDGE: It is unusual for small business owners to have an accounting background, which is often a cause for concern, given that failing to keep records up to date can seriously impact the survival of a business. However, there are easy-to-use software packages that will take the pain of accounting away from the business owner, leaving you time to focus on running and growing your business.

PLANNING FOR FUTURE GROWTH: Many small business owners want to grow their business, however as it expands the basic needs of the business may change. This is particularly true in relation to accounting software and I would advise that small business owners consider the future growth of their company before investing in new technology.

Software should be easily scalable and have a clear upgrade path so that it can easily accommodate changes as your business grows.

A LACK OF TECHNICAL KNOWLEDGE: It is necessary to embrace new technology in order to make the most of your business, yet many people struggle in this area. There are courses available to get you on track, and also many vendors will offer support from their team of experts to keep you on track and out of trouble.

TRAINING AND CONSULTANCY: This is a simple question of whom do you turn to for help. Starting out on your own can be a lonely journey and I would encourage small business owners to seek out professional support. Many accountants specialise in providing such services and can add significant value to a small business.

VAT CONFUSION: Many people are unaware of the difference between the cash or accrual methods of accounting for VAT. So put simply, the accrual method means that you pay tax when the invoice is raised, even if you have not received the payment, while the cash basis allows you to pay VAT on sales when you receive payment from your customer. Getting professional advice on such issues could improve cash flow for your business.

CHANGES IN GOVERNMENT LEGISLATION: Small businesses can often be unaware of government incentive schemes which can be of benefit to them. Take for example the PAYE online filing (payroll year end reports) incentive scheme that was introduced by HM Revenue & Customs (HMRC) department. According to an MYOB survey, 27% of small businesses in the UK were still unaware of the cash-back incentive for filing PAYE returns online two months before the deadline. Small business owners should use the services of their accountant to keep up to date with changing legislation.

3.0

RESEARCH

WHAT'S IN THIS CHAPTER

■ Once you have got an idea for a business and are
sure you're made of the right entrepreneurial stuff,
the next step is to start planning your venture to help
you gain any investment you may need and to make
sure everything is in place for a successful launch.
Find out as much as you can about the market you
propose to launch into, your potential customers and
any rivals that are already trading in your chosen
area. This information will tell you whether your idea
is viable provide key data for your business plan and
prove invaluable when you start up. So read on find
out how to approach market research…

What is market research?

Properly targeted market research is the key to a thriving business and can make the difference between success and failure, say experts. Market research can be a cost-effective way of discovering what your customers want and matching products and services to this demand. Even better, it can help a business grow by keeping you up to date with current trends and with what your competitors are doing. Knowing the state of the market and how to improve your position within it can revolutionise your businesses but this can only be achieved by carrying out proper market research. 'Unfortunately, most companies shy away from market research, and then they wonder why they don't succeed,' says Simon Wieremiej, spokesperson for the British Market Research Association (BMRA).

If you are looking to start a company, now is the time to realise the importance of effective market research. Once you come up with the business idea you'd like to pursue, it pays to carry out the necessary research into the potential viability of your venture. First, it will provide key material for your business plan, which is an essential part of attracting the investment you may need to launch your business. Second, it would help you assess the chances of success of an activity that is likely to take up a lot of your time and money.

Just because there may be a lot of companies already succeeding in the area you'd like to enter, doesn't automatically mean you are on to a winner. The competition may be too fierce and there may not be a demand for what you are offering in the specific location you plan to launch your version of the business. Equally, if your 'eureka' moment has produced a highly original idea that you think could make a good business, there may be little or no competition around, but this could be for a very good reason. In either case, marketing research can help provide the answers.

> "Most companies shy away from market research, and then they wonder why they don't succeed"

> "If you are looking to start a company, now is the time to realise the importance of effective market research"

One key area you need to look at is demand:

- Do customers want what you plan to offer them, and if not is it simply down to their profile in the particular location where you planned to launch?
- If there is demand, can you put a figure on it?

You also need to examine the competition:

- What other companies are offering something similar to what you are proposing?
- How successful are they?
- Can you improve on their offer, or strategically differentiate your offer from theirs, while maintaining demand?

Other research can provide key information on pricing, location, size of premises and more. Securing these data early on not only shows potential sources of investment that you are serious about your proposal, but also reassures them that you are organised and motivated, making them more likely to part with their cash. And, of course, it also increases the chances of your launch being a success, if after carrying out the research you decide to go ahead.

! TIPS

THREE FACTS ABOUT MARKET RESEARCH

! It's one thing recognising the importance of market research and quite another carrying it out properly

! Of those companies that do conduct research, many simply don't approach it in the right way

! This can be just as dangerous as not doing any research at all, as it produces inaccurate results, which can lead to the wrong business decisions being made and false confidence on the part of the entrepreneur

For many small businesses, the cost of commissioning a market research agency can be prohibitive, so you will most likely want to conduct the basic market research yourself. You should be aware that it covers a great deal more than the lady who stops you in the street with a questionnaire in her hand. Ultimately, depending on the market you're considering entering, you may find that carrying out the research yourself is too complex and time consuming, and that calling in the experts can save you money through producing more accurate results and allowing you to concentrate on your core skills. Initially, though, for the purposes of informing your business plan and providing an early indication of the viability of your venture, your own research could be enough.

Looking for trends

Before guiding you through key market research techniques, here are some useful official startup statistics, published by the Department for Business, Enterprise and Regulatory Reform (BERR), which offer a key insight into the types of business that are on the increase or decline opposite. This information is a useful starting point for you to make a quick assessment of the viability of your idea before embarking on more thorough research, while also informing you of the most popular sectors for business startups. When looking at the sector you intend to enter, consider not only how many businesses were started in the current year, but how it compares with the previous year. Is it a growing market? If so, has that now been fully exploited and will it drop in the coming year? If it's less than in the previous year, why is that? Also consider the changes to the total number of businesses that occurred during the current year. For instance, while around 9,300 new manufacturing businesses were started in 2006, around 10,700 ceased to operate with both figures down 0.3% on 2005. If you're looking to enter a market that's losing businesses, you will need to consider why this is so and research which particular firms are suffering and why. Evaluating the statistics doesn't mean that you shouldn't enter into a sector that is shrinking, but it should alert you to whether important changes are afoot. In addition, you should think about the outside influences that are likely to have affected startup

> **Evaluating the statistics doesn't mean that you shouldn't enter into a sector that is shrinking, but it should alert you to whether important changes are afoot**

Table 1

Enterprises registering and de-registering for VAT by industry, UK, 2006

Thousands

	Registrations		Deregistrations	
	2006	change on 2005	2006	change on 2005
All industries	182.2	0.5	143.1	−0.5
Agriculture, fishing	3.9	−0.1	6.0	1.4
Mining, energy, water	0.2	0.0	0.2	0.0
Manufacturing	9.3	−0.3	10.7	−0.3
Construction	22.9	0.1	15.5	0.5
Wholesale, retail, repairs	34.7	−1.1	29.6	−1.6
Hotels, restaurants	19.2	0.0	13.9	−1.0
Transport, communication	8.6	−0.3	6.8	−0.2
Finance	1.6	−0.2	1.5	0.1
Business services	68.1	1.0	47.5	0.9
Education, health	2.9	0.6	1.5	0.0
Other services	10.9	0.7	9.9	−0.3

Source: BERR Enterprise Directorate (Statistics Team)
1: Where there has been a very small change of 5 businesses or less this is reported in the table as 'no change', in absolute numbers and is denoted as * in the percentage change column

business figures. For instance, how much have the fish, agriculture, hotel and restaurant trades been affected since the foot and mouth epidemic?

National startup statistics are important to consider, but are by no means relevant to every situation. For instance, trends may vary in different parts of the country and at different times. The local economy will also affect your chances of success. Unless you're about to launch on a national scale, probably the most valuable research you can do is to investigate what need exists for your business locally. Look how many other similar businesses are in the area and target places with few companies offering the service or products you're looking to launch, or where there's room for competition, either in terms of better quality service or on price.

There's also the argument that trends should be made and not followed, and there's some truth to this. The telecommunications industry is full of very young bold, and now wealthy, individuals who proved a lot of sceptics wrong, and it can pay to be at the forefront of the latest movement. However, over-confidence can also be perceived as arrogance or naivety, and it's always worth checking the state of the markets even if you then choose to ignore them. Anyone walking into a bank confident about launching in manufacturing but oblivious to the current difficult market in the sector shouldn't expect to be taken seriously.

> **Trends should be made and not followed**

Doing it yourself

A good place to start assessing the potential of your startup idea is the internet. Choose a number of keywords that people who would need your idea would use when looking for companies that provide your potential product or service. Remember to keep a note of these words and phrases as they will prove useful in the future to help with optimising your website. Internet searches should throw up the range of companies across the UK that you will be competing with if you launch. If there are none, you have an original idea – but is there a market for it? If there are lots of competitors, is there room for you? To find this out, assess the

> **There's no better way of testing than by using the services and products directly**

local competition, what they are offering and whether you can improve on this. You can get much of this information from company websites, initially.

Depending on the business you're proposing to launch, in the next level of assessment, get out of the office and check out the competition first hand, either personally or by enlisting the help of others. There's no better way of finding the quality of the competition and how successful they are than by sampling it. For example, if you plan to launch a restaurant or catering business, you need to check out rival establishments for the following:

- How good is the food?
- Is the wine list special?
- Is the service up to scratch?

Also, you should find out your rival's unique selling proposition, and whether you could match it. If you're worried that you are too well known in the area, ask your friends to help out.

If you do your marketing research fully enough, you should be able to organise your business in a way that gives you a clear advantage afterwards. You can even play detective and go on a stakeout to observe how busy your rivals' premises are, and can even subtly question customers about what they are looking for in this kind of business – these after all will be the people you are hoping will buy from you!

You can also investigate the performance of your rival companies by tracking down their annual accounts at Companies House. Although the data are likely to be at least a year old, you can source turnover and profit and loss details, which will give you an idea of how successful each business is. If your rivals are having problems, try to find out why this is so. It could be simply that they are not very good, or that there are simply too many companies offering this service in the area, or that the service isn't in demand.

Finally, there's always room for some background reading either through the local papers, or by visiting the public library. Check out whether your rivals make the most of free editorial coverage, and whether you could dream up a newsworthy item to interest a news editor.

CASE STUDY
MY WORLD JOURNAL
AND THE PRICE GAP

Having come up with an original idea for a business in a niche market, entrepreneur **Iain Row** set up My World Journal, an online service that allows travellers to create a website dedicated to their adventures and experiences. 'One of my best friends went travelling, and didn't want a leaving present – he had no room in his rucksack and felt it was heavy enough already,' explains Iain. 'I was working as a freelance web designer at the time, so I decided to make him a website that he could update easily from anywhere in the world. Setting it up cost about £1,500 initially, which I was able to cover by reinvesting the small profit I'd

made from the freelance web design, so I never had to borrow any money.'

Everything seemed to be pointing towards a successful launch of the new business, but Iain suffered a blow that many firms never recover from – he simply couldn't get any sales. It took Iain six long months to get his first sale – a depressing barren spell, which he admits caused many sleepless nights. However, advice from a friend alerted him to the problem, and also to the fact that he should have done more research before launching.

'First, I halved the price at the suggestion of a friend, who was himself travelling around the world,' recalls Iain. 'As he pointed out, a night in a hostel cost less than my cheapest product! I was able to drop the price because the marginal cost of each journal is very low, the fixed costs set the price, and you need the volume to recoup them. Then, I offered a free seven-day trial. The main problem was that, as a unique product, no one had ever seen a World Journal before. Most people have never had their own website, and are understandably reluctant to pay for something that might not be worth the money. The free trial allows them to experience all the features, and see how easy it is to use, with no commitment.

I should've done better research on prices before I started,' he admits. 'I approached it from the wrong angle – I was charging businesses £40 an hour for web development, so giving people a website for the same price per year seemed like a bargain to me. However, my customers obviously thought differently. Also, it took me far too long to realise that I needed to offer a free trial. I'm still kicking myself about that – I got my first sale within a week of implementing it.'

Iain has managed to turn things around since those difficult days, and My World Journal is now thriving.

CASE STUDY
PRIDE VALLEY FOODS
CUSTOMER TRIAL

Pride Valley Foods was founded in 1990 by **Hossain Rezaei**. The firm supplies speciality breads to some of the biggest suppliers in the country, including Tesco and Marks & Spencer. Based in Seaham, County Durham, the business now employs 250 staff and has, on average, doubled in size every year.

Rezaei attributes his success to research and planning. Before he launched the business, Rezaei researched the market and made sure that his product would be a hit with customers. Instead of making the product and then selling it to retailers, Rezaei went to the customers to find out which breads they would buy. 'People think that marketing is selling. It isn't. It is finding out what the customer wants and selling it to them,' he says. Armed with detailed market research, Pride Valley was in a position to go to the major retailers and say this is what your customers want.

'If you have the research to back it up, they can't not put it on the shelves,' says Rezaei. 'It is finding out what the consumer wants, making it and then they are bound to pick it up. You can't sell a luxury item to someone who doesn't want to pay for it. There is no point in trying to sell a cappuccino for £3 to someone who wants a plastic cup and a coffee for 25p.'

While Rezaei had the financial clout to carry out some extensive research, it doesn't need to cost a lot. It may simply be a case of adding a couple of weeks to your start and having some friends or family standing in the high street observing what is selling and what is not. 'It is the cheapest thing to do and it is the most important thing to do,' says Rezaei.

The cost of setting up a business can run to thousands of pounds and if it is going to be the main source of your income, you can't afford to start without having done the research. Once he was certain that the product would find favour with the customers, Rezaei then started to plan his company's growth.

Some pubs and restaurants, for example, thrive by being media-friendly. Could you dream up some publicity stunts of your own?

Primary research

Long-winded questionnaires are likely to put respondents off, and will distort the response

Primary research is research that you can conduct yourself or commission someone else to do for you, instead of using information that is already published. You can carry out research into your market and competition using the internet as mentioned previously, or through direct contact with your potential customers. The latter falls into two broad types: quantitative research, which focuses on a broad cross-section and produces a numerical result, such as '36% of the target audience think this', and can produce useful figures to throw at a potential investor; and qualitative research, which is more in-depth, often using a smaller, but representative, sample, and discovers not only what people do, but why they buy a certain product, how they feel about it and how they would like to see it improved.

An example of qualitative research is a focus group. You gather a small number of people who represent a cross-section of your target market for a discussion with an assigned leader to assess their opinions of the product or service you'll be offering. If this can include giving the focus group members first-hand experience of that product or service, their opinions will be better informed. To entice people to attend a focus group, you will need to give them some kind of inducement, such as a small payment or gift. A simple direct survey of your target audience (the bigger sample, the better) is an example of quantitative research, where you either send questions out to a database (either by post or through email), go doorstepping or ask people in the street.

Michael Warren, former director general of the Market Research Society (MRS) and now a freelance researcher and consultant, emphasises that it is misleading to suggest that one kind of research suits certain goods and services better than others. 'Qualitative and quantitative research are complementary to each other, and should be used together,' he advises. 'Qualitative research, in particular, can be used to give a greater understanding of the figures.' The key to success for both qualitative and quantitative research, though, is the kind of questions asked and how they are put across. So a properly devised questionnaire can be an invaluable marketing tool, as long as you avoid the common pitfalls. A good market research agency with experience in your sector can help with this, because you need to take care in drawing up the questions. Alternatively you can consult marketing guides for advice, but bear in mind that this is something of a skill and getting it wrong can mean you would have wasted any effort you put into doing the research.

Simon Wieremiej, spokesperson for the BRMA, says questions such as 'Would you buy this product?' can give misleading answers. 'The answer might be "Yes", but they could mean that they would pay £1 whereas the price might actually be £10,' he explains. So avoid closed questions with yes/no answers, as you're likely get more information by eliciting a fuller response. Warren is equally cautious. 'In sectors such as fast-moving consumer goods, where market researchers are trying to explore the image of one client's products against those of its rivals, it is usual for respondents to be asked about other products, some of which they may never have used,' he says. 'You might ask them about a range of variables, including smoothness, price, levels of satisfaction, but you have to be careful about what you compare the product to. Asking people how a new car, say, compares to a Rolls-Royce really gets up respondents' noses because they have probably never driven a Rolls.'

ACTION POINT
KEY STEPS TO DOING YOUR OWN RESEARCH

Whichever type of primary research you decide to undertake, there are a number of factors you should bear in mind before you start:

KISS (KEEP IT SIMPLE, STUPID!)

Long-winded questionnaires are likely to put respondents off, and will distort the response – the only respondents may be those with nothing better to do that day, which may not be your target market. 'Telling them that a survey will take five minutes is likely to get a better response than one lasting 25 minutes,' says Warren. 'If it does last longer than that, it is bad for the industry and not good for your product image.'

CHOOSE A REPRESENTATIVE SAMPLE

It's no good working hard on a producing an good questionnaire, if you present it to the wrong people, so you need to make sure that your 'sample' represents a cross section of your potential customers.

CIRCULATE THE QUESTIONNAIRE APPROPRIATELY

Via the internet is usually the best way to do this, unless you are a retailer or caterer, when you can hand them out to your customers.

OFFER A PRIZE DRAW FOR COMPLETED QUESTIONNAIRES

Remember that a low response rate will distort figures, and often people need an incentive to complete questionnaires, because they take up valuable time.

RESPECT CONFIDENTIALITY

The Marketing Research Society's Code of Conduct specifies that respondents should not be misled over what they are being asked about. Do not use their responses for follow-up sales. The customer who completes a questionnaire in your restaurant will not take kindly to telephone calls the next morning.

Secondary research

Secondary research is information others have acquired and already published which you may find relevant, as mentioned earlier with respect to BERR startup statistics or Mintel business sector reports. Access to this secondary market research data may be yours for the asking and cost you only an email, letter, phone call, or perhaps a nominal fee for copying and postage. Much of it is entirely free and available to search for on the internet. Good sources include websites of trade associations, government departments and market research firms, which will usually charge for general market profiles and more specific information.

Many websites, sponsored by a variety of organisations, can provide you with the business information you'll need at the beginning, a jump-off place for more in-depth research for your business and marketing plans. Many industries are blessed with an active trade association that serves as a vital source of industry-specific information. Such associations regularly publish directories for their members, and the better ones include statistical information that tracks industry sales, profits, ratios, economic trends and other valuable data. Find out about and contact possible associations, and visit their websites to see what information is available. When in doubt, call or email the industry association offices and communicate with the managers.

Industry-specific business magazines can offer a wealth of information on your proposed venture and your market. Aside from the major general-interest business publications, such as *Business Week* and *The Economist*, many specialty publications look at specific industries. Tim Berry and Doug Wilson's book *On Target: The Book On Marketing Plans* advise 'specialism is an important trend in the publishing and internet businesses. Dingbats and Widgets may be boring to the general public, but they are exciting to Dingbat and Widget manufacturers who read about them regularly in their specialised magazines. The titles are an important medium for industry-specific advertising, which is important to readers as well as advertisers. The editorial staff of these magazines have to fill the space between the adverts. They do that by publishing as much industry-specific information as they can find, including statistics,

> "Industry-specific business magazines can offer a wealth of information on your proposed venture and your market"

KIRSTY'S STORY
AS FOCUS GROUPS GO,
THEY WERE REALLY USEFUL

To refine her product, **Kirsty McGregor**, founder of parenting website Entertainthe
kids.com, decided to arrange around nine special preview evenings attended by
childcare experts to get feedback on her site, to make sure it was right for her target
market.

'We spent days on end collating address lists, stuffing envelopes, and sticking
stamps to send out a 7,000 mailing inviting those who work with children (nurseries,
kids clubs, childminders, football clubs, primary teachers, tutors, etc) to our preview
evenings. There were some good ideas voiced by the attendees, many of which we
incorporated into the site prior to the launch.

'It was incredibly nerve-racking. I'm normally so confident, and have such a strong
belief in the site. But just prior to every preview evening start time I got so nervous.
Would anyone show up? What would they think of it? Would they tell us something
that we hadn't realised that would make the site useless, or certainly not as good
an idea as we thought it was? Your self-confidence plummets, so you have to pull
yourself up by the bootstraps, smile and wait to see what happens.

'On the whole they have been very positive, although we had a real wobble one
evening when at 6.30pm, the start time, no one had arrived. Thankfully that wasn't
the case by 6.40pm.'

forecasts and industry profiles. Consulting these magazines or websites
can sometimes produce a great deal of business and market forecasting,
along with key economic information.' Spending time researching the
relevant media now will pay dividends later.

If you don't know which magazines focus on your business area,
the best place to start looking is on the internet. For traditional printed
directories, several good reference sources list magazines, journals and

other publications. They also offer indexes to published articles which you can use to search for the exact references you need. These will be kept in the reference section of most libraries. Once you have identified the right magazines, contact the editorial departments using their website, phone number and published contact information. Use the indexes to identify useful published information. When you find an index listing for an article that forecasts your industry or talks about industry economics or trends, jot down basic information on the publication and ask your local library if it has a copy or contact the title directly. Many business magazines will send back issues free, or allow you to go into their offices and consult them there.

Market research agencies

Sharing the cost of the survey with other organisations can save money

For many startups, the costs of using an agency may be prohibitive, and good ones are likely to start at four figures, according to **Michael Warren**. But those costs should be set against the real benefits to your business of getting right the product, the retail layout or new restaurant. Good market research should pay for itself and, as with anything, there are also ways to keep costs down.

First, shop around. The BMRA offers a free helpline and a free service through its website to help you select a market research agency. Contact three or four, outline what you need, then compare prices and service. A good agency should have detailed proposals about ways to carry out the research and should also be happy for you to contact existing or former customers for testimonials.

Sharing the cost of the survey with other organisations, who have their questions included in the same questionnaire, can also help to cut costs.

When approaching an agency, be clear from the outset about what you want to discover, whether it is testing a new product during development, or gauging customer needs and people's responses to different products. Going to a market research agency with a definitive set of objectives, and a good sense of how you will use research results to improve your business, can make the agency's task much simpler.

Understanding your competition

As mentioned previously, finding out about your competition is a key part of the market research you need to carry out before starting up. But collecting information isn't enough, it's also vital that you gain an in-depth understanding of your potential competitors. It's important to know whom you will be competing with for your potential customers' time and money. What are their strengths and weaknesses? How are they positioned in the market? A good competitive analysis varies according to what industry you are looking at and your specific marketing plan and situation, but there are some common themes.

Begin by thinking about the general nature of the competition in your type of business, and how and why customers seem to choose one provider over another:

- Price or billing rates
- Reputation
- Image and visibility
- Are brand names important
- How influential is word of mouth in providing long-term satisfied customers?

For example, competition in the restaurant business might depend on reputation and trends in one part of the market and on location and parking in another. Alternatively, for the internet and internet service providers, speed of connection and response rates to problems might be important. Meanwhile, a purchase decision for a car may be based on style, or speed, or reputation for reliability. For many professional service practices, the nature of competition depends on word of mouth because advertising is not completely accepted and, therefore, not as influential. Is there price competition between accountants, doctors and lawyers?

Next, think about the factors that make the most difference for your business and why:

- How do people choose travel agencies or florists for weddings?
- Why does someone hire one gardener over another?
- Why would a customer choose Starbucks over the local coffee house?
- Why select a Dell computer instead of one from HP or Gateway?

This type of information is invaluable in understanding the nature of competition. Compare your product or service in the light of those factors of competition. For example:

- As a travel agent, your agency might offer better airline ticketing than others, or perhaps it is located next to a major university and caters to student traffic. Other travel agents might offer better service, better selection, or better computer connections.
- The computer you sell is faster and better, or perhaps comes in fruity colors. Other computers offer better price or service.
- Your graphic design business might be mid-range in price, but well known for proficiency in creative technical skills.
- Your car is safer, or faster, or more economical.
- Your management consulting business is a one-person home office business, but enjoys excellent relationships with major personal computer manufacturers that call on you for work in a vertical market in which you specialise.

In other words, you should know how you plan to position yourself in the market. Why would people buy your product or services instead of the others offered in the same general categories? What benefits will you offer at what price, to whom, and how will your mix compare to others? Think about specific kinds of benefits, features and market groups, comparing where you think you can show the difference. Describe each of your major competitors in terms of those same factors. This may include their size, the market share they command, their comparative product quality, their growth, available capital and resources, image, marketing strategy, target markets, or whatever else you consider important. Make sure you specifically describe the strengths and weaknesses of each competitor, and compare them to your own in terms of service, pricing,

! TIPS

WHERE TO FIND KEY MARKET INFORMATION

! The internet
! Trade associations
! Government departments
! Local libraries for reference directories
! Industry magazines
! General interest business titles
! Market research firms

reputation, management, financial position, brand awareness, business development, technology, or other factors that you feel are important. Consider the segments of the market in which competitors operate and their strategy. How much are they likely to affect your business, and what threats and opportunities do they represent?

As indicated earlier, you can find an amazing wealth of market data on the internet. The hard part, of course, is sorting through it and knowing what to keep. Access to competitive information is variable, depending on where you are and the nature of the competition. Competitors that are publicly traded may have a significant amount of information available, as regular financial reporting is a requirement of every serious stock market in the world. Wherever your target is listed for public trading, it has to report data. Competitive information may be limited in situations where your competitors are privately held. If possible, you may want to play the role of a potential customer and gain information from that perspective. Industry associations, industry publications, media coverage, information from the financial community, and their own marketing materials and websites may be good resources to identify these factors and 'rate' the performance and position of each competitor.

CASE STUDY
THE TARGETED APPROACH

For the Six Continents pub company, a change in the make up of drinkers led to it developing a new bar concept. It's hard to imagine a city centre in the UK without an All Bar One, a Pitcher and Piano or a Slug and Lettuce. Love them or loathe them, these modern, spacious, wood-decked bars, filled with smart young professionals, have become a permanent fixture on the UK pub scene. Over the past decade or so, and seemingly from nowhere, this new breed of pub has emerged to dominate city-centre drinking. It's a spectacular business success story, but what are the reasons behind it and, more importantly, what can you as a small business learn from it?

'The first All Bar One opened in December 1994. It was a time of major change in the British pub market, following the gentle, long-term decline of traditional pub goers,' explains **Bob Cartwright**, communications director for Six Continents, the company behind the All Bar One chain. With the traditional customer base of predominately male, blue-collar pub drinkers shrinking, pub companies such as Six Continents realised they had to attract new types of customers. One group in particular stood out – women.

'Shifting social attitudes were changing the role of women at this time. They were taking around 80% of new jobs in knowledge-based businesses and there was a dramatic shift in the age at which they were marrying and having children,' explains Cartwright. These young, women professionals, combined with an ever-expanding group of professional men, had formed a new pub-going market – and it was clear that the existing pubs weren't equipped to serve it. 'We needed female-friendly pubs that young professionals of both sexes would want to visit. From this we came up with some ideas that seem very obvious now, but which were quite revolutionary at the time.'

For a start, the buildings broke the traditional pub mould, with spacious saloons and large windows instead of the usual frosted glass frontage. 'This was so people could walk past and see immediately whether it was the sort of place they would feel comfortable in,' says Cartwright. Behind the bar, things changed as well. 'Beer had always been the traditional pub drink. We decided to have a large choice of wine, displayed very clearly and available to buy by the glass or bottle,' explains Cartwright. 'We also compiled a large [food] menu that

would be attractive to both men and women.' In short, everything about All Bar One was designed with its target market in mind – a lesson that small businesses would do well to take on board, according to **Nick Shrager**, member of the National Council of the Institute of Business Advisors.

'I always explain that you need to focus down on who you want to sell to. Most people starting a business are like drunks with a machine gun,' he says. 'They want to sell to everyone, but this isn't necessarily a good idea. When I owned a pub, I wanted to sell a drink to everyone that walked in. But the fact is that not everyone wants to drink in the same bar as drunks or families with kids, for example. All Bar One focused very much on who their market was and went for it.'

4.0

PLANNING AND FINANCE

WHAT'S IN THIS CHAPTER

- By this point you should have carried out research into the viability of your proposed venture, including having examined your market and looking at customers and competition. With all this data to hand, and convinced that your company will be a success, you now need to start planning the business properly. The best way to do this is to prepare a business plan, which will prove valuable not only in securing any necessary funding, but also in helping you run the company after launch. This can be one of the most daunting aspects of starting up a business, because so much can ride on it. However, if you approach it carefully and logically, and clearly understand each key element, you'll have little to worry about. Read on for a definitive guide to drawing up your business plan and the various types of finance it could help secure…

Why write a business plan?

If there's one thing life teaches us, it's that you can never plan for everything. But that doesn't mean you shouldn't try. Having a well-researched and logical business plan will not only get your venture off the ground, but also keep it on track when it is up and running.

- In the first instance, unless you have a strong plan, you're unlikely to secure any funds and your idea could fall at the first hurdle. Your plan will serve as a structured form of communication to your investors, whether it's the government's Business Link service, the banks or even family and friends, and it will provide reassurance as well as a means for everyone, yourself included, to measure your business' performance.

- Writing a business plan will help you to prioritise what exactly needs to be achieved and by when. Do you need to find premises for your business before you hire staff? Should you be talking to wholesalers before your product has been finished? The answers will be different for each business, but it certainly helps if they are clear in your mind. 'If objectives are clearly flagged up, they are more likely to be achieved,' says **Tim Berry**, president of business planning software company Palo Alto.

- By using your business plan to prioritise key tasks, you can also use it to plan your cash flow. It's vital to establish just how much you intend to spend and when. Whether it's to buy stock, order uniforms, lease equipment or whatever, unless your finances match your requirements at the right moment, your business could stall.

It ought to be clear by now that compiling a business plan should be at the top of your 'to do' list. If you're in a partnership or part of a potential management team, then establish early on whose job it is to write one, and then the same individual should be assigned the task of making the business stick to it. How far ahead to plan will again come down to your own aims and the type of business, but a year, broken down month by month, will be a minimum.

> **It's vital to establish just how much you intend to spend and when**

CASE STUDY
PRIDE VALLEY FOODS AND THE CAREFUL PLAN

Pride Valley Foods was founded in 1990 by Hossain Rezaei. The firm supplies speciality breads to some of the biggest suppliers in the country, including Tesco and Marks & Spencer. Based in Seaham, County Durham, the business now employs 250 staff and has, on average, doubled in size every year. Rezaei attributes his success to research and planning. In the previous chapter, you found out how he went about researching his idea.

His next job was to plan his company's growth, for which he used the Tick Tree method. Starting from the first branch on the tree, Rezaei borrowed a small amount and built the business gradually. Each of the steps must be completed on time and within budget. He illustrated his approach with a household example. If you want to decorate a room in your house, you plan a timetable outlining each of the steps. The first step is to remove the furniture, then you may need another person to help you move it and perhaps need somewhere to move it to. You may need to budget for removal costs, such as £50 to hire a van and the time it will take to move the furniture. Only then can you move on to the next stage.

With Rezaei's business, the figures are larger but the principle is the same. 'You have to borrow £10,000 and then deliver what you said you would do. When you have done that you can go back and borrow more. A lot of people fail because they go straight to step two or three and they haven't got the track record, the experience or the market knowledge,' he says.

This careful planning also ensured that when Pride Valley's factory was destroyed by fire and insurers initially refused to pay out on the policy, Rezaei kept the business running. While keeping sight of his original plan, Rezaei moved back to old premises, handed customers over to competitors and returned to his backers with an emergency plan. Within six months, his business was back on track because Rezaei planned a series of steps to get back to his original plan.

Rezaei believes that any business will succeed or fail on the basis of the three Cs – capital, character and capability. What he didn't add to the list was careful planning – but this has undoubtedly been the key to the success of Pride Valley Foods.

Once you've established responsibility and a timeframe, you need to decide on certain criteria on which your business' success will be determined and how these can be achieved. For instance, it could be hitting a given number of sales by a set date through an aggressive marketing campaign, or expanding to three more product lines through extensive market research. Whatever these achievement criteria turn out to be, you need to think long and hard about them without making too many assumptions. Consider your business failing in two or three years' time and try to imagine the reasons it might do so.

> "Whatever achievement criteria you choose, you need to think long and hard about them without making too many assumptions"

Preparing data for your business plan

Market research will help you create an informed and detailed business plan, which will not only help you gain investment, but also act as a template when you start up. Here is the key data you'll need to compile before you start, some of which you'll be able to get from your market research, discussed in the previous chapter:

Decide the legal structure of your startup

While, understandably, the focus of most entrepreneurs is on their 'idea', it is vitally important that the operational and logistical requirements are not neglected. For example, decisions regarding whether you intend to trade as a sole trader, partnership or limited company are very important. Prior to deciding, enlist the help of a local accountant or Business Link office. You'll find the characteristics of the options in the next chapter. Similarly, issues such as understanding your VAT obligations, registering a trademark or trade name and drafting employment contracts have to be covered.

Manage the numbers

Whether you like figures or not, having a thorough understanding of 'the numbers' that impact your business is a crucial component to running a successful business, particularly at the planning stage. At the outset, it will be important to understand:

- Your startup costs
- Your break-even point
- Your funding requirements
- Your cash flow forecast for the following months.

Identify the right people

Along with financial predictions, the people entrusted with putting the plan into action will be subject to particular scrutiny by potential financiers. Regardless of the entrepreneur's/founder's skill set, he or she will invariably need help. While many non-core activities can be outsourced, certain functions, such as sales, will need full-time attention. You should outline the various skills required to run the business, price them into the model, and also identify any gaps and prospective candidates to fill them.

Clearly define and articulate the customer benefits

Many entrepreneurs fail to clearly articulate the benefits of their new venture. As a result, the term 'elevator pitch' was introduced into modern lexicons as a proposed solution to this. An elevator pitch is your idea, supported by your business model, company solution, marketing strategy and competition, all stated in the length of time it takes for a short elevator ride. This simple idea seeks to force entrepreneurs to think carefully about the language they use when describing their new venture (particularly technology ones). It is also used to remind them that they should remain customer-focused and ensure that they concentrate on describing the benefits.

Get a mentor

Many startup entrepreneurs are paranoid that their idea will be taken and often behave irrationally prior to launch. Usually the idea is closely guarded and only discussed with close confidantes. However, these confidantes (often family or friends) find it difficult to pose sufficiently rigorous questions, because they don't want to offend or they lack the relevant experience or judgement to critically analyse the new venture. Hence, an idea with serious flaws, which could have been rectified early on in the process, can progress before the wheels come off at the most important phase. It is highly recommended that the entrepreneur engages an independent mentor or plan reviewer at an early stage. This person can help hone the idea before it is presented to financiers or bankers.

Key elements of your plan

On a basic level, the plan should at the very least give a description of what your company will sell or the service it will offer, the buyers you will be selling to and just how you'll be filling a gap in the market by touching on pricing and existing competition. For your own benefit, as well as others, it must contain details of how exactly you intend to meet your key objectives, as well as sales forecasts, target dates and who, apart from yourself, is to be responsible for this. Then comes the boring, but just as necessary part. Include a financial analysis that shows clearly where your sources of finance will be coming from (and be honest), a profit and loss forecast, cash flow and balance sheet projections. The key to all this will be striking a balance between covering your business in enough detail, while at the same time keeping the plan clear and concise enough for it to be useful. The most successful business plan will be the one you refer to time and time again, and not the one just sitting on a shelf gathering dust once you've begun trading.

! TIPS

CHAPTERS TO INCLUDE IN YOUR BUSINESS PLAN

- ! Executive summary (including mission statement)
- ! Products and services (detail on your offer)
- ! The market (customer and competitor analysis)
- ! The proposition (why customers will buy from you)
- ! Marketing strategy (how you will get your message across)
- ! Sales strategy (how you plan to convert interest into sales)
- ! Financial data (sales forecast, cost base, profit estimates)
- ! Management and personnel (profiles of key people behind the business)
- ! SWOT analysis (strengths, weaknesses, opportunities, threats)
- ! Ownership and legal structure (shareholders and whether limited, partnership or sole trader)
- ! Summary (brief overview and roundup)

Your business plan should be prepared to a high standard, be verifiable (meaning that you need to be able to back up your statements with facts) and avoid jargon or general position statements. It should offer the reader a combination of clear description and analysis, including a realistic SWOT (strengths, weaknesses, opportunities and threats) test of each area. This will demonstrate to investors that you are realistic about your company's prospects. So make sure you have a full appreciation of the risks, and you know how to grab your market share – all of which, of course, should have been covered in your market research. Here's a guide of the key features of your plan.

The length

The length of a business plan depends on individual circumstances. It should be long enough to cover the subject adequately and short enough to maintain interest. Unless your business requires several million pounds of venture capital and is highly complex, the business plan should be no longer than 15 pages. The British Venture Capital Association (BVCA), the members of which you may well be pitching your plan to, recommends erring on the side of brevity. If investors are interested, they can always call to ask for additional information.

The look

The plan should look professional. Ensure there are no typing, grammar or spelling mistakes. Use graphs and charts where appropriate and titles and subtitles to divide different subject matters. While the aim is to make the plan look good, you should avoid expensive documentation, as this might suggest unnecessary waste and extravagance.

The company

The business plan should detail all the important aspects of your company. It should include information about the market and customers, products or services, the strength of the management team – and if there are any gaps in talent, identify how you will fill them. The plan should also explain how products will be made or services provided. Realistic financial projections should be outlined and you should provide different scenarios for sales, costs and cash flows for both the long and short term.

'What if's and ways out

A number of possible scenarios should be presented, along with how your company would cope in the different situations. These 'What if?' questions will show how your business will react to or counter the effects of an unexpected drop in sales or an increase in costs. The business plan should also detail potential exit strategies.

The executive summary and mission statement

The last thing to be written is the first part of the business plan: the executive summary. This is the most important section and summarises in

> While the aim is to make the plan look good, you should avoid expensive documentation

two pages what you have written in detail in the following 10–15 pages. This is where, among other things, you lay down the company's mission statement – a few sentences encapsulating what the business does for what types of client, your aims for the company and what gives it its competitive edge. The mission statement should combine the business' current situation with your aspirations.

As with the main part of the business plan, the executive summary should be clearly written and powerfully persuasive, yet it should balance sales talk with realism in order to be convincing. It should be no more than 1,000 words and should also state the company's legal status.

Forecasting your sales

> **Sales should close the deals that marketing opens**

Developing your sales forecast isn't as hard as most people imagine. Think of your sales forecast as an educated guess. Forecasting takes good working knowledge of your business and is much more of an art than a science. Don't think you aren't qualified to forecast if you don't have business training, because if you can run a business, then you can forecast its sales. Most people can guess their own business' sales better than any expert device, statistical analysis or mathematical routine. Experience counts more than any other factor.

A business plan should usually project sales by month for the next year, and annual sales for the following three years. This doesn't mean businesses shouldn't plan for a longer term than just three years, it simply means that the detail of monthly forecasts doesn't pay off beyond a year, except in special cases. It also means that the detail in the yearly forecasts probably doesn't make sense beyond three years. It does mean, of course, that you still plan your business for five, 10, and even 15-year time frames; just don't do it within the detailed context of business plan financials. Break your sales down into manageable parts, and then forecast these different elements. Estimate the figures based on line of sales, month by month, then add up the sales lines and add up the months, presenting your estimate graphically in a table or chart. Although charts and tables are great, you still need to explain them. A complete business plan will usually include some discussion of your sales forecast, sales strategy, sales programmes and related information. The text, tables, and charts together will provide some visual variety and ease of use. Remember to position the tables and charts near the text covering the related topics.

Near the sales forecast you should describe your sales strategy, which should deal with how and when to close sales prospects, how to compensate sales people, how to optimise order processing and database management, and how to manoeuvre price, delivery and conditions. It should answer questions such as:

- How do you sell? Through retail, wholesale, discount, mail order or over the phone, for example.
- Do you maintain a sales force?
- How do you train your sales people, and how are they compensated?

> **Make sure you discuss important assumptions in enough detail, and that you explain the background sufficiently**

Don't confuse sales strategy with your marketing strategy. Sales should close the deals that marketing opens. To understand the difference between marketing and sales strategies, think of marketing as the broader effort of generating sales leads on a large scale, and sales as the efforts to bring those sales leads into the system as individual sales transactions. Marketing aims to build the business' image, customer awareness and propensity to buy, while sales involves getting the order.

Your business plan text should summarise and highlight the numbers you have entered in the sales forecast table. Make sure you discuss important assumptions in enough detail, and that you explain the background sufficiently. Try to anticipate the questions your readers will ask. Include whatever information you think will be relevant and that your readers will need. Details are critical to implementation and your business plan should include specific information related to sales programmes.

- How is this strategy to be implemented?
- Do you have concrete and specific plans?
- How will implementation be measured?

Business plans are about results, and generating results depends in part on how specific you are in the plan. For anything related to a sale that is supposed to happen, include it here and list the person responsible, dates required and budgets. All this will make your business plan more real.

SWOT analysis

> **SWOT is an easy, understandable way of identifying key issues and communicating them to others**

SWOT analysis is a method of describing your future company in terms of those factors that will have the most impact on the business. Strengths and weaknesses are internal factors, such as the quality of your product or the skills of your management, whereas opportunities and threats are external factors, which may include the development of a whole new market (opportunity) or the arrival of a clutch of new competitors (threat). SWOT is an easy, understandable way of identifying key issues and communicating them to others, and to make things even simpler to grasp, the typical SWOT analysis is done on a four-cell grid:

Strengths	Weaknesses
•	•
•	•
•	•
Opportunities	Threats
•	•
•	•
•	•

Sometimes it helps to start without the grid and list any issues at all that might affect the business – internal or external, real or perceived. Then, when the flow starts to dry up, organise the chosen items into the SWOT categories. Here's a guide to help you complete the categories.

Strengths

In the first box list all the strengths of your company:

- Why should you succeed?
- What will you do well?
- Why will customers do business with you?
- What distinct advantages does your company offer?

The important consideration is honesty. Avoid being too modest, but also make sure that you are realistic. Any SWOT analysis is essentially subjective, but try for a third-party viewpoint: what strengths does the outsider see? A jump-start trick, especially for a group SWOT session is to begin by brainstorming adjectives that characterise your business, writing them down as quickly as people say them, and then using those words to construct a more considered profile of your company's strengths. If you're the sole proprietor or the prime mover in the business, try starting with a list of your own positive personal characteristics.

Weaknesses

A weakness is something that could seriously impede your company's performance – a limitation or deficiency in resource, skills or capabilities. These could be factors that you will be able to address on launch. For example, a weakness could be a lack of awareness in the marketplace compared with your competition, which means you'll need to promote your company heavily to raise its profile, ideally before you launch the business or immediately after. Also, although you may list your personal knowledge of the market as a strength, the fact that the company will initially be heavily reliant on you could be seen as a weakness. If you can spot the key weaknesses of your proposed venture now, you can address them in time for the launch, and it shows investors that all-important element of realism in your approach. So don't try to disguise weaknesses, simply acknowledge them and ensure you have a strategy in place to tackle them.

Opportunities

Under opportunities think about where the openings are for your business, or the customer needs are not being met by your competitors. You'll probably start with marketing issues, presumably because your business fills a niche or can compete effectively, but do include all the possibilities. For instance, think of the interesting trends in your business sector – in terms of not only markets but also in technology changes, the legislative and regulatory environment and social patterns.

Threats

> **It's important to include a couple of worst-case scenarios... to consider how possible damage may be overcome**

Threats are key impediments that your company will face on launch. What are the more apparant obstacles in your way, both actual and potential? Obvious candidates would include a sudden rush of bad debts or a slack sales period leading to cash flow problems. But try to think further than that:

- What is your competition doing that could take business away from you or stunt your company's growth?
- How might your competitors react to any moves you make?
- What trends do you see that could wipe you out or make your service or product obsolete?
- Might technology changes threaten your products or services?
- What happens if a key customer goes under before paying a sizeable invoice?

It's important to include a couple of worst-case scenarios. Weighing threats against opportunities is not a reason to indulge in pessimism, but rather a question of considering how possible damage may be overcome, bypassed or restricted.

Using SWOT data

Once you have the results of your own SWOT analysis and at least one (but preferably more) from another source, you can combine them on the grid. Then sort each category first by relative importance. Then re-sort them in terms of reality – this an interesting exercise, which might well require some soul-searching. For example, ask yourself what evidence you really have for saying that customers will choose your product over your competitors'. Finally trim the categories to around no more than five or six items each per category, homing in on the really critical issues. You can use this as the basis for some strategic planning. This cut-down SWOT summary and a description of your sound strategic approach to address the points listed should appear in your business plan. This will cover how you plan to:

> **A SWOT analysis helps identify the critical issues in any situation and organises them in a way that enables you to come up with a sound strategic approach**

- Build on the strengths
- Minimise the weaknesses
- Seize the opportunities
- Counter the threats.

Using swot analysis to clarify your business goals

After a SWOT analysis you might see things in terms of answers to these four questions:

- How can strengths be used to take advantage of opportunities?
- How can strengths be used to avoid or defuse threats?
- How can weaknesses be overcome to take advantage of opportunities?
- How can weaknesses be overcome to counteract or minimise threats?

Remember to try to be objective at all times when writing your strategy approach.

ACTION POINT
FOUR KEY RECOMMENDATIONS FOR A FLAWLESS SWOT ANALYSIS

BE COMPREHENSIVE: This means picking up small details. A minor weakness could be too few filing cabinets, while a major threat could be a decline in the value of sterling following an election. Of course, this could also be an key opportunity if there was a rise in currency value instead.

BE PREPARED: Put real effort into background preparation and gathering information. Be self-critical, but don't be too defensive. SWOT analysis is there to stimulate ideas and not stifle them.

INCLUDE OTHERS: SWOT works well in group sessions. To get a real brainstorm going you need more than four people, but to keep it manageable limit numbers to around 10.

TEST YOUR ANALYSIS: Ask an outsider (your accountant, perhaps, or family member) to conduct the same exercise and compare their views with your findings. The more people who look at your SWOT analysis, the more ideas you are likely to get.

The people

> If you are launching solo, the people section will initially revolve around your skills and experience

Anyone who runs a real business knows that none of the areas covered by a business plan can be tackled without people. Why then do so many business plans feel that it's sufficient to insert an appendix with the CVs of the managers? This token gesture does not give any feel for how the business will be run, what the potential gaps in expertise may be or what essential skills will be needed in the future. It all comes back to strategic planning versus day-to-day fire-fighting.

If you are launching solo, the people section will initially revolve around your skills and experience. But this model can still help you to draw up a list of the kind of people you will need to meet your projections for the business, either at start up or beyond, which will show that you have a clear understanding of what is required to realise your vision. Here is a model that might help you to analyse the 'people' section of the plan.

- Draw up a table with four columns, headed (a) People, (b) Experience, (c) Skills and (d) Functions.
- Make a list of all the people who are involved in your business in column (a) and summarise their experience and skills in columns (b) and (c), so that you can clearly see who you have on board and what they each bring to the business.
- Make a list of the areas of sector and functional expertise required for the business and see who is ideally placed to fill each of these roles. Are there any functions that can't be undertaken by the people who are within the team and, if so, how do you propose to fill these gaps?
- Draw up another table showing the business in three years' time. How will the management team be different? What steps will you need to take to both keep existing staff satisfied and recruit new staff of sufficient calibre to deliver your ambitious future plans as described in other sections?

Businesses change over time, and it is unusual for an early-stage company to have a full management team. Generally an entrepreneur will endeavour to fill many roles, some of which they will be particularly unsuited to. Why not explore in the business plan what roles could be performed better by others, such as a finance director, sales director and even the chief executive? How are you going to afford people of sufficient calibre to deliver what you want? Perhaps you will need to raise some further finance to cover this at a later date. One of the most valid reasons for raising equity capital is to pay for people who are good enough to take a company to a higher level, and yet generally entrepreneurs leave such recruitment too late.

The mission statement

An effective mission statement should be able to tell your company story and ideals in less than 30 seconds, and, as such, it can be one of the more challenging elements of your business plan. The readers should be able to gain a clear understanding of what your company's about from the mission statement, so it's vital to think it through very carefully. Essentially, it should only be around three to four sentences long, defining what your company is, what it does, what it stands for and why, and it is often best developed with input from everyone involved in the launch. Rather than explaining how great you are and how wonderful your company will be it should be descriptive, succinctly describing your business along with its vision and values – kind of a brand statement.

It can help to examine other companies' mission statements, but don't be tempted to copy any, because it's vital that the mission statement is original and accurately reflects your business, not someone else's. You should also make sure that you believe in your mission statement, as it will provide the basis for your business going forward, inspiring both you and your future employees to success. Therefore, if it's a lie, it can be demotivational for your employees and put off customers once this becomes apparent.

The executive summary

The executive summary presents the highlights of your business plan, and even though it opens the document, it's often the final part to be completed – for obvious reasons. The executive summary is the doorway to your business plan, so it's important to get it right or your target readers will go no further. As a general rule, for a standard plan, the first paragraph should include:

- Business name
- Business location
- What product or service you sell
- The purpose of the plan

Mission control: Example mission statements from famous companies

IBM

'At IBM, we strive to lead in the invention, development and manufacture of the industry's most advanced information technologies, including computer systems, software, storage systems and microelectronics.

We translate these advanced technologies into value for our customers through our professional solutions, services and consulting businesses worldwide.'

Amazon.com

'To be the most customer-centric company in the world, where people can find and discover anything they want to buy online.'

Apple Computers (1984)

'To produce high-quality, low cost, easy-to-use products that incorporate high technology for the individual. We are proving that high technology does not have to be intimidating for non-computer experts.'

Sainsbury's

'Our mission is to be the consumer's first choice for food, delivering products of outstanding quality and great service at a competitive cost through working faster, simpler and together.'

Although your statement needn't necessarily be this short, you should try to make it as brief and punchy as possible.

! TIPS

WRITING YOUR PLAN

! Write from the audience's perspective – tell them what they need to know

! Research the market thoroughly – it proves the viability of your business

! Understand the competition – and how you'll beat it

! Pay attention to detail – it shows you really care

! Focus on the opportunity – talk it up, but be realistic

! Ensure all key areas are covered – be comprehensive

! Make sure your figures add up – they won't take it seriously otherwise

! Write a killer executive summary – it's the bit that gets them interested

! Get reviewed – ideally by an experienced independent source

! Implement the plan – don't leave it on a shelf and forget about it

Next, highlight important points, such as projected sales and profits, unit sales, profitability and keys to success. Essentially, you should include the news you don't want anyone to miss. This is a good place to put a 'highlights' chart – a bar graph that shows prospective sales, gross margin and profits before interest and taxes for the next three years – as well as drawing attention to them in the text. As you are starting up, one of the main purposes of your plan is likely to be to secure investment, so say this in your executive summary, and specify how much investment is required and the amount of equity ownership offered in return. It's also a good idea to add highlights of your management team and your competitive edge.

If you're looking for a loan, say so in the executive summary, and specify the amount required. Leave loan details out of the summary.

Getting people to read your plan

Many business plans are technically perfect, because most people recognise the importance of the document in securing essential finance and other support vital to getting a business off the ground, and therefore do the required research, working hard to make sure it's well presented in the right format. However, despite this, many business plans still fail, because often they need to show more than technical excellence. You may find that even though you have included the necessary sales forecast, SWOT analysis and mission statement, still no one wants to read your plan. That's because investors are looking to be inspired. They receive lots of business plans and want to find something out of the ordinary. Here are some tips that could provide the key to unlocking a target reader's interest and encourage them to venture beyond the executive summary.

The more you know about the reader and their requirements, the better equipped you will be to give them what they want – and so get what you want. The bank manager, the equity provider and whoever else you may be pitching your business plan to are likely to all have different needs and concerns, but will probably have one thing in common: they are busy, short of time, impatient and hassled. So spoon feed them. Make their lives easier and they will appreciate it. Once you have excited the finance provider with your vision, give some background about the business. Don't make assumptions about what they know. Just because you know so much about your company, your ambitions and your plan, doesn't mean they also do. Tell them who you are, how you got into this position of writing the plan, and engagingly unfurl your vision for the business. In short, put it all in perspective. Frame the plan, and the reader will have some reference points straight away.

Once they know two things – where you came from and where you are going – next comes the fun bit: can you explain what your value proposition is to your customers in no more than 30 seconds or a few

> **Investors are looking to be inspired**

> **Tell them who you are, how you got into this position of writing the plan, and engagingly unfurl your vision for the business**

lines of text? If you can, you are in a very small minority of entrepreneurs – even some of the successful ones have never managed it – which means you've already achieved more than most. Succinctly summarise who will buy your product or service and why they will buy. How many will they buy? Why will they continue to buy over time? Why will they buy from you rather than someone else? In short, what value are you really delivering to your customer?

It can often help to test yourself. For example, bore your friends with your proposition, or if you get the chance, try it out on prospective customers, and once you have it off pat, get it down in writing. It will be one of your most valuable assets. If all this sounds quite simple on paper, remember that many have found it impossible to achieve in practice. But after all the time spent researching your market, working through your sales forecasts, constructing your SWOT analysis and other relevant details and then committing them to paper, you may just crack it. And working on producing a killer executive summary will be well worth the effort, as it could prove decisive in gaining the investment you need to launch your company.

Checking and pitching the plan

> **You must be prepared to adapt the plan as your market or customer base changes**

Once you've made the final checks are happy with the content and visual presentation, it's time to prepare your pitch to possible investors, which you will then need to practise until you're confident that you will be able to get across the key points professionally and effectively. If you are using a business angel network, which match young businesses with private investors, there should be plenty of advice on offer. Remember that business angel networks see many companies a year and they will know exactly what a business angel is looking for. Local agencies such as Business Link can provide advice on how to structure and present your

KIRSTY'S STORY
I PREPARED A FANTASTIC BUSINESS PLAN

Co-founder of the website Entertainthe kids.com, **Kirsty McGregor** was 10 months into the planning process with five months left before launch when she got a pleasant surprise…

'The process took this long because we still had "day jobs", family life and other commitments, and wanted to give ourselves the best chance of surviving the rocky road that most startups face in their first few years. So we took our time, did lots of research and planning, and used the most professional approach we could.

'Once I had the idea for the site, I discussed it with my brother Ross who was just finishing a degree in e-business. He thought it was great too, but we needed to put some numbers down – I had no idea if it was financially viable. The two biggest costs I thought we would have were the website development itself, and the marketing costs to promote the website address to the general public – or more particularly to our target market of parents and carers. We drew up a shortlist of some website designers we wanted to talk to, emailed them a synopsis and asked them to quote for the work. Although two didn't even get back to us and the two that did weren't particularly impressive, at least we had ball-park figure.

'Then we started thinking about marketing – there was really only one place for us to go in my opinion. My old employer had an in-house marketing company that I knew very well and really respected. When we got talking to them about our idea in general, they actually recommended a website designer to us. They'd worked with him several times before and he also designed and managed their own site, which I knew was pretty good. Word-of-mouth recommendation (from someone you trust) is so much better.

'We'd pretty much resigned ourselves to the fact that, at this very early stage, we weren't going to get any funding from a bank or business angel, so thought we'd have to fund the startup ourselves. Of course, we'd looked at the likely costs, and I'd prepared some draft projections. I wrote a fantastic business plan (if I do say so myself) and enclosed three sets of projections, worst case, most likely case and best case, and we submitted it initially to three high-street banks: HSBC, Barclays and RBS. The first two turned us down, both really due to the same thing – it was too speculative for them. However, RBS finally met with us, and lo and behold, agreed to provide us with a loan, that was pretty much on an unsecured basis – not quite as much as I'd requested, but I wasn't arguing!'

ACTION POINT
COMMON BUSINESS
PLAN MISTAKES

While including the necessary items in a business plan is important, you also want to make sure you don't commit any of the following common business plan mistakes.

PUTTING IT OFF: Too many businesses make business plans only when they have no choice in the matter. Unless the bank or the investors want a plan, there is no plan. Don't wait to write your plan until you think you'll have enough time. It should play a key role in the development of your business, creating a strategic framework to build your company around, and not just created in response to a specific need, such as securing funding. This is why it is essential to review your plan regularly – it should be an organic document that develops as the business grows and as the influences on it change, such as marketing conditions.

CASH FLOW CASUALNESS: Most people think in terms of profits instead of cash. When you imagine a new business, you think of what it would cost to make the product, what you could sell it for, and what the profits per unit might be. We are trained to think of business as sales minus costs and expenses, which equal profits. Unfortunately, we don't spend the profits in a business. We spend cash. So understanding cash flow is critical. If you have only one table in your business plan, make it the cash flow table.

IDEA INFLATION: Don't overestimate the importance of the idea. You don't need a great idea to start a business; you need time, money, perseverance and common sense. Few successful businesses are based entirely on new ideas. A new idea is harder to sell than an existing one, because people don't understand a new idea and they are often unsure if it will work. Plans don't sell new business ideas to investors, people do. Investors invest in people, not ideas. The plan, although necessary, is only a way to present information.

FEAR AND DREAD: Although preparing a business plan can seem daunting, if you approach it carefully and strategically, and have carried out the necessary research into the viability of your business beforehand, there is no need to fear anything – in fact fear and dread could mean you put it off until the last minute and then don't dedicate the time and energy to it that it deserves. There are also plenty of resources available to help you get it right.

SPONGY, VAGUE GOALS: Leave out the vague and the meaningless babble of business phrases (such as 'being the best'), because they are simply hype. Remember that the objective of a plan is to secure results, and for results, you need tracking and follow up. You need specific dates, management responsibilities, budgets and milestones. Then you can follow up. No matter how well thought out or brilliantly presented your business plan may be, it means nothing unless it produces results.

ONE SIZE FITS ALL: Tailor your plan to its real business purpose. Business plans can be different things. They are often just sales documents to sell an idea for a new business. They can also be detailed action plans, financial plans, marketing plans and even personnel plans. They can be used to start a business, or just run a business better.

DILUTED PRIORITIES: Remember, strategy is focused. A priority list with three to four items is focused. A priority list with 20 items is certainly not strategic, and rarely, if ever, effective. The more items on the list, the less the importance of each.

HOCKEY-STICK SHAPED GROWTH PROJECTIONS: Sales grow slowly at first, but then shoot up boldly with huge growth rates, as soon as 'something' happens. Have projections that are conservative, so you can defend them. When in doubt, be less optimistic.

plan. Try to run through the plan with any business contacts that you have, as they may spot something that you hadn't noticed. Asking friends and family to help can also be useful.

When the business plan has been prepared and it has received input from a financial adviser, the next step is to put it in front of investors. At this point, it is worth considering only sending a copy of the executive summary. This has the advantage of saving costs and increasing the chances of receiving attention. Response times to the business plan will vary, but can take as little as a week. If the answer is 'No', you should find out the reasons why and then consider incorporating those ideas into a revised business plan, changing and strengthening the management team or carrying out further market research before approaching other potential investors.

And remember, the business plan is a living document. Don't think of it as a fixed route and be prepared to adapt it to suit your audience. Even if you are in an established business, you must be prepared to adapt the plan as your market or customer base changes or if disaster strikes.

Raising finance

One of the key uses for a business plan when you're stating up is to help you secure the necessary finance to launch your business. If this is the primary function of your plan, make sure that you clearly state how much money you need and why, based on the details you're presenting. Although banks remain the most common source of initial finance, it pays to bear in mind all the options available, and adapt your plan accordingly. For example, you may arrange finance in return for a stake in your business – known as 'equity' – rather than it simply securing a loan. In such as case, you need to include how big a stake of your company you're prepared to forfeit for the amount of funding you need. Here are the range of finance options open to you.

> **Banks are the commonest source of initial finance but there are other options**

Debt finance

> **As the loan is secured, the cost is usually less than other more risky types of borrowing**

Debt finance is simply borrowing money to buy the things you need to launch your business, and then paying it back in some way. Although many small companies are now financed by the founders themselves, when people think about raising money, their first port of call is generally the bank, from which a loan is the most typical form of debt financing. Generally it has to be repaid at an agreed interest rate and within a specified period of time. The interest rate can either be variable or fixed.

Typically the loan is secured against an asset. This means that if the business fails to repay the loan, the lender has the right to claim the asset. An asset could be a house or other premises or some equipment owned by the business. If you are unwilling to put personal possessions like your house on the line and your company has insufficient assets, a bank is unlikely to lend you money. Often a bank will also expect some financial commitment from you personally, such as a percentage of the amount you're requesting. As the loan is secured, the cost is usually less than other more risky types of borrowing. However, a bank loan also locks companies into a payment schedule, which may cause cash flow problems for small businesses. You will have to show how the money will be repaid, and details from your business plan should help.

The straightjacket of making a set payment at what may be a fixed interest rate can also cause a lot of problems for fast-growing companies that consume capital very fast. For these reasons, loans are more suited to tried-and-tested business models that offer good prospects for profitability.

Debt finance can also take the form of an overdraft. This is generally used to fund working cash flow rather than capital expenditure, and is repayable on demand, while exceeding the agreed limits can be expensive. Increasingly banks are offering term loans to small businesses as an alternative to using an overdraft facility. In particular, it allows the banks to impose a regular repayment schedule over a fixed period of time and to see the amount of credit gradually reducing.

Other types of debt finance that are growing in popularity include leasing, a way of borrowing to buy specific equipment or machinery, or factoring and invoice discounting, where the small business borrows against sales as a means of freeing up cash. Invoice discounting involves a company loaning you a large percentage of the money for each invoice as soon as it is raised, which is then repaid plus a commission fee when payment is received from your customer within a specified time period. Under factoring, the company will also chase the debt for you, for a slightly larger commission payment. Each method provides a way around cash flow problems for new or small companies, and they can prove particularly useful for those businesses that have a large outlay for each job or if they use a lot of suppliers. In fact, there is a vast range of different debt financing tools and each business should find the one that is right for them. Using them creatively and wisely can help to reduce the reliance on a bank.

So, if your business needs some working capital, but the amount fluctuates, an overdraft is probably best for you. The interest rate is agreed in advance and you only pay interest for the time and amount that you are overdrawn. But if your business needs longer-term finance, in particular for a specific purchase or planned expenditure, you should look to take a loan that can be repaid over a set period. There are many reasons why debt finance could suit your business – it is accessible, flexible and tailored. Debt finance will be the first option for most small businesses, and whether it is loans, overdrafts, leasing or invoice discounting, the company is borrowing against reserves rather than giving someone ownership of shares. One key reason that most businesses will borrow money rather than sell shares in their business is that debt finance is usually available from organisations in smaller amounts than equity, and unless the company is very large it will be too small for formal equity.

> **There is a vast range of different debt financing tools and each business should find the one that is right for them**

Equity finance

This is where you give up a stake in your business in return for money. Many small businesses actually use equity finance without even realising it. As Bank of England figures show, some 61% of businesses are launched with either personal capital or that of friends and relatives. That can be an equity arrangement where friends and family take a stake in the business in return for their funds. The big advantage of equity finance is that it never has to be repaid and there is no interest rate paid on the money. Equity investments are true 'risk capital', as there is no guarantee of the investor getting their money back. The investment is not tied to any particular assets that can be redeemed from the business and, should the business fail, an equity investor is less likely to get their original investment back than other investors.

The return from an equity investment can be generated either through a sale of the shares once the company has grown or through dividends, a discretionary payout to shareholders if the business does well. However, the reason that firms will give you cash in this form is that they will take a share of the business in return, therefore gaining some influence over it. Formal equity finance is available through a number of different sources, such as business angels, venture capitalists or the stock markets. Each varies in the amount of money available and the process of completing the deal.

Business angels are usually individuals who invest in companies they think have the potential to make them money, and are typically looking to write a cheque for a minimum of around £25,000 – any smaller amounts are not usually appropriate because the fixed costs are too large. Venture capitalists are organisations set up to invest in companies, and prefer to deal in figures higher than business angels.

However, because all equity investors are prepared to put up risk capital in return for a share in a growth business, if your business cannot support growth rates of at least 20% a year, you may not be able to attract equity funding. It is this control and the prospect of a high return if your

> **The big advantage of equity finance is that it never has to be repaid and there is no interest rate paid on the money**

business is successful that attracts this type of investor. It is also these factors that many business owners are wary of – they are reluctant to give up control of their company. Those businesses that have fast growth potential, such as IT or internet companies, are often reluctant to give away equity as it is likely they will need further cash injections as they grow, which would further dilute their stake in the business.

Many companies shy away from equity financing because they see it as relinquishing control. However, you can gain more than just money from the deal. Companies also sell the equity for 'valuable consideration' (or expert advice) – in return they will usually get expert help, as investors are keen to make sure the business is a success. And many companies are giving up effective control if they rely on an overdraft as a major source of finance, as paying back the loan can heavily influence how the business is run.

> "Explore the many different options that are available and investigate each one so that you can find the right finance to suit your purpose"

Other ways to fund your business

YOUR OWN MONEY

This is one of the most common ways of funding a business and if you have the money readily available it can be beneficial. There is no waiting around and virtually no red tape involved. However, if something goes wrong and you have nothing to fall back on, you could face a severe knock-on effect. Your business' fate is in your own hands.

THE FOUR FS

The four Fs are: founder, family, friends and foolhardies. If your own money is not quite enough, you may choose to seek help and next stage funding from friends and family. Those involved may ask for something in exchange, such as a stake in the company, but this is up to your own discretion. Written guarantees and/or legal documentation may also have to be drawn up.

Whatever you do, make sure that you plan for every eventually. Unfortunately, most people don't enter a business partnership thinking about what can go wrong, but just like a marriage, divorce can happen to anyone and at any time.

EXPERT OPINION

How to impress the bank manager

It is often said that if you fail to plan, then you plan to fail and this is certainly the case when it comes to running your own business.

Preparing an effective business plan can make all the difference between success and failure. Besides being a great way of capturing the long-term objectives and financial goals for your business, your business plan can be used to convince prospective lenders, investors and customers that you have thought through your ideas and that they are dealing with a business which has good potential.

So, when it comes to preparing a business plan what are the requirements and exactly how can you impress your bank manager?

Be comprehensive

This is one of the most important components of a good business plan. Your bank is interested in more than just the numbers. You need to include details of the proposed business, such as key staff, business assets, finance and a competitor analysis. You will need to demonstrate that you know your business, what makes it tick, what your core experience is and how you are going to use your skills and abilities to make a success of the business.

Be realistic

Be realistic about the assumptions you make within your plan. A plan that is too optimistic won't stand up to close scrutiny. One that is too pessimistic will put potential investors and financers off. Professional plans should be built on realistic assumptions.

Be clear & concise

Your business plan should be written in clear, straightforward language. Many people reading your plan will be pressed for time so don't make them work too hard. For the purpose of selling your idea to your bank manager, keep it short so it's easy to read and understand. Start off with a really strong executive summary, this should capture their interest and encourage them to read more.

Know your business

It is critical that you understand every aspect of your business plan in order to field any questions easily and professionally.

Don't plan too far ahead

Your plan will undoubtedly change in the first 12 months of trading, as you learn more and more about your business customers and competitors. For most start up businesses, a 12 month plan is ideal as you refine your business model.

Act on your plan

A good business plan is an action plan. It will influence every aspect of your business's operations. It should be used to monitor the progress of the business, if you are underperforming against your plan you need to understand where and why as soon as possible so you can take action to correct it.

Used in the right way, a business plan is an essential tool. However no business plan should be set in stone, you should regularly review it and revise it as your business develops.

There are various tools available that can help you create your business plan, take time to find the right template that works for you. One option to consider is a new software planning tool from Sage. Sage Planning for Business. can guide you through the planning process, it will help you to think through and document all aspects of your business and could help turn your business ideas into a professionally presented business plan.

Once you are ready to start trading, Sage Planning for Business can integrate with Sage Start-up (a financial management software package) to allow you to track the progress of your business against your plan to see how you are actually performing..

Lloyds TSB Commercial has teamed up with Sage, one of the UK's leading suppliers of business management software to bring you:

- A complementary copy of Sage Planning for Business software.
- A 90-day free trial of Sage Start-up. This is free for the first 90 days. Then if you become a business customer of Lloyds TSB Commercial, you'll have the option to subscribe at an exclusive discounted rate – about 50% less than what it normally retails for in its first year.

With help from their Business Advisors and free planning software from Sage, Lloyds TSB Commercial can help you prepare at the start of your business journey. To download Sage Planning for Business visit www.lloydstsb.com/sage.

To find out more about how Lloyds TSB Commercial can help get your business off to a great start: call 0800 022 4358, or visit www.lloydstsb.com/10steps

This article is produced for information only and should not be relied on as offering advice for any specific set of circumstances.

Calls may be monitored or recorded in case we need to check we have carried out your instructions correctly and to help improve our quality of service.

Lloyds TSB Commercial is a trading name of Lloyds TSB Bank plc and Lloyds TSB Scotland plc and serves customers with an annual turnover of up to £15M.

Sage Planning for Business and Sage Start-up software is licensed for use by Sage (UK) Limited and is subject to the terms and conditions set out in the Sage Licence Agreement. Lloyds TSB Bank plc makes no guarantees in relation to any Sage product and you should ensure it meets your requirements. Lloyds TSB Bank plc is not legally responsible for any damage caused by the use of the software or services provided to you by Sage (UK) Limited.

Business Plan Pro® 11.0 –
the fastest and easiest way to write a business plan

So, you need to write a business plan. Why? Well you began doing some research into your business idea, and noted that nearly every single thing you read about starting a new business includes the action **'write a business plan'**.

Why is this so?
Because the benefits of compiling a business plan are numerous – not least, the fact that committing your thoughts to paper **dramatically improves your prospect of getting started in the first place.**
A business plan also helps you gain a holistic view of the business and helps you to devise a strategy to ensure a successful launch for your idea regardless of whether you are an entrepreneur, business student or someone looking to launch a new product in an existing company. Business planning also helps you manage cash flow so as to ensure you stay on top of your company's financial position from Day One!

> *We believe that using Business Plan Pro® is the fastest and easiest way to write a business plan.*

Having decided to produce a business plan, there are three main ways to write one:
1. Pay someone to write it.
2. Write it yourself using Microsoft® Word and Excel.
3. Write it using a task-specific software product such as **Business Plan Pro®** 11.0.

If you, like many entrepreneurs, are time rich and cash poor, option one quickly removes itself from the equation, given the cost of having someone write a plan for you.

You are then faced with the choice between using **Business Plan Pro®** and building everything yourself, from scratch, in Microsoft® Word and Excel. Why are we not recommending other business plan software options? Because **Business Plan Pro®** is the best business-planning software available – without exception.

Palo Alto Software (the maker of **Business Plan Pro®**) has a proud history and has been making the best-selling business-planning software available for many years. There are also extensive lists of testimonials and independent reviews on the website, all corroborating this view. By all means, you can consider other software options; however, we are confident that your own analysis will reveal that **Business Plan Pro®** stands head and shoulders above the alternatives.

When it comes to using Word and Excel there are undoubted benefits – not least the fact that they are 'free' in the sense that they are bundled on most PCs. The interface is also familiar, given the popularity of their use. However, while these tools are excellent when you know exactly what you need to produce, **they offer negligible assistance when it comes to producing specific content, such as that required for a business plan.** If the purpose of the business plan were simply to jot down a few notes to keep you on track, they would suffice. However, if you intend to circulate the business plan to peers, colleagues or prospective investors, you will need to produce a plan worthy of your name. After all, you are the author!

Facing a blank screen with a flashing icon is not a nice place to be in. With **Business Plan Pro**® help is available at every step ensuring you have someone to hand hold you through the process if need be. Here are some of the reasons why we believe that using **Business Plan Pro**® is the easiest way to write a business plan:

> *Business Plan Pro® is designed specifically to help you write a business plan with the least amount of hassle.*

1. Offers significant time saving
Business Plan Pro® was designed to help you write a plan as efficiently as possible. It comes with extensive help, lots of examples and expert advice.

2. Provides the structure
Business Plan Pro® walks you through a list of specific tasks, step by step, in stark contrast to the blank screen and flashing

cursor you face when you create a new document in Microsoft Word.

3. Includes hundreds of examples
Business Plan Pro® includes over 500 full sample business plans so you can browse plenty of examples to help give you ideas.

4. Ensures you do not leave out any sections
Over ten years of history means that we know what sections to include, where they should appear in the document and what you need to put in them.

5. Makes the numbers part easy
We recognise that while compiling the financials is an essential part of any plan, it is a very challenging area for many people. We have simplified this process with the inclusion of easy-to-use financial wizards and automatic calculations, linking together all the financials from Start-up costs to Sales Forecast to Personnel Expenses to Cash Flow to Profit and Loss.

6. Free Support Available
Alongside the extensive in-product help, we also offer a free UK support line and comprehensive help facility on our Paloalto.co.uk website e.g. Help Index, Email and Instant Messenger.

7. Signposts relevant resources at appropriate points
The software also includes links to relevant local U.K. resources where you can read specific advice on any areas with which you need further assistance, including

trademarks, company formations, and more.

8. Designed specifically for producing a business plan

Whereas Microsoft® Word is a general purpose tool, **Business Plan Pro®** is designed specifically to help you write a business plan with the least amount of hassle.

9. Risk free

The time saving alone will easily justify the small cost you will need to pay for **Business Plan Pro®** (RRP £79.99) However, you can avail of our 60-day money-back guarantee if you are still unsure as to whether it will benefit you.

10. Increases your chances

Finally, for most people a business plan is written for a specific purpose, such as securing funding. You should give yourself every chance of succeeding by producing the best quality plan that you can.

Why believe us?

While this recommendation is clearly from our perspective, the risk is essentially negligible. You can try out the best-selling business-planning software and avail of the money-back offer if it is just not for you. Our websites contain numerous independent reviews and testimonials that we have gathered over the years. In the U.K. you'll find us powering the business planning software used by banks such as Barclays. Try **Business Plan Pro®** today from as little as £79.99 (inc VAT) – we are confident you will not be disappointed.

> *Give yourself every chance of succeeding by producing the best quality business plan that you can.*

Further information

Business Plan Pro® is available from Amazon.co.uk, Borders (Oxford Street, London) and from our Paloalto.co.uk website. Please visit Bplans.co.uk and Paloalto.co.uk for more information.

5.0

SETTING UP

WHAT'S IN THIS CHAPTER

■ There are essentially three legal or accounting structures recognised for starting a business. You can go it alone by being a sole trader, team up to form a partnership or operate a limited company. Before you launch, you need to decide which is the best structure for you, then go through the necessary processes to officially register your business. If a partnership or limited company is for you, then you're also likely to need to open a business bank account, and the relationship with your bank manager could be crucial to your success. Read on to find out the pros and cons of the various business options, how to set up each one and the best way to deal with your bank…

Limited companies

There are two types of limited company – those that are publicly traded on the stock market (known as a public limited company or 'plc') and those that are privately owned (identified by the abbreviation 'ltd' at the end of their name). Most likely your startup will not be starting life on the stock exchange, so this chapter will focus on limited companies that are privately owned.

A limited or limited liability company is very different from a sole trader to business. Registering and running a limited company requires more legal administration than a sole trader business or partnership. However, if you are a sole trader or partner, you can be held personally liable for your business, meaning that any outstanding debts can be met from your personal assets. In a limited company, it is the business itself that shoulders the liability as opposed to the individuals who run it. This is because a limited company is a separate legal entity to the company directors (discussed below). Profits and losses belong to the company, and the business can continue regardless of the death, resignation or bankruptcy of the shareholders or people who run it.

Limited companies pay corporation tax on their profits and company directors are taxed as employees in the same way as any other people who work for the company. Your personal financial risk is restricted to how much you have invested in the company and any guarantees you gave when raising finance for the business. However, if the company fails and you have not carried out your duties as a company director, you could be liable for debts, as well as being disqualified from acting as a director in another company.

Before you can start trading, you need to officially register your limited company, decide on the company officers and choose a name for your business. Then, once you've filed the correct documents with Companies House, you are ready to start trading. Here's a guide to each step.

> **In a limited company, it is the business itself that shoulders the liability as opposed to the individuals that run it**

Contact

Companies House
www.companies
house.gov.uk

Registering your company

Although it is possible to register a limited company yourself, unless you've done it before you are probably going to need to engage the services of either a solicitor, accountant, chartered secretary or a company formation agent. Formation agents, such as the National Business Register, use their own software that works directly with the Companies House systems. If you want to register your company electronically (most are registered this way) you will need to have the specific Companies House electronic interface – hence the need for a formation agent. However, you can still deliver the physical documents directly to Companies House without the need of a formation agent or specific electronic interface.

Fees for formation agents can cost anything up to around £200 depending on the level of service you require. A key advantage of using a formation agent is the advice they can give you on the compiling of the necessary documents and the right structure for your business. Companies House does not provide this service when registering, so if you are unfamiliar with the process it's advisable to get help to avoid errors. Going through the registration process yourself can be time-consuming, especially if you make a mistake, and Companies House staff will not advise you about specific matters, such as the content of the required memorandum and articles (more about these later). Alternatively, you could also get assistance from an online registration company. The standard service usually costs £80–£100 including fees, but since some documentation needs to be posted, registration takes three to eight days. This option is usually cheaper than using a formation agent, although you won't receive the same level of personal service.

Finally, you can buy an 'off the shelf' company, receiving a ready-made limited company that has designated company officers listed on the paperwork. You simply transfer your name, and the names of any other company directors, to the company once you receive your documentation. The process can be completed on the same day, and many accountancy firms have several ready-made limited companies that they can sell to you. This is the quickest option, and with the exception of registering the company yourself, can often be the cheapest too.

It has never been easier to register a limited company due to recent key developments, according to **Simon Harrison** at Complete Formations, one of the UK's leading online company registration agents. 'While accountants and solicitors still play a role in registering companies, particularly for their corporate clients, their involvement in incorporations for individuals has undoubtedly reduced,' he explains. 'A typical modern scenario might be where a private individual uses an accountant for advice on what type of company to incorporate, based on an assessment of tax position and plans for the future. The individual might then go away to form the company themselves through a formation agent and save themselves money in the process.'

The costs of incorporating a company have also reduced due in part to greater competition between formation agents, and their development of more efficient internal systems, which have automated some of the manual tasks. 'Examples of this include batch printing of incorporation documents and providing more controls and guidance over what customers can and should enter on the online registration forms,' says Harrison. 'This, in turn, results in less support costs dealing with repetitive issues. It is now possible to purchase an electronic company formation for as little as £24.99 plus VAT.'

Another significant change in the way in which companies are registered today is the manner in which the eventual directors, secretary (if the option is taken to have one) and the subscribers are appointed. 'Previously, accountants, solicitors and company formation agents typically used nominees to act as the shareholder and company officers at the time a company was incorporated,' says Harrison. 'Once the company was successfully formed, the purchaser's officers would be appointed and the nominees would resign. This practice often caused issues when the purchasers then went to open a company bank account and the nominees were still shown on the Companies House register, which might not have yet been updated to reflect the new ownership and management appointments.

'With the exception of ready-made companies, where the use of nominees is still commonplace, the expectation for most companies incorporated today is that the first appointees will be those which the

> " A significant change in the way companies are registered today is the manner in which the eventual directors, secretary and the subscribers are appointed "

purchaser requests. This does mean that more time must be spent by the purchaser at the pre-formation stage, entering details of their directors and shareholders. Once the company has been set up, however, there is not then the requirement for this task to be undertaken in order to take ownership of the business.'

The necessary documents

If you get professional help registering your company, which will save time and avoid errors, then you are unlikely to be dealing directly with these documents, but it's still a good idea to get to know them. When registering a limited company, four documents must be provided to Companies House. These are described below.

1. MEMORANDUM OF ASSOCIATION

This document sets out:

- The company's name
- Where the company's registered office is located in England, Wales or Scotland
- What the company will do. This can be as simple as: 'to conduct business as a general commercial company'.

2. ARTICLES OF ASSOCIATION

In this document you set out the rules for running your company. You must state how shares will be allocated and transferred, how the directors, the secretary and your meetings will be governed. The standard document used is Table A of the Companies Act. However, if you choose an amended version of Table A, you must submit this version when registering. Once your company is incorporated you can only make changes if the holders of 75% of the voting rights in your company agree, so it pays to get this right at the outset.

3. FORM 10

This document gives details of the first director or directors, company secretary and the address of the registered office. Company directors

When registering a limited company, four documents must be provided to Companies House

must also give their name, address, date of birth, occupation and details of other directorships held in the past five years. Companies based in Northern Ireland should use Form 21.

4. FORM 12

This document is the statutory declaration of compliance with all the legal requirements of the incorporation of a company. It must be signed by one of the company directors or the secretary named on Form 10 or the solicitor forming the company. The signing of the document must be witnessed by a solicitor, a commissioner for oaths, a justice of the peace, or a notary public. Companies based in Northern Ireland should use Form 21. Form 12 must not be signed and dated before any of the other documents are completed, signed and dated.

WHERE CAN I GET THESE DOCUMENTS?

Form 10 and Form 12 can be obtained for free from the Companies House website. The Memorandum and Articles of Association can be obtained from legal stationers, accountants, solicitors or company formation agents.

COST OF SUBMITTING THE DOCUMENTS

The standard fee to register a limited company is £20, but a same-day service costs £50. If the registration documents are filed using the Companies House software filing service, the fee is £15 for standard and £30 for same-day registration. However, to file electronically you must either purchase the suitable software, develop your own or go through an agent.

Company officers

If you set up a limited private company, you appoint company officers, who are simply the formally named directors and company secretary, as stated in the Articles of Association described previously. Usually, as the founder of the company, you would be one of the directors, along with the people with whom you may have launched the company. One of

It is a legal requirement for company officers to be in place at all times and for their names and current addresses to be written on the registration documents

the directors could also be appointed company secretary, although this could be someone who is not a director. All companies used to have to appoint a company secretary, but this is no longer the case. It is a legal requirement for company officers to be in place at all times and for their names and current addresses to be written on the registration documents. If there is a change in company officers, you must inform Companies House straight away. All private limited companies must have at least one director. The following sections provide a rundown of the official roles of your company officers.

DIRECTORS

Company directors must manage the company's affairs in accordance with its Articles of Association and the law. Generally, anyone can be appointed company director and the post does not require any formal qualifications. However, there are a few exceptions. You are prohibited from being a company director if:

- You are an undischarged bankrupt or disqualified by a court from holding a directorship
- You are under 16 (this only applies in Scotland).

Company directors have a responsibility to make sure that certain documents reach the registrar at Companies House. These are:

- Accounts
- Annual returns
- Notice of change of directors or secretaries
- Notice of change of registered office.

Directors who fail to deliver these documents on time can be prosecuted and are subject to fines of up to £5,000 for each offence. An average 1,000 directors are prosecuted each year for failing to deliver accounts and returns to the registrar on time. So unless you are particularly knowledgeable about company facts and figures, it's a good idea to appoint an accountant to help you prepare these documents. Your accountant will also advise you on the necessary information you need to keep hold of and prepare, such as invoices, receipts, etc.

"
If documents aren't delivered on time to Companies House, you can be prosecuted and fined up to £5,000 "

COMPANY SECRETARY

The duties of a company secretary are not specified by law, but are usually contained within an employment contract. For private limited companies, the secretary is not required to have any special qualifications, but this is not the case if you decide to change your company to a public limited company.

The main duties of a company secretary are to:

- Maintain the statutory registers, which means updating the details on the business held at Companies House when necessary. For example, if you relocate or appoint or lose a director.
- Ensure statutory forms are filed promptly
- Provide members and auditors with notice of meetings
- Send the registrar copies of resolutions and agreements
- Supply a copy of the accounts to every member of the company
- Keep or arrange minutes of meetings.

With limited companies now no longer needing to appoint a company secretary by law, few will probably do so when launching, with the administrative duties being covered by the directors. These do not take up much time at all. In fact, once your company has launched, there is unlikely to be much to do on this front for a couple of years at least, barring submitting accounts and annual returns and recording the content of director meetings, unless you relocate or change directors over this period. Your accountant will be there to help with accounts and returns, and can also offer general advice on the official roles of company officers, as can your solicitor.

Sole traders

If you want to literally go it alone in business, you are… er… not alone! A massive 74% of all British businesses have no employees, according to the latest Department of Trade and Industry figures. So you could say that sole traders pretty much drive the UK economy. The popularity

Sole traders pretty much drive the UK economy

of this type of business reflects the ease with which you can start sole trading: registration is straightforward, record keeping is simple and you get to keep all the profits after tax. Starting small by sole trading is a way to test your chosen market, and many companies are born this way, but there are pitfalls. If your business fails, for example, you will have to pay for that failure out of your own pocket.

Sole trading is defined as when an individual is the only owner of the business and has complete control over the way it is run. The law makes no distinction between the business and a sole trader. This unlimited liability means that any business debt can be met from the owner's personal wealth if the business fails, and the business usually ceases on the owner's retirement or death. A sole trading business is usually small in size, with a low turnover, and few, if any, employees. But there were an estimated 4.7 million active businesses in the UK at the start of 2007, according to the latest government statistics, and more than 3.5 million of these are class zero businesses – that is without employees (BERR Directorate Analytical Unit – Enterprise Directorate: Small and Medium Enterprise Statistics for the UK and Regions).

Most sole traders operate in the service sector, including photographers, plumbers, hairdressers, shops, real estate agencies and bed and breakfast hotels. Some 24.5% of the UK's 3.5 million class zero businesses are in the construction sector, with 24% in real estate and a significant number in business-related services (BERR Directorate Analytical Unit – Enterprise Directorate: Small and Medium Enterprise Statistics for the UK and Regions).

"Most sole traders operate in the service sector"

Getting down to business

Contact

National Business Register
0121 678 9000
www.national businessregister.
co.uk

You need to fulfil certain legal requirements before you can open for business. If you are going to trade under a name different from your own personal name, you must display the name or names of the owners and an address where documents can be served on all business stationery and at your premises. So you will need to design letterheads, business cards and signage accordingly.

A business name means the name of your business if it is different from your own name. It is not compulsory to register a business name, but you can do so with the National Business Register. You also need to be careful about choosing a name, since the wrong one can get you into difficulties. Certain words and expressions such as 'international', 'federation' and 'registered' are restricted under the Business Names Act 1985 and the Company and Business Names Regulations 1995. Companies House and the National Business Register have lists of these words and details of how to obtain approval to use them. In addition, your business name cannot be the same or too similar to that of another business, trademark or company. If it does conflict, you could face legal action from its owner. Check phone books, trade journals and magazines to ensure against clashes, and you can run free name checks against all these via the National Business Register, the Trade Marks Register and the Patent Office, as well as the limited companies names index at Companies House. To be absolutely sure that you can use a name, contact a solicitor to perform the checks or register your name with the National Business Register, which will then do the checks for you and ensure no one copies it the future or passes it off as their own.

You must register as self-employed with Her Majesty's Revenue & Customs (HMRC) within three months of starting up or face a £100 fine. The three-month limit starts from the last day of your first month of trading.

Legal issues

A sole trader business is simple to set up legally, although certain trades may need a licence. These include nightclubs, taxi and car hire, restaurants, pet shops, indoor sports venues, adult shops, street trading, hotels, pet kennels, nursing homes, waste management, weapons sales and money lending. You can get a licence from the relevant local authority for most of these. To make sure you are on the right side of the law, refer to the relevant Acts of Parliament:

To make sure you are on the right side of the law, refer to the relevant Acts of Parliament

- The Trade Descriptions Act 1972 means that it is a criminal offence to knowingly make false or misleading claims – verbal or written – about goods or services you offer. This covers areas such as ingredients, place of manufacture and customer testimonials, as well as associating yourself with a brand without being entitled to.

- The Sale of Goods Act 1979 dictates that the goods you sell must be of satisfactory quality, match your promises of performance and be as you describe them.
- The Supply of Goods and Services Act 1982 commits you to undertake the services you offer with reasonable care, skill, time and cost.
- The Data Protection Act 1984 directs you to register the source, nature and purpose of any personal data you keep about individuals, except data used for internal administration such as payroll. Registration forms are available at post offices.
- The Consumer Protection Act 1987 holds you liable if you supply a faulty product causing damage or injury unless you can show that not enough was known about its dangers at the time of supply. To protect yourself under this Act, offer an estimate first and a written quote only when you have properly assessed costs.
- The Price Marking Order 1991 makes it compulsory to put the price of goods offered for sale in writing.

You should also consider any legislation relating to environmental and health and safety requirements, as well as checking the planning and building regulations relating to your premises. Local authorities and the Department for Business, Enterprise and Regulatory Return should be the first ports of call for this.

Tax and sole traders

As a sole trader, your profits are taxed like any other income by the HM Revenue and Customs (HMRC), and as you are self-employed, your tax will be self-assessed. The amount you owe is calculated after business expenses and personal allowances have been deducted. Your income will fall under tax Schedule D, and as you will be paying income tax twice a year, it makes sense to put money aside. As a self-employed person, many of your business expenses can be deducted from your taxable income, such as overheads on your premises, travel, delivery costs and trade association subscriptions, but you will have to pay capital gains tax if you sell or give away any assets. You will also be paying National Insurance Contributions (NICs).

If your income rises above a certain level, you will have to apply for value added tax (VAT) registration. This means you will be collecting VAT from your customers and paying it to HMRC less the VAT you have paid out in the course of conducting your business. The increase in popularity of online businesses had led to an increasing number of people setting up part-time businesses for additional income to their main job. As a result, many are unsure what they have to declare for tax purposes and at what point they should register as self-employed. HMRC rules stipulate that all e-traders must be registered with it so that their income can be taxed.

What defines an e-trader?

You are an e-trader if you:

- Sell goods that were bought with the intention of re-selling them
- Sell items you made yourself for a profit
- Sell or buy on behalf of others for financial gain
- Receive payment for a service.

If you do any of the above, then you must register as self-employed with HMRC within the three-month deadline mentioned earlier. With regards to eBay, it is extremely unwise to delay registering, as HMRC carries out checks on online auction sites to root out members who process a high number of transactions.

ACTION POINT
KEY THINGS TO DO AFTER SETTING UP AS A SOLE TRADER

Once you've set up as a sole trader there are a few other things to consider that will help you and your new business.

BANKING: You can operate your sole trading business from your personal bank account. You must, however, be able to distinguish your personal spending from that of your business for tax purposes. You can also run separate bank accounts and major banks are keen to get you on board for the future custom you may bring. Shop around for a bank that best suits your needs.

INSURANCE: Ensure your business will keep working even when you are not by insuring it. As a sole trader, unless you employ staff or make alternative arrangements, your business will come to a standstill if you fall ill, have an accident or go on holiday. So shop around for health and medical insurance tailored to small businesses with self-employed owners. Check to see if subsidised insurance schemes are offered by your trade association or local chamber of commerce. You should also consider taking out disability insurance to cover you for time off through illness or injury. But check the qualifying period – some policies with lower premiums won't pay out until after an excess period of three months.

PENSIONS: Although putting aside money for the future may be hard for you right now, a pension plan is well worth considering. And not just for the financial security it will offer you in retirement – investing in a pension scheme can be tax-beneficial too. Everyone in the UK can get a basic state pension if they have built up a record of NICs for a quarter of their working life. But only those with a record of NICs for nine-tenths of their working lives are entitled to a full state pension, so self-employed people need to make further arrangements. Sole traders should also contribute to a private pension scheme. Many pension schemes on the market are designed for the self-employed, and several of these allow you to pay a lump sum, take a break from payments for a year or even make withdrawals.

TAKING ON STAFF: As a sole trader you might want to take on employees to help with your growing business. There are no restrictions on staff numbers, but you will have to deduct pay-as-you-earn (PAYE) tax from wages and pay it to HMRC each month. You will also need to make some summaries for employees and HMRC annually, as well as when a staff member leaves your employment. As a sole trading employer you will be responsible for your employees' Class 1 NICs and your employer contributions. These are calculated as a percentage of an employee's wage. You will also need to consider statutory sick pay, equal opportunities and health and safety conditions, as well as employment terms and contracts. And remember that if you have taken over a business, you must uphold employees' existing terms of employment.

Business partnerships

Collaboratively owned or acquired firms are probably more successful and grow faster, and in certain important sectors, such as hi-tech, collaborative ventures may actually predominate. This is when two or more people combine to form a business unit. Each partner receives a percentage of the return of the business, depending upon how much they invested. As with sole traders, all partners are also responsible for all the debts incurred by the business. This doesn't only apply to debts you have incurred as a partner but to those of any partner. This means in a partnership you need to pay particular care to the conduct of your fellow partners, because creditors will take your personal assets to pay off debts incurred by any of the others if necessary.

When considering what format the business should take, partnerships need extra attention. One of the most fundamental issues is to draw up a partnership agreement. 'We require all business partnerships to visit a solicitor (through our pro bono legal advice set up) and have a legal partnership agreement in place before we can finalise funding,' says

One of the fundamental issues is to draw up a partnership agreement

! TIPS

SUCCESSFUL PARTNERSHIPS

For a successful partnership, co-owners need to:
! Have the same shared visions, aspirations and objectives for their firm
! Have similar or compatible personal values
! Have clearly defined responsibilities and roles.
! Have complementary skills and knowledge
! Have mutual respect for the other's competence
! Have mutual trust in the other and for the other's honesty
! Be good at working as a team
! Be tolerant of the other's weaknesses

Contact

The Prince's Trust
www.princes-trust.
org.uk.

Elaine Thatcher, business support manager for The Prince's Trust in London.

Such an agreement forces partners to think about issues such as the structure and roles of each person involved, as well as the likely exit routes for the partners, according to **Thelma Quince**, who recently completed a study into 390 businesses in East Anglia. This can ensure that there is a mechanism for valuing and buying one partner's shares. 'It is a bit like a marriage and divorce. No one wants to think about the fact that it could go wrong,' says Quince. But partners can address the issues in less confrontational ways by asking what each partner wants to do when they are bored of the business. One of the common factors with collaborations that weren't successful in Quince's study was mutual respect. 'If you lose confidence in the competence of your partner and start to worry about whether they can do the job, that can be fatal,' she warns. A number of threads ran through the accounts co-owners gave as to why collaboration had failed (see box below). Quince found that mostly the collaboration failed when personal, individualistic or selfish goals started to take precedence over the collaborative, shared goals. 'One partner attempted to take control and focused on personal gain rather than long-term growth of the business,' was one comment.

Why collaborations can fail

- Differences in personal values
- Differences in personal objectives
- Differences in objectives and visions for the firm
- Loss of respect for the competence of the other
- Failure to communicate effectively
- Failure to reward effort justly
- Loss of trust in the other

The price of conflict

According to Quince, partnerships can be highly successful, but a high proportion of co-owning teams are likely to experience conflict leading to the departure of one or more of the original owning team. When this happens it can have severe effects not only on the business, but on partners' personal lives. Quince's research revealed that in 42% of the firms founded collaboratively by people who were not related or married to each other, the original owning team had fragmented, leaving only one of the original co-owners. Meanwhile, 41% of the 106 co-owners taking part in the study reported that they had prior experience of an unsuccessful collaborative relationship.

In their accounts of failed relationships the co-owners described three main adverse effects of the conflict. Only three claimed the conflict had not adversely effected themselves or their business, with just two of these feeling that, in the long term, the outcome of the conflict had actually been beneficial. Most, however, told a very different story. For nearly 40%, partner conflict had hit their businesses badly in a number of ways, including: lost revenue, which in eight cases sunk the firm; poor morale among employees; suspicion and lack of cooperation between co-owners; and even personal effects on partners, such as financial loss, lack of self-worth and marriage break-ups.

So although many partnerships work, they can be prone to conflict, which anyone thinking of starting up this kind of business must bear in mind. Meanwhile, a carefully constructed partnership agreement can help increase the chances of a harmonious and successful long-term relationship between partners.

The consequences of conflict

If you needed any further evidence of the need to approach partnerships with caution, here are personal comments on the fall out from partner disharmony by a number of people who contributed to Thelma Quince's study of 390 businesses in East Anglia:

- 'Disharmony at board level led to unnecessary risk and confusion of direction'
- 'Challenged my reason to go on'
- 'Staff morale declined'
- 'The board was unable to make decisions about things that mattered – views were too diverse. Performance suffered through inertia and the company became loss making. The team collapsed and this came close to causing the collapse of the company.'
- 'It caused an early sale of the company at the wrong time and at a disadvantageous price'
- 'The additional financial commitment was difficult to sustain'
- 'My marriage broke up shortly after the break up of the company'

From the owners who had once collaborated, but now found themselves in sole ownership came other stories of attempted suicides, nervous breakdowns, divorce, attempted assaults and one sad case of attempted murder.

CASE STUDY
HOLROYD HOWE AND THE JOINT EFFORT

Being a successful entrepreneur is often viewed as essentially a solo experience, with the hard decisions, particularly in the formative days of a business, agonised over by the man or woman at the top. The idea of forming a partnership is often dismissed by budding business owners. Even those that take the plunge with a co-founder can find that ideas and personalities clash to the point of breakdown.

However, Holroyd Howe is a business that could be used as a living and breathing example of how partnerships can, and do, work. Founders **Rick Holroyd** and **Nick Howe's** eponymous firm is well on its way to becoming the premier independent contract caterer in the UK.

Holroyd freely admits that he probably could not have done it without Howe, underlining the joint effort that has gone into building the venture.

'I don't think that either of us would've wanted to embark upon setting up the business alone, that's probably been one of the strengths of the business, 'Holroyd explains. 'It was always my intention to start with someone else because I probably wasn't the full ticket in terms of running all aspects of the business. It was important to have someone who complemented me in terms of skills.'

Holroyd rejects the idea that compromise has played a vital role in their relationship, insisting that the duo arrive at the best approach after discussion, rather than fudging the issue.

'It's amazing how the vision has been almost identical,' he says. 'But the way we see things are at the opposite ends of the spectrum – we're very different characters.

'It's very important to put your individual views to one side. Every decision we've made has been for the good of the business, and not for ourselves individually. We've seen startups that have lasted six months or a year and I think it's because egos get in the way – you can't afford to let that happen.'

Pros and cons of partnerships

These are the advantages and disadvantages of collaboration cited by almost all of the 106 co-owners in Thelma Quince's East Anglian study.

Why you should collaborate

- Being able to share the burden
- Having access to more skills, knowledge and experience
- Better, more effective decision-making
- Being able to look at problems from different perspectives

...And why you shouldn't

(These were the most important disadvantages of collaboration seen by the co-owners in Quince's study)

- Less autonomy and not always getting your own way
- Differences in personal aims and objectives for the firm
- Decision-making can be slower
- Collaboration often means a loss of spontaneity

Banking on success

There are many factors to consider when choosing a bank

Whether you decide to be a sole trader, set up a partnership or run a private limited company, you will need a good relationship with your bank. And although it has never been easier to switch banks, taking time to decide on the right one (and bank manager) for you at the outset can save problems later that could adversely affect your business. If you are a sole trader you can keep a personal account, but need to make it clear what incomings and outgoings relate to your business. If you launch a partnership or limited company, you will need to set up business bank accounts.

There are many factors to consider when choosing a bank. Interest rates and charges will obviously play their part, but it's also essential to look at the quality of service you will receive from your bank manager. After all, this is the person who you will deal with on a regular basis and the person you will need to approach for funding. So you need a manager who will understand your business and one whom you can trust.

When looking at banks, don't be afraid to ask to speak to the manager who will be dealing with your account, and when you do, make sure your needs are met. To help you find the right bank manager, Allied Irish Bank (GB) has put together a list of questions that you should be asking:

> **You need a manager who will understand your business and one whom you can trust**

- Do you really understand my business and industry?
  Every industry has slightly different needs and you want to be sure your bank understands what's important in your industry.

- How long have you been in your job?
  Ideally, you don't want to keep having to build relationships with different bank managers; continuity is key.

- Can I reach you whenever I need to? Or will I speak to someone working in a call centre whom I have never met?
  There is no substitute for having a contact who intimately understands your business and what you want to achieve. Not so easy to do over the telephone.

- Are you able to make a quick decision when I need one?
  We all know that if you really need to extend your overdraft for a short period you need a quick decision. Having to jump through lots of 'hoops' just eats up your valuable time, and few businesses can afford that.

- Will I have one point of contact who understands who I am and, as importantly, knows about my business?
  The Model-T Ford approach to service is no longer good enough – one colour does not suit everyone.

- Can I speak to companies you currently work with in a similar industry for a reference?
  There is no substitute for third-party endorsement. All banks say they deliver great service, but do they really? You need to find out.

- Will you provide more general business advice when I need it?
  Getting the basics such as a cheque account, credit card, etc is simple, but businesses require far more. They want a bank that will deliver much more value.

- How are you rated in the industry?
  Have they won any awards recently, for instance? Again, third-party endorsement can be a powerful method with which to judge the success of an organisation.

- Do you have the name of a company in your patch that you helped to grow?
  Most businesses have similar aspirations – to grow and to improve profitability. Banks play a major role in helping to turn ambition into reality. You need to know that the bank you select can help you achieve your business objectives.

Remember, when it comes to choosing a bank, the more questions you ask, the more likely it is that you will enjoy a long and fruitful relationship.

What banks offer businesses

Before you start comparing different business bank accounts, it's worth knowing what products and services they may offer, what they involve, and deciding on the ones that are most critical to your business.

Bank facilities

- Deposits: Paying in cash and cheques
- Withdrawals: Taking out cash through an ATM or at a branch
- Payment by cheque: Use of a business chequebook, which can sometimes be personalised with your company logo
- Automatic money transfers: Direct debits and direct credits
- Night safe: For depositing money when the bank is closed
- Balance enquiry and statements: For keeping track of your finances

Payment cards

- Company debit card: This will debit an amount immediately from your business account. In most cases the transactions are free and there is no annual fee.
- Company credit card: A charge card (such as Barclaycard or MasterCard) that can be issued to key members of staff. Repayment made monthly from your business current account (usually interest-free credit). There is usually a fee per transaction, an annual fee or both.

Borrowing

- Overdraft and loan facilities: Short-term financing, subject to an application procedure. May also provide access to the government-backed Small Firm Loan Guarantee scheme.
- Asset finance: Leasing and hire purchase facilities to enable you to buy equipment
- Factoring and invoice discounting: Short-term borrowing against the value of unpaid invoices
- Commercial mortgage: Funding to help buy a business. Often up to 80% of the purchase can be financed by the bank.

Other features

- Deposit accounts: A lot of banks have business deposit accounts with higher interest than a current account for any reserve funds your business may have.
- Merchant services: If you want to accept credit and debit card payments from customers, you will need a merchant account. This is provided by a bank but to get one you will often need two years' trading history and audited accounts. Once set up, you will be charged an annual fee plus a percentage of every transaction.
- Insurance: The larger banks will often offer their customers insurance cover for business interruption, health, loan repayment and more.
- Support: Most of the larger banks offer resources and support to help you run your business. For example, you may be assigned a relationship manager who will offer business advice. The bank may also provide seminars, educational literature or bookkeeping software.
- Introductory offers: Many banks offer special introductory offers to startups. This is usually a period of free banking for 12–24 months.

ACTION POINT
MANAGING YOUR
BANK MANAGER

Although it is important to ensure you have a bank and a bank manager capable of giving you what you want, it is a two-way relationship and there are a number of things you can do to get the most out of it, as **Christopher Jenkins**, managing director of Wingrave Yeats, a leading London accountancy and management consulting firm, points out.

KEEP BUSINESS AND PERSONAL ACCOUNTS APART: It's not always a good idea to keep your business account at the same bank as your personal account. Resist the temptation of the one-stop borrowing concept. You don't invest without spreading risk, so don't borrow without doing the same.

KEEP YOUR BANK REGULARLY INFORMED: Don't go and see the bank only when you need something – no one likes to be constantly confronted with tales of doom and gloom, or even worse, thinly veiled gestures of optimism. Get in contact or make an appointment to visit when you have good news and when you don't need to borrow more money. Get them excited about your business, enthuse about it and go away without asking them for more cash. Equally, if you are having any problems that could affect your ability to make a loan payment or stay within your overdraft limit, give your bank manager plenty of warning. You will find your bank far more receptive and willing to help you out of your predicament if you let them know of any issues as far in advance as possible.

BE PROFESSIONAL: Bankers are an intelligent breed of people, so make sure any figures or information you present is correct and consistent with the story you told them last month. One thing that you can be sure of is that everything goes on file and, quite naturally, has a horrible habit of being thrown back at you when you least expect it. Don't let your accountants/financial advisers do it all for you, but don't go anywhere without them. Bankers can spot a report that has been written by a professional but signed off in your name. They want to know that you as the borrower understand and believe what you are telling them. However, don't take the risk of trying to forecast for the bank without professional help. There is nothing worse than sending off a profits and losses forecast and cash flow estimate, which hasn't been reconciled to a balance sheet and which would show negative debtors in year two.

CONSIDER WHAT THE BANK WANTS TO SEE: If your bank is not fed regular information, then it can only resort to what can be gleaned from your account. Bankers examine average balance calculations from your statements and also highs and lows on the account. What makes them really twitchy is what they often refer to as 'hardcore borrowing' (where the account is constantly up against the limit). What they love are wide swings from full utilisation of the facility to occasional credit balances. They also compare your company statistics with comparable industry standards. It pays to look at the trend of your own account before you step into the lion's den, and have pre-prepared answers to the questions they are bound to ask.

Lending usually comes with nasty little things called covenants, which are certain financial limits that your company must adhere to. For example, not allowing particular balance sheet items or ratios to fall below or go over an agreed figure. It is easy to monitor these covenants and rather than letting the bank do so, include a calculation in your monthly management accounts that you send them.

MANAGE YOUR TOTAL BORROWINGS: Be careful with your capital expenditure. Try out asset finance (leasing and hire purchase facilities to help you to buy equipment), leasing and rental deals rather than outright purchase of equipment and technology goods. While they may look expensive, they are 'off-balance sheet financing', which does wonders for your covenant calculations. Also consider other forms of maintaining cash flow, such as using a factoring company to collect and manage your invoices, and at all times, try to minimise the bank's perception of risk in lending to you, increase their confidence and enthusiasm to lend by promising them no more than you know you can achieve, and then delivering above forecast, understand what they can and can't offer and then structure your request so that it's watertight in banking terms.

EXPERT OPINION

Choosing the right IT and communications supplier can be important in running your business

BT offers advice on getting the best phone and computer services:

Fixed line, mobiles, broadband: getting the basics right

The sheer number of different providers for landline connections, mobile calls and broadband internet can leave startups feeling swamped. For many, the way to cut through this jungle of choice is to search for the cheapest deals. But while every business should be careful to manage its expenditure, there are other important considerations.

Fixed line

- Do you need staff to have their own direct numbers? Or will a single number be more suitable?
- What other features might you need? Can your provider offer voicemail, three-way calling and divert calls to a user's mobile?
- Make sure your deal includes 'call capping' – so that, for example, calls to

other UK landlines cost no more than 5p per hour.

- Look out for discounts based on usage – so the more your business uses the phone, the lower the per minute charge.
- Ask your provider if they offer the tools to let you monitor things like missed calls, engaged calls and call waiting times. These data can be vital in helping you to grow the business.
- Make sure you work with a landline provider that can guarantee quick and effective help if things go wrong.

Mobile

- Ask if your provider offers a tariff that provides free mobile calls between employees and free mobile calls back to the office.
- Can the overall number of monthly minutes on your tariff be shared across your users?
- Would your team benefit from wireless access that lets them connect to the internet when out of the office?
- Ask your provider if they offer a combined voicemail service – including all your landline and mobile messages on one number.

Broadband

- Make sure the monthly download limits are suitable. For example, design companies are likely to need far higher download limits than management consultants because graphics tend to be large file sizes.
- Think about the applications you will need to protect your business. Is virus protection included as standard? Can your supplier provide a business firewall?
- Does your supplier offer mobile broadband so you can work anywhere at anytime?
- Look for a supplier that can provide broadband business tools. For example, can they design and host your company website; do they offer tools to allow you to sell products via your website; is business email provided – so you can access emails from wherever you are?

A one-stop shop

A useful way to cut down some of the complexity, and to make it easier to get these key purchasing decisions right, is to use a supplier capable of meeting all your landline, mobile and broadband needs.

- **Saving time** – Using a single supplier means benefiting from a single contact number when you need help or advice. Meanwhile, receiving one bill for all of your phone and internet usage can be a valuable time-saver.
- **Saving money** – Typically, suppliers that are able to meet all of your requirements will also offer discounted packages if you use them for landline, mobiles and broadband. Meanwhile, some suppliers will also offer tools that allow you to analyse your fixed and mobile spend by type of call, time of call, calls made by specific users or departments, so you can identify opportunities for further cost efficiencies.
- **Getting better advice** – Working with a single supplier means that they will gain a clear picture of your communications needs and challenges. This knowledge can prove invaluable in advising your business as it grows and evolves.

For further advice about what technology can do for your business, and getting it right from the outset, visit the BT Business Insight website (www.bt.com/insight), a unique online resource for small businesses.

EXPERT OPINION

BT gives advice on protecting and maintaining your computing system

Security

Most people are familiar with the importance of protecting IT systems from threats such as viruses, hackers, and junk email (known as 'spam'). Whether protecting your intellectual property, customer details or financial information, it is essential that your business uses the correct software and processes to keep it safe.

- **Software:** Your supplier should be able to advise you on, and provide you with, software to prevent viruses infecting your system, to stop spam clogging up your in-boxes and to guard against other risks such as spyware and malware.
- **Firewall:** Every organisation should use a firewall, a 'virtual' barrier that is designed to block potentially unsafe data entering your system.
- **Processes:** Your employees play the most important role in keeping your system safe. Your IT supplier should be able to provide clear, detailed guidance to help you ensure that staff do not expose the company to security threats.

Support and maintenance

This is perhaps the key ingredient. A recent survey conducted by YouGov found that 77 per cent of small business owner-managers spend up to nine hours every week maintaining IT and communications systems. This is time that could be spent winning and consolidating business. Make sure that your supplier will set up, or 'configure', your computers when they are delivered. Computers should also come pre-loaded with all the relevant software. If you have technical problems, is there a dedicated 24/7 support number that you can dial to get issues resolved immediately?

If you are leasing the computers, will they be automatically upgraded after a fixed period of time? Technology evolves quickly; you don't want to be stuck with out of date computers or software. Can you get advice on developing your infrastructure? As your business develops, so will your IT needs.

Free business services

The internet has had a profound effect on all of us, particularly when it comes to free services. In the past, these have tended to be developed for consumers but free business-grade applications and services that solve a wide range of problems are now available for business users too. Many people think this sounds too good to be true but free business services and applications are available from even the biggest service providers and vendors, including BT Business. Users have to register to use them but have no commitment to pay for the services in the future. The option that is open to them is to upgrade the products to get more functions or services for a small monthly subscription.

CASE STUDY
DESIGN AND PRINT CENTRE AND THE UNEXPECTED BONUS

Building a strong relationship with his business bank has helped **David Miller** through the tough couple of years of starting Design and Print Centre. Although launching a design and communications agency into a crowded marketplace, a strong business plan, incorporating the benefits of working virtually from a cost and billing perspective, helped secure the necessary investment.

Managing to attract an unsecured loan for £40,000 to launch his business from Lloyd's Bank, which meant that he and his fellow directors did not have to secure their homes or any other personal assets against the borrowing, Miller was determined to run a tight ship to avoid further borrowing that may need securing.

'This was difficult initially as cash was tight, but if we were approaching our agreed overdraft limit I simply told my bank business adviser, who was prepared to let us exceed it for a limited period if necessary,' he explained. 'Keeping him informed was key.'

What's more, regular meetings with his bank meant that his adviser understood his business and its market.

'This led him to putting us in touch with some of his clients who might be able to use our services, which I never expected,' said Miller.

6.0

FINDING A NAME

WHAT'S IN THIS CHAPTER

- Choosing a business name is one of the most important things that you will have to decide upon when starting a business. And it's also one of the very first decisions that you will have to make. There's a lot more to it than simply going for something you like, from practical reasons of recognition to legal factors. Until this point you could get away with not naming your company or having a name that's inappropriate from a business sense, but before you submit a business plan to anyone, you'll need to get it right. Read on for tips and examples that should help you choose the right name for your business...

What's in a name?

In a completely sane and rational world, a company with a strong product, service, or niche idea could expect to make a healthy profit. However, it takes more than that to get across to customers the benefit of using your business instead of your competitor's. The name is the first thing that any potential buyer is going to notice and, in this respect, is more important than your sales pitch or even your end product. You might have the best idea in the world, but if people are going elsewhere because your competition 'looks' more attractive, then no one will ever know.

As the name is the entry point to your business and, superficially, the only differentiator between you and your competitors, customers will make instant judgements on where they want to part with their cash. Therefore, it's essential that you strike the right tone with your business' name. However, successful companies do not just have good names, they develop a brand. And, in time, brands can literally sell themselves. Company branding specialist, **Jim Fowle**, of Red Mullet Design, says: 'When starting a company, your brand is of vital importance. Branding is not just a memorable logo, but also an effective, memorable name that can really help people remember you. This can be portrayed strongly visually as well. In the initial stages, we find it's good to envisage your name and branding, making sure it's recognisable, simple and reflects your business.'

Easier said than done. After all you want to stand out from your competition, but you also need to be taken seriously. When you're choosing a business name it's essential to remember that this is a name that you will have to say dozens of times each day and it is something you will be known by. Make sure that you like how it sounds and how it looks before committing. 'Initially, in the early stages, the best option is to be experimental,' suggests Fowle. 'Sometimes it's easy to get too clever and lose sight of what you are trying to achieve. It is about getting the balance of a good name and having good branding at the same time. This encapsulates the perfect package.'

> "The right business name can offer a real advantage in the battle for customers"

It's tempting to incorporate your own name into your business' moniker, although Dave's Cabs or Hutchison Landscape Gardening hardly screams originality. A safe and trustworthy method is to link your business' name to the area in which you operate – customers associate such firms with strong local roots and a friendly approach to the public. Therefore, the Acton Sandwich Shop or Govan Records would be perceived to be well-established, reputable businesses. Humour or a nice play on words is an effective way to stand out from the crowd. While a fish and chip shop called Your Plaice or Mine or a hairdressers named Hair Today, Gone Tomorrow would elicit predictable groans from passers-by, puns can be used for good effect, as long as they are not overly cheesy or digress from what image you are trying to convey for your firm.

> **" Names should be snappy, original and instantly informative as to what your business does "**

There are essentially three kinds of business name

Descriptive
These describe what the business does, or may be named after the owner. For example: Design and Print Centre.

- Pros: Provides information about your business or who runs it
- Cons: Can lack creativity and be less memorable

Associative
These aim to create positive associations in customers' minds. For example: Ocean Fish Bar.

- Pros: Can help to generate a positive image of your company
- Cons: If not original or creative, they can come across as clichéd

Abstract
These may have no meaning at all, and could be just words joined together. For example: Shoon (shoe shop).

- Pros: Easier to be original and can attract attention
- Cons: Provide no information about the company

Ideally, names should be snappy, original and instantly informative as to what your business does. Customers should be drawn to a name that stands out from the crowd, but also find it trustworthy and professional.

What you can and can't call your business

Words or expressions deemed to be offensive are not allowed by Companies House. You will have to exercise your own judgement as to what such words include, but chances are that swear words or phrases generally considered insulting will not be not permitted. There are also phrases that are deemed to be 'sensitive' and you will have to gain permission to use them. These phrases can be classified into five main groups, and include words that:

- Suggest your business is of national importance, such as British, Scottish, national or international
- Depict a special status or authority such as association, chamber of commerce, council
- Describe a particular function, such as a charity or trust
- Refer to a specialised activity, such as surveyor or chemist
- Give the impression that your business is connected to the government or the Royal Family.

Limited companies

If you are starting a limited company then your company name must end with Limited (or Ltd). Also, this word must not appear anywhere else in your name, so 'Limited Ltd' is not allowed. Once you have chosen your name and it made sure that it complies with the rules, you can apply to have it registered at Companies House.

Contact

Companies House
www.companies
house.gov.uk
....

! TIPS

YOUR BUSINESS NAME CHECKLIST

When you choose a name for your business, make sure it:

! Is not already taken

! Has no negative connotations

! Reflects what your business stands for

! Is appropriate and appealing to your audience

! Has the potential to be memorable

! Won't be able to limit your business in any way

! Has a meaning that can be transferred overseas if necessary

! Is easy to say and spell

! Can be owned and protected as your trademark

! Can be registered as an internet URL or web address

(Source: More Th>n Business)

Sole traders

If you are a sole trader then you can trade under your name and/or your business partner's name if you have one. However, this is not obligatory and you can be far more creative if you wish. Sole traders, however, are not allowed to use Ltd or plc (private limited company) in their name, as it describes the business incorrectly.

Checking for originality

When you're choosing a business name make sure that you **can** use that name and it isn't already being used. To spend money publishing stationery or setting up your website could be an awful waste if another company with your prospective title already exists. Making a few simple checks before you do any of this is a good idea. The Companies House website is one good way to do this – just go to www.checksure.biz and see what's available before choosing a business name. However, as sole traders do not have to register with Companies House, they will not show up on this search. So you should also check local phone books, business directories and run some internet searches on your chosen name. If you find there is a sole trader on the other side of the country who is using your name, then this may not be a problem, but if the company is local or national then you will have to choose again.

You also need to check if your proposed name isn't too similar to a name that someone else has registered as a trademark. The easiest way to do this is via the Patent Office website – again simple checks now will save you time and money later.

If you are setting up your own website, checking out available domain names is also well worth your time. Many companies pick a different name for their website than the name they use to do business. But this isn't the best scenario if your company is going to be web-based. See the section on domain names below for more details.

Contact

Patent Office
www.ipo.gov.uk

A great name is good marketing

A creative name plays a huge role in setting a small business apart and getting it noticed

The small business insurance company More Th>n Business conducted a survey into the impact of business names on potential customers. First, the company asked for nominations for the most creative company name, with entries coming not only from the companies themselves, but also their customers, giving a clear indication of just how much attention a great company name can attract. Once a list of the best names had been compiled, they were then tested on the general public. Three-quarters of those surveyed admitted to being influenced by a catchy name, while 58% said it would make them remember the business. In fact, they were found to be most important to the younger people, with three-quarters of 18–24-year-olds stating they would notice and remember a shop with a humorous name. 'Our research confirms what the UK's most creative business owners already knew – that the right business name can offer a real advantage in the battle for customers,' says **Mike Bowman**, head of insurance at More Th>n Business. 'With over 400,000 new startups each year, it is becoming increasingly difficult for business owners to settle on a catchy yet original name, but the research shows that it's definitely worth putting in the time and effort to get the right name.'

Citing the great marketing potential of a good, creative business name, Bowman, adds: 'A creative name plays a huge role in setting a small business apart and getting it noticed. Small businesses and independent high street retailers may not have massive marketing budgets, but this doesn't mean there is a lack of creative flair.' More Th>n Business awarded the title of most creative British business name to Aisle Alter Hymn, a wedding shop for gay and lesbian couples in South Shields. However, remember that you don't have to use a pun to achieve a memorable name, but if you're in an industry where it's hard to market your unique selling point, it may just help you stand out from the crowd, as William the Concreter would probably agree.

ACTION POINT
WHERE TO START LOOKING FOR A NAME

GET FRIENDS AND FAMILY TOGETHER FOR A BRAINSTORM: It helps to canvass opinion and your nearest and dearest is as good a place to start as any, according to small business insurance company More Th>n Business.

EXAMINE WHAT COMPETITORS ARE CALLED: Do you think the names of your competitors work? By checking them out you should know the standard you're up against, and although you can't copy any and would be ill-advised to choose a similar name, you may be inspired by good ones.

THINK OF GOOD BUSINESS NAMES THAT STAND OUT IN YOUR MIND: Beyond your competitors, you can also get inspiration from famous companies without directly copying them.

USE THE INTERNET, PHONE BOOK, MAGAZINES AND BUSINESS DIRECTORIES TO RESEARCH: You can pretty much carry out all necessary investigation from home using handy sources of information.

CHOOSE AT LEAST 10 NAMES: Then you can whittle these down to a shortlist of three or four by checking which of your possible names are available – remember that many will already be taken. Once you have your shortlist of available names, use family and friends in the elimination process and make sure each of the names generated stands up to the checklist on page 167.

The top 20 creative business names

Here's a rundown of the best business names in the UK, following a survey by small business insurer More Th>n Business:

1. Aisle Alter Hymn (UK's first wedding shop for gay, lesbian and heterosexual couples in South Shields, Tyne & Wear)
2. Battersea Cods Home (fish and chip shop in Sheffield, South Yorkshire)
3. Mad Hakkers (hairdressers in Leven, Fife)
4. Mr Bit (window cleaners in Derby and Coventry, West Midlands)
5. Only Foods and Sauces (takeaway in Walsall, West Midlands)
6. Spruce Springclean (window cleaners in West Byfleet, Surrey)
7. Tree Wise Men (tree surgeons in Wallington, Surrey)
8. Vinyl Resting Place (second-hand records shop in Croydon, Surrey)
9. Walter Wall (carpet sales in Exeter, Devon)
10. Plaice Station (fish and chip shop in Manchester)
11. William the Concreter (concrete suppliers in Hastings)
12. Carter, Whey and Tippet (refuse collection service in London)
13. Dustin Often (cleaning service in Leicester)
14. C Thru Cleaning (cleaning service in Middlesex)
15. Give Us A Break (window fitters in Leicester)
16. R Soles (Bootmaker in London)
17. Floral and Hardy (gardeners in Hayes, Kent)
18. Sarnie Schwarzenegger's (sandwich shop in Liverpool)
19. Abra-Kebab-Ra (kebab shop in Dublin)
20. Wok This Way (Chinese takeaway in Glasgow)

There are also some other serious contenders, including north-east entertainers Amps and Decks and arborists Tree Amigos. Then there's Pimp my Pet, Fishcoteque, Pain in the Glass, Junk and Disorderly, Curl up and Dye, Spice Boys, Bubble n Chic and The Head Gardener. Can you guess what these businesses do?

CASE STUDY
THE NAME THAT HAS EVERYTHING

Arguably, there's no better way to attract a potential customer's attention than putting a smile on their face. Make someone laugh and they'll automatically have positive associations with your company, and if the amusing name also cleverly says what you do, you could be on to a winner. **Judy White** runs a one-woman ironing and laundry business in Bristol and won an award from *Yellow Pages* for the name of her company Crease Lighting, which was inspired by the popular song from the musical *Grease*. 'I came up with the name because I am a massive *Grease* fan,' she says. 'I even wear my hair like Olivia Newton John does in the movie.'

Not everyone takes the naming of their business to such extremes, but the clever thing about Crease Lightning is that it's not just highly amusing, it also reminds people of an incredibly popular movie that's both funny and entertaining. Although humour is a good trick for getting your business noticed and loved even before anyone has even bought anything from you, it only works if its appropriate and positive. There is a funeral directors in Twickenham, south-west London, called Wake and Paine, but presumably that's simply the names of the proprietors, as humour is certainly not the right route to take when naming such a business. The professions from legal to architectural also need a more serious approach, as often do many tradesmen, especially builders, who need to engender a feeling of trust. So remember that humour is not for everyone.

Your domain name

Today, the vast majority of companies need a website, and the name you choose for your web address is just as important as your main registered name. That's because your website should lie at the heart of your marketing strategy, and attract as many customers as possible. If it is isn't doing this, you are missing out on a major online marketing opportunity, particularly at a time when more and more people are using the internet to research the businesses they want to buy from. Of course, if your business exists solely online, your web address could be your registered company name as well, but sometimes it can be useful to have a separate registered name – in which case it's back to the start of this chapter for you.

Just like your registered name, your domain name should describe the nature of your business or reflect your main one to create brand awareness and encourage repeat hits – that is the number of times a customer clicks onto your website – and online sales. It is the central ingredient for successful online marketing and, if appropriate to the market, your name could be spread without you even having to do anything. Names can include letters, numbers and hyphens, so there are a several ways to distinguish yourself from the competition. For example, if your company is called John Smith Printers and the .com and .co.uk names are already taken, use your imagination to create an alternative. This could be perhaps jsprinters.com or jsprint.com. Although johnsmithprinters.com would be the obvious choice in this case, often the shorter the web address the better, as it can be easier to remember and be keyed in more quickly, while still reflecting the company and what it does.

You don't always need a name that directly states what you do. Having a unrelated catchy name can sometimes work to your advantage. Take Amazon.com, for example. The name is not directly linked to the products the company sells. However, Amazon has built a reputable brand around a totally new name that stands out from the crowd.

What makes a successful domain name?

Before attempting to buy any domain name, you will have to pose yourself some serious questions: How easy is it to recall the name? What about the visual appearance of the name, and how it will appear on any documentation you produce – as it needs to be there along with your main registered name (if it's different) and all you other contact details? It will also affect your personal business email address, which, of course, is a key way for people to contact you. As it needs to make an instant impression on the customer, keep it short, recognisable and consistent with the brand you plan to establish.

If in doubt, remember the acronym RAIL:

- R (Recall): How easy is it to recall the name?
- A (Aesthetics): How does the name look and how will it appear on business cards and company literature?
- I (Impressions): First impressions are crucial, so choose your name carefully
- L (Length): Web addresses are limited to the 26 letters of the English alphabet, 10 numerals and a hyphen – 37 characters in all. When picking a name, less is more. A short name is preferable to a long one.

Lesley Cowley, operations director at Nominet, the internet registry for .uk domain names, confirms the length of name is crucial in customer retention. 'There is no standard in the length of a domain, but the rule of thumb is the shorter the better,' he says. As it is becoming increasingly difficult for customers to find what they are looking for, your name will also have to be easily picked out by search engines, which is an increasingly popular route people take to locate a specific website or a selection that offer the service required. If you keep your domain name short, simple and catchy, it can be found, accessed and remembered more easily.

There are companies you can pay to make your business more attractive to search engines, and they provide a service called web optimisation or search engine optimisation. This can be expensive and,

> *If you keep your domain name short, simple and catchy, it can be found, accessed and remembered more easily*

> *When choosing a name it is vital to consider the email address you will have as well*

these days, it's not really possible to fool search engines like it was in the past, so be wary of companies that offer a foolproof service, as websites that are spotted by search engines as trying to use underhand means to jump up the rankings are blacklisted – a marketing catastrophe. However, there are some companies that offer a kosher service which will involve them helping you to track down keywords and phrases that your potential customers would use to locate your service, and then cleverly build them into the content of your site, perhaps donating a page each to the main keywords and phrases. Your domain name can help here too, as it will be a little more attractive to search engines if it is descriptive – although this is only a minor factor compared to keyword association. Ultimately, search engines want to be sure that when someone searches for a particular service, they deliver relevant company websites. So if your company has lots of appropriate content about what you do, including perhaps advice and other relevant information, and is full of the necessary keywords, then this will help greatly.

As briefly touched on earlier, another key consideration when selecting a name is your email address, which people swap all the time as a way of staying in touch for business as well as social reasons. So it is vital that these are memorable and descriptive. So when choosing a name it is vital to consider this as well. It is a means by which you are remembered, contacted and will gain repeat hits or sales, not just a name.

Choosing a domain name

"The best and most highly regarded name is still .com"

Once you have chosen a domain name you will have to think about and research the possibilities of the ending. Will it be .com, .org, .net or something more unusual? This depends on a number of factors, including the nature of your business, whether you are national, or international or both, and what is important to you and your customer base. The suffix .com is the broadest option, but as **Nick Saalfeld**, group editor of CompuServe UK, says, if you can't register .com, then simply go elsewhere. 'You have two big choices, .com and .co.uk,' he explains. 'These are the most desirable. However, with the uptake of alternative names, such as .net and .uk, .com is slowly becoming less desirable.'

Whatever the experts say, though, the best and most highly regarded name is still .com. It is globally and universally recognised, so if you can register it, as well as .co.uk, do it sooner rather than later. Even if you don't use the UK name, by registering it you will keep others from copying your name and it will protect you from the competition. In theory, the more names you own, then the better the chance you have of maintaining that brand as yours and yours alone. Unfortunately, today – with websites launching pretty much at the same rate as companies, and with some businesses having more that one website to perhaps target a specific sector – the short names are becoming scarce and fading fast. This means it's even more important to think as creatively as possible when deciding on both your main company name and that of your web address.

'Although there's very little status in suffixes today,' says Saalfeld. 'A British company should aim to own .co.uk and .com addresses, both of which imply a corporate entity, with .co.uk specifically identifying you as British.'

Registering a domain name

Assuming that no one has beaten you to it, anyone can register a domain name. Nominet, the internet registry for .uk domain names, encourages companies and individuals to register a domain via an internet service provider – or ISP. This is because the majority of ISPs are Nominet UK members who can register on your behalf. Once you have registered with an ISP, they will then submit the application to Nominet, ensuring a more thorough and secure process. However, be aware that contractual terms, charges and service levels of ISPs vary greatly, so it's worth shopping around to find the best deal. Some companies offer domain registration, while others include free webspace and email addresses or more specialist options. As with every business agreement you enter into, never forget to read the small print, and ask to see copies of the terms and conditions for domain name registration, as well as your right to move across to another ISP if you are unhappy. If you don't register with an ISP, there are around 6,000 companies who have domain registration facilities.

> **As with every business agreement you enter into, never forget to read the small print**

Contact

Nominet www. nom.net.org.uk

Nick Imrie of Domainnames.com, says: 'The key rule is that you get what you pay for, and it is often worthwhile paying the extra to deal with an up-front, reputable company that won't let you down.' There are some online packages and ISPs that will offer you a domain name for free, such as Microsoft's Office Live. However, you may still wish to register the domain name independently, because, as Imrie points out, you are likely to get a better service, so it's worth checking the options available and comparing what's on offer in each case.

Once you have decided upon which company is going to register your domain name, the process is generally swift and painless. First, you will be asked to pay a fee to secure your domain. Second, the company will send you a template of your registered domain name to the network information centre (NIC). Each country has its own NIC, which is where all the details of registered domains are held. Third, if your registration is accepted, the company you have chosen will set up a domain name system (DNS) entry. Essentially, this means assigning your name to a name server that collates and keeps all registered names, so that your domain can be found on the internet. The process takes between two and three days. Once these stages are complete, you will be live on the internet and can use your name.

Cost of registering a domain

As mentioned above, there are a variety of packages on offer when it comes to registering a domain name for your business. Some are cheaper than others and it often depends on what other services are included, such as whether you go for simple registration or choose any additional support services. Nominet's Cowley has seen a great deal of variation in the cost of domain names – from free of charge to £200 for .co.uk names – but this depends on levels of service and support. Prices will vary, depending on what your business needs, but there is an average price you will pay for single domain name registration, which is around £10.

If you have a portfolio of names, for example 10 separate domain names you'd like to use, you may need the services of a domain name manager. This is a relatively new entrant to the dotcom scene, and for a relatively small fee Domainaudit.com, which offers this service, will manage and maintain your domain assets. **Niamh Cullen**, marketing manager for Domainaudit.com, explains: 'Due to customers complaining about the amount of confusion they suffered after they had registered their domain names, we started the company. For just over £100 we can almost instantaneously register, manage and give you updates on the names you own, when they are up for renewal and who owns the names you want.'

How much would you pay for a domain name?

Throughout this section, you'll have noticed an emphasis on the originality of your domain name. Obviously this is to avoid confusion with other companies, and because you can't register exactly the same name as another business. However, you may find that the company that has registered the name you want doesn't actually do anything like what your business does. If that is the case, then it's probably because it's function is to register and sell domain names – and this can be big business. If you ask many companies how much they paid for their domain name, many will say £5, perhaps £15 or a little more. But if you thought that the name you had chosen was absolutely key to your business, perhaps because you only planned to trade online, and found that it was being sold, just how much would you be prepared to pay? Would you go as far as spending £560,000? That price tag doesn't cover the cost of creating the website, nor does it include the cost of web hosting. For a cool half million, all you get is a domain name – a highly popular one, of course, but, that's right, just a name. And the domain name in question, according to web hosting site 123-reg.co.uk, is cruises.co.uk. Apparently, it was bought by website cruise.co.uk, and is going to be used to host 'the UK's largest cruise community'.

An online presence is pretty much vital these days no matter how small your business is. It's no surprise then that entrepreneurial minds set to work on how to make a profit out of your need for a domain name. It's

> **If you ask many companies how much they paid for their domain name, many will say £5, perhaps £15 or a little more**

Contact

123-reg.co.uk
www.123-reg.co.uk

standard to pay around £10 for a domain name, and there are currently around six million co.uk domains, but as more companies go online, the demand for particular words or phrases is only going to increase. And to cash in on that demand are the clever people who have already snapped up the popular domains to sell for a profit later on.

So what about the most expensive domain name ever purchased? Well sex.com has got to be up there, which allegedly went for a whopping $12 million. And there are lots of alleged examples that similarly dwarf the official .co.uk domain name purchase record (see box), proving just how important a name can be.

The world's most expensive domain names

- sex.com ($12 million)
- porn.com ($9.5 million)
- business.com ($7.5 million)
- diamond.com ($7.5 million)
- beer.com ($7 million)
- casino.com ($5.5 million)
- korea.com ($5 million)
- asseenontv.com ($5.1 million)
- seo.com ($5 million)
- shop.com ($3.5 million)
- altavista.com ($3.3 million)
- loans.com ($3 million)
- vodka.com ($3 million)
- creditcheck.com ($3 million)
- wine.com ($2.9 million)
- creditcards.com ($2.75 million)
- autos.com ($2.2 million)
- express.com ($1.8 million)
- seniors.com ($1.5 million)
- tandberg.com ($1.5 million)
- cameras.com ($1.5 million)
- vip.com ($1.4 million)
- scores.com ($1.18 million)
- chinese.com ($1.12 million)
- topix.com ($1 million)
- wallstreet.com ($1 million)
- rock.com ($1 million)
- poker.de ($957,937) (this is the world's most expensive non .com name)

(Source: www.16thletter.com)

CASE STUDY
EASY JET AND THE
SIMPLE APPROACH

Startups.co.uk has a number of interesting video interviews with successful entrepreneurs, and one of the shortest and most interesting is the owner of easyJet's account of where the name of his company came from.

In classic abstract style, **Stelios Haji-Ioannou** called his company Stelmar, which was an amalgamation of Stelios Maritime. The reason he wanted to incorporate his name was to stamp his own personal credentials on the company. 'I wanted to achieve something specific and for it to be known as Stelios' company and not my father's,' he says. In the same vein, Stelair was the working title for the airline he planned to set up, once again trying to involve his name in the business. But then he changed his mind. 'I decided that I shouldn't be so self-centred,' he says. 'And it was also difficult to pronounce... I also decided that the brand had to be extendable over several industries.' There were also considerations of longevity behind his decision to call this business easyJet, as well as consideration for his shareholders. 'I'd like to think that the more mature easyJet companies can carry on independent of me,' he says. 'I think people would still like to fly easyJet, whether I'm in charge or not. Certainly outside shareholders would like to think that that's true.

'How can you operate a business that is so focused on its founder that it can't run without him?' he asks. 'You have to give outside shareholders the confidence that your business has a future without you.' However, he believes that although companies should not be totally dependent on a single person, it is important to have a strong, recognisable personality at the helm. 'It is good to put a face on your business when you start up,' he says. 'People like to read about people, not companies. Therefore, the media talk about people and not companies. If there is a strong personality behind a company, then the media are more likely to talk about it.'

So with easyJet, you could say that Stelios has managed to get the perfect mix of strong brand and strong leader, without the latter overshadowing the former.

DON'T START A BUSINESS!

without going to the National Business Register free start-up website

• advice • help • support • searches

www.start.biz

free info pack
0870 700 8787

National Business
REGISTER

freedom

Want to break away from the herd and go it alone? If you've got a great business idea, we can help you realise your dream. Get connected today and find out how.

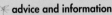 advice and information
 social networking
 your gateway to business success

Shell
liveWIRE
supporting bright young business

REGISTER NOW AND MAKE IT HAPPEN AT www.shell-livewire.org

Think business potential

think IP

Do you have a brand to protect? **think Trade Marks**
Invented something innovative? **think Patents**
Artistic or creative? **think Copyright**
Shape or form to protect? **think Designs**

The UK Intellectual Property Office is the Government agency responsible for IP in the UK. If you need help and advice on Trade Marks, Patents, Copyright or Designs then contact us on:

08459 500 505
enquiries@ipo.gov.uk
www.ipo.gov.uk

For Creativity and Innovation

18 months free business banking for start-ups.

Thinking Of Starting A Business?

Finally An Amazingly Simple Way To Attract More Customers, More Quickly – And It Doesn't Cost A Single Penny!

Many new business owners think marketing is just advertising or selling. The more cynical consider that marketing is getting people to buy things that they don't really want!

If this is how you think of marketing, you may be missing a trick.

See your business "through your customer's eyes"

For many people, looking at their business in this way is a complete change.

The usual starting point is to develop what we want to sell and then set out to find people to buy it.

Adopt a different mindset

Effective marketing reverses this process. It requires an outside-in approach – a mindset that puts the customer at the centre of everything the business does. After all without customers, we don't have a business.

So, you may ask, how do we get inside their heads? The answer is simple – just ask them! Ask the right questions to make sure we really understand what they want.

No need for big surveys or expensive market research

Just speak to your customers – or prospective customers if you haven't started the business yet. Think of the people who would be interested in what you have to offer. Ask them what they want most for their business or for themselves.

Now make a list of all the possible things your customers could want from your product or service, and get them to rate what's most important on the list. Now use that information in your marketing.

Here's what successful businesses do

Look at the example of successful weight loss companies. They know full well what their customers need – to lose weight by having a strictly structured eating plan. But those companies market what the customer wants – "Eat anything you want, even chocolate and cakes - our system makes it easy." By tapping into the wants, they give their customers what they need – namely weight reduction, overall fitness and improved eating habits.

What do your customers WANT? How can you re-frame what you offer to satisfy them?

Finding out what they want and giving it to them will get you more customers, more quickly, more easily – and doesn't cost a penny!

Five Tips To Jump-Start Your Marketing

There's more to marketing than placing an advert, producing a brochure or designing a website. These five tips can make a difference and help you get results.

Focus on your customer

Yes, I know, you hear this all the time – and yet many of us still start by developing what we want to sell and then find people to buy it. Effective marketing starts with your customer – after all without customers, we don't have a business.

Target your marketing

Trying to be everything to everyone is costly and ineffective. Find that gap in the market that only you can fill and focus all your efforts there. Identify your ideal customer, aim at them and you will achieve success.

Fish where the fish are

Are you talking to the right people in the right places? Focus your marketing where you are likely to be seen by the highest number of potential customers. If your customers only read the Sunday Times, that's where you should advertise and if they shop at 'Cheap Charlie's' don't go for distribution in Harrods!

Everyone likes to buy

Help your customer to buy by making it easy for them to do business with you. Check out your sales processes – are you putting barriers in their way, with complicated forms or no contact details?

Ask for the order – Always!

Do you know that over 90% of people in business fail to ask for the order. In all your marketing simply ask your customer to take action and tell them EXACTLY what to do next.

Helen Murdoch has spent 25 years discovering the secrets of successful marketing. Better still, she reveals those secrets in an amazing **FREE** report titled "How To Get More, More, More From Your Marketing". The report guides you step-by-step to get the results you want but can't achieve by yourself. Claim your **FREE** report now. Simply go to **www.hmmarketing.co.uk** and download your personal copy.

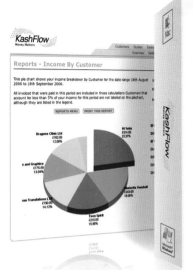

BT Tradespace

Make your business the obvious choice.

Stand out for **FREE*** by advertising on BT Tradespace.

Joining the BT Tradespace community is the FREE and easy way to raise your business's profile online.

- Make your Tradespace site as unique as your firm by adding photos, videos, blogs and podcasts.
- Use the Tradespace networks to get people talking.
- Benefit from BT's marketing and promotion of Tradespace to drive thousands of potential customers to your business.
- Extend your reach by being listed on search engines like Google.

Visit www.bttradespace.com

External

Case Study

BT Tradespace boosts internet trader's sales

Connecting buyers and sellers

Through her company, Hedgepig, Lyn Hill started selling unusual gifts and homeware – innovative and niche products that chain stores did not stock – from her home in Lancashire. Initially Lyn used a website and the Google AdWord services, but that proved to be an expensive combination and Lyn did not feel that Hedgepig was getting the search engine profile that she would have liked. Then Lyn heard about BT Tradespace, an online community that brings small businesses and individual sellers together with potential customers.

Rocketing sales conversions

The basic Tradespace service offers advertising for up to five products and entry into one sales category, together with an individual blog space. Lyn recalls: "The effects were immediate in terms of search engine ratings: Hedgepig quickly found its way towards the top. In my first two months with BT Tradespace I saw 2,000 high quality visitors and my sales conversion rate went up from five per cent to 15 per cent."

In addition to providing a range of powerful and easy-to-use online marketing tools, BT Tradespace provides interactive features such as blogs and members' ratings. Lyn was particularly impressed by the BT Tradespace image sharing facilities. "The quality of the online images that I am able to use on Tradespace is actually better than on my website, and that helps to drive sales," she says. "Now I have taken the full BT Tradespace service for just £15 a month, and I'm advertising Hedgepig's full product range and using several sales categories."

Quick and easy

BT Tradespace is designed to make things as easy as possible for its customers. Lyn recalls: "It took me about 20 minutes to start trading on BT Tradespace; it's that quick and you don't need any IT knowledge at all. It's dead easy to interconnect my web site and my BT Tradespace presence." That means, for instance, that Lyn can link people to her BT Tradespace blog.

Lyn concludes: "In its first year, the company turned over less than £20,000 but I expect that to at least triple by the end of its second year, accelerated by Hedgepig's presence on BT Tradespace. BT Tradespace is saving me hundreds of pounds every month and both my family life and my business benefit enormously."

About the BT solution

BT Tradespace Basic is free to register (www.bttradespace.com). It allows traders to build a profile, describe their company, and upload up to five photos. Subscription to BT Tradespace Contact additionally enables members to advertise and sell unlimited items; post unlimited photos, podcasts and videos; and promote their business on as many relevant channels as they like. It also allows customers to call them free and receive their business card via SMS text and email from anywhere in the world.

> "In my first two months with BT Tradespace I saw 2,000 high-quality visitors and **my sales conversion rate went up** from five per cent to 15 per cent."
>
> Lyn Hill, Owner, Hedgepig

IT • communications • support

Bringing it all together BT

7.0

PRODUCT PREPARATION

WHAT'S IN THIS CHAPTER

■ Once you've decided on the business you want to run, carried out the necessary research into its viability and put together your business plan, perhaps also having secured early stage finance, it's time to make sure you have the necessary elements in place to be able to launch effectively. Depending on your business, this can range from finding the right premises to recruiting staff, looking at key issues such as pricing and insurance along the way. Read on to find out the areas you need to consider addressing before you're ready for the off. This is the largest section of the book, because there's a lot to cover…

Searching for the right premises

Finding the appropriate home for your business can be time consuming and, once you've found the ideal place, it can then be a key expense for your company. It can, however, cost you very little if you can simply rent a desk in another company's premises, or it can take up hardly any of your time in searching for the right space if you decide to work from home. So before you do anything else, you need to decide the kind of premises you'll need to launch your business.

If your business dictates that you are going to need dedicated premises to operate from, then knowing which type of property you need – office, workshop, shop, etc – is merely the beginning. You also need to consider the location and available transport links, and then ask yourself questions such as how important common areas are to you and what standard of facilities you need, such as bathroom, storage, meeting room, kitchen, delivery access and so on.

> **One overriding factor dominates looking for premises, and that's cost**

Determining what do you need

One overriding factor dominates the priorities of startup businesses looking for premises, and that's cost. No one ever has enough money, so there is an overwhelming temptation to go for the cheapest property. This is often a mistake that can take decades to rectify – and even bring a promising business to its knees. Ironically, some firms swing too far in the other direction, committing themselves to a heavy initial outlay because they believe image is vital – and image does not come cheap. Finding the right premises is the real secret. That can, and will, vary enormously according to the type of business. But there are some general rules that apply to any operation.

LOCATION

Shops need passing trade, but high street premises are expensive. Do you need passing trade or will customers come looking for you? Rents fall quickly within yards of main roads. Offices are even more flexible, particularly if most business is done on the phone. Manufacturing and storage relies heavily on access, so think about how vans and lorries will deliver and collect goods. What's more, nearby parking can be important, and as traffic restrictions tighten, public transport may be even more so.

SIZE

Size is a crucial factor. Health and safety laws provide basic guidance on how much space is needed per office desk or manufacturing process, but it will pay you to allow for growth. After all, the whole point of business is to expand, so try to be flexible. Yes, this will cost more, but today's outgoings must be balanced against the prospects of tomorrow's earnings.

Growth

It is crucial to consider restrictions on potential alterations in how premises may be used

Every small business aims to become a big business, but this prospect can be choked from birth if the wrong decisions are made. Building in flexibility at the start can be important. Can a building be physically altered internally, such as knocking down walls, extending outwards or upwards? Is there spare land next door for expansion?

Landlords obviously hold the whip hand, and it can be important to make agreements from the outset about what will be allowed and how much extra will be charged on top of the cost of rebuilding or alteration. Planning rules must also be considered, as local authorities are not always open to discussion about the future of premises. They may have rigid rules about increasing density of development, or buildings may be in a conservation area or near housing, in which case it will be much more difficult to consider changes.

Even where no physical changes are required, it is crucial to consider restrictions on potential alterations in how premises may be used. Lease conditions and planning rules are usually quite specific about what goes on within a building. For example, you can't change a shop to an office, or vice versa, without permission from the local authority and landlord. In fact, even switching from one type of shop to another can sometimes fall foul of planning restrictions. So you'll need to cover all the options and regulations before signing on the dotted line.

CASE STUDY
IGLU.COM AND THE INCUBATOR SAVIOUR

Richard Downs started to put together his business plan for iglu.com while a full-time MBA student at London Business School (LBS). The original plan was based on selling property on the internet, but was quickly focused on the holiday ski market to take advantage of the correlation between skiers and internet users, as well as the fragmented nature of the market. Having met his partner, Emmanuelle Drouot, iglu.com needed to be ready in time for launch at the impending Ski Show.

As the countdown began, the company was lucky enough to find a home in the newly created LBS incubator, which provides basic office facilities for startup companies. This gave them the time to focus on the business rather than hunting for suitable office space. The website was completed at 2am on the morning of the show, explains Downs, who notes that even half a week spent looking for office space would have been disastrous. 'If we had missed the ski season, we would have been marginalised. The market opportunity would not be there,' he says, noting that a 12-month delay would have seen competitors steal the top slot.

The space offered by LBS is scaleable and is charged by the number of people. This makes the incubator relatively inexpensive for companies of two or three, but relatively expensive for larger groups. 'If a company is successful and grows, there is an economic impetus to move out,' says Downs. iglu.com, which currently consists of a team of eight, is preparing to do just that as it has outgrown its original needs. The company is moving as a private tenant to another part of the building and hopes to keep a close association with the incubator and be on hand to provide advice to other companies starting. 'The other benefit is the network – being in an area with people in the same industry to throw around ideas,' says Downs.

Other factors to consider

On top of your company's specific requirements, there are other issues you will need to consider before making a final decision on the premises to go for.

USE OF PREMISES

Most leases overflow with restrictions on how buildings can be used. This is partly to protect the landlord's investment by, for instance, preventing dangerous or noisy activities. There may also be covenants from the original ground landlord on types of business activity, as well as local planning restrictions. Sub-letting is commonly denied without the permission of the landlord. If a lease contains too many of these caveats, it can restrict your ability to pass on the lease to another tenant when you want to move on.

> **If a lease contains too many caveats, it can restrict your ability to pass on the lease to another tenant**

REDECORATION AND REPAIR

Designating when, where, and how often redecoration and repair should take place, and who should do it can be a crucial factor, particularly for older premises, where hefty costs may be involved. Furthermore, many modern leases load most of these onto tenants, and landlords usually demand power to carry out the work at your expense if it is not done on time and to a required standard. Tenants also face what are called dilapidations schedules at the end of their lease term, where the landlord can demand payment where premises haven't been kept in good condition.

ALTERATIONS

Structural changes and extensions are usually restricted. Internal changes require negotiation and may need clearing when the lease ends.

LENGTH OF COMMITMENT

A tradition has grown up in the UK for long leases. At one time, these ran for as long as a century, but the term has gradually been eroded to between 10 and 15 years. These generally apply to new buildings or those in high-demand city centres, however. Much shorter terms can be found – or negotiated – nowadays, as landlords adjust to conditions where tenants are unwilling to commit themselves for such long periods. Three to five years is generally considered a good compromise between a landlord seeking security of investment and small businesses unsure of their future. For financial reasons, a landlord may prefer to maintain the lease length at 10 years, but allow a break clause. This effectively means the tenant can leave after, say, three or five years. On the other hand, it also means that the landlord can demand this break even when a tenant does not want to move, causing expense and disruption.

SECURITY OF TENURE

Many businesses may feel more secure with longer leases. They are usually assured of this by the 1954 Landlord and Tenant Act, which gives them the right to a new lease when the existing one expires. But sometimes these restrictions do not apply. Serviced premises are one example, along with a sub-lease situation or older buildings in temporary use pending redevelopment.

Others may seek the freedom to get out of their commitment. Watch out for restrictions on sub-letting or assigning a lease, which are common, as landlords usually like to keep control of who is using their buildings. Be aware that this may involve you paying someone a premium to take on the responsibility for a lease. One crucial factor when taking on an assignment, which means paying a fee to the existing leaseholder to take over their lease, is whether that lease is subject to an archaic rule called 'privity of contract'. Until the law was changed in 1996, a tenant remained responsible for rent and other charges even after assignment of the lease to a new tenant.

Alternatives

There are options outside renting premises through a traditional lease.

SERVICED OFFICES

Serviced offices are becoming common as more investors plough into this growing sector. This involves a contract rather than a lease, running for terms ranging from a few hours to several months. The charges may appear high compared with usual rents, but include all services such as heating, lighting, security and business rates. Offices sometimes come complete with furniture and carpets.

SERVICED INDUSTRY

The serviced industry sector is growing as landlords find it more difficult to attract tenants to older industrial space. The same terms apply as serviced offices, with an all-in monthly charge for rent and services.

Before you start the search

Having decided on the building details, you must feel ready to start your search. But before you do, bear in mind that while landlords used to give few choices, today's business environment is less certain and the market has responded by providing a range of options to suit. You should consider your business' financial model, and decide on your growth plans and the amount of money you want to spend. This will give you guidance on the services you want the landlord to include in the package, those you wish to pay for and the length of the lease term that suits you best. Before you set off, calculate your budget including one-off costs for items such as furniture and IT equipment, as well as ongoing costs such rates and service charges.

Shop search

Location can define your image, bring in other business and other contacts

Location is an important consideration for all new businesses, but for a retail shop, it's absolutely crucial to get it right. If there's one thing that commercial estate agents know about business premises it's the old adage: location, location, location… Your location, whether it is a high street, a shopping centre or an office block, will determine your business activity. But location can also define your image, bring in other business and other contacts. So what does that actually mean:

Things to consider before you secure the space

There are many ways to find potentially appropriate units – through commercial agents, online searches, local newspapers and even just walking around. Then comes the really important stage – the viewings. At this stage try think about questions that go beyond the obvious:

• Can you control the room's temperature?
• Is the building well maintained and water tight?

Once you've found the property that meets all your criteria (including, of course, your budget):

• Check out the landlord before you agree to take the space
• Talk to other tenants in the building to establish their reputation, and ask for a copy of their 'customer service charter', as you need to know how responsive they will be if anything goes wrong. If they don't have one, take that as a warning sign!
• Clarify what the monthly payment covers (for example rent only, or are some utilities included)
• Confirm what services the landlord is contractually obliged to give.

Before signing the first offer that you are presented with, try to negotiate, because you may be able to achieve a rent-free period, for example. Finally, rethink the whole process to help you finally decide if this is the right space for your business and for your customers.

This will be your last chance to change your mind without it potentially costing you money, so you need to ask yourself a number of key questions:

• Are you sure you can afford both the direct and indirect costs?
• Are you happy with the landlord, do you understand the deal and what you are committing to?

Once you've done your homework and you feel confident that you're getting a fair deal, you should move to secure the space.

- Where should you position your business?
- Should you head straight for the high street and aim to directly attract customers as they walk past?
- Should you locate on the edge of town or just off the main shopping avenue, because there are better parking facilities?
- Or should you head out of town altogether and follow the larger stores into a retail park, but pay more rent?

There are two main principles to bear in mind when thinking about the above questions: what sort of business you are and what sort of customers you are going to be targeting. Then comes the most important factor – market research and the four main areas you should consider:

- Population
- Accessibility
- Competition
- Costs

> **We studied what kind of people were shopping in the area**

These factors will determine where you locate. For example, if you run a sandwich bar or café, are the customers in the high street the ones who will buy take-away snacks? Can they afford your prices? What is the footfall or number of passers-by that walk in or past your shop? How visible is your store next to your competitors, and how accessible is your business?

Jo-Anne Bayliss, joint founder of People, a fashion shop in Kings Heath, Birmingham, knows all about researching your business for the ideal location. She believes that a knowledge of the area is crucial. 'We had lived in the area for four years and were seconds from the location,' she explains. 'We also knew that this area contained a lot of creative and young people, and that they would buy our products. This stretch of road also contains several gift shops, there is an existing customer base and shopping here saves a trip into town, even though this street is only a five-minute walk into Kings Heath high street.' When researching their location Bayliss and her co-founders used several methods and techniques. 'The library was very useful and told us how many people lived in the area, where people were employed and what was going to be built in the near future, for example', she says. 'We also carried out a questionnaire in the street, asked friends, studied what kind of people were shopping in the area, as well as counting them as they passed by. What's more, we consulted a business adviser who gave us more information on the area, such as bus routes and that Kings Heath is the second busiest area in the city.'

Getting the right help

The cost, time and plethora of potential problems makes the whole business of buying, leasing and selling property a minefield. At best, it can absorb huge amounts of your time, and at worst, it can lead to bankruptcy before you're even off the ground. So it's advisable to take specialist advice from a chartered surveyor or a valuer. Just as lawyers know the law, surveyors know bricks and mortar. There are different types of surveyor and valuer who can help:

- One group are effectively agents and know all about availability, rents and prices. It may be worth employing one to find the right space rather than traipsing around those selling or leasing.
- Building surveyors specialise in the nitty-gritty of construction. They can organise a new-build or inspect existing buildings for potential faults.
- Another skill lies in analysing the average 40-page lease a landlord will expect. Or they can take over negotiations on rent reviews, rating appeals and planning applications.

Use an expert with letters after their name. Several professional organisations award these, such as the Royal Institution of Chartered Surveyors (RICS) and the Incorporated Society of Valuers and Auctioneers (ISVA). Ask in advance how much it will all cost. Then, after taking a deep breath, consider how quickly such fees will be saved in making the right choice or winning a cut in the asking rent.

Contact

Where to go for further help:
- **Royal Institution of Chartered Surveyors (RICS):** information Centre: 020 7334 3838/3842/3819; Rent Review and Lease Renewal Helpline: 020 7334 3806
- **Dispute Resolution Service:** Surveyor Court, Westwood Way, Coventry, CV4 8JE; tel: 020 7222 7000 or 01203 694757; fax: 020 7334 3802
- **Commercial Property Leases in England & Wales:** *Code of Practice.* Available from the RICS Bookshop; tel: 020 7222 7000; or by mail order from: RICS Books, Mail Order Department, Surveyor Court, Westwood Way, Coventry, CV4; www.rics.org.uk
- **Incorporated Society of Valuers and Auctioneers (ISVA):** tel: 020 7235 2282; www.isva.co.uk

CASE STUDY
GRAFTERS AND
THE LUCKY BREAK

Don Ferguson's business Grafters rescues and recycles valuable resources, such as glass, steel, aluminium, slate and textiles, while cleaning and demolishing properties for housing authorities in Liverpool. It uses a yard to store and recycle raw materials, as well as an office to run the business. Ferguson managed to save between £200 and £300 a week for the first six months by getting free premises.

Ferguson's free premises were in Crawford House, a disused territorial army barracks owned by the Granby Toxteth Development Trust. The trust is a non-profit making organisation designed to help local residents. Local business adviser Dave Petterson enquired about Grafters moving into Crawford House. The deal was done on condition that Ferguson kept the premises in reasonable condition. Despite being run down, it provided Grafters with office space and large, open areas to store materials before they were sold. Unfortunately, the yards were not secure and some of the salvage equipment went missing. Ferguson was forced to reconsider his premises when a fire destroyed much of the property in the yard and decided that he needed more secure premises instead.

Ferguson was lucky again with his business premises. He now pays for his yard, but has free office space on the same premises, provided by a friend who is based there. The new yard is much more secure as it is not shared, and has gates and a security guard. Getting free premises helped Grafters start up without getting into debt – the business is now firmly established and Ferguson has plans for expansion.

CASE STUDY
CHELSEA FLOWERS AND
THE PREMISES NIGHTMARE

Amanda Johnston had worked as a florist since leaving school. For a long time she had had her eye on a vacant shop in her local high street and made the leap to setting up her own shop when offered a loan to get started. However, the dream shop that she had always wanted soon turned into a nightmare. Johnston knew straight away that the shop would be a good place to sell flowers. It was on a main thoroughfare with a lot of passing traffic. The high street was always busy in the afternoon and the shop even had parking outside. 'It was an ideal position and I knew the area really well,' she explains.

Amanda's father then offered to help if she could get the premises she wanted. After a visit to the bank, Johnston visited the local enterprise agency and The Prince's Trust and managed to secure a £3,000 loan. She then set about securing an assignment of the lease from the existing leaseholder who was using the premises for storage, meaning she would take over their lease. 'My solicitors were talking to their solicitors and it seemed open and shut,' she explains. With the loan from the Prince's Trust secured, Johnston started to advertise her new business, Chelsea Flowers, in the local paper using the high street address, but with her home telephone number. However, two years down the line the property is still empty and a court case is looming. Johnston wanted to get the lease checked by a legal clinic run by the Trust. Although the lease was approved, Johnston was advised to get a surveyor to check what repairs might be needed on the property.

The inspection showed that £5,000 was needed to bring the property back to good order. The existing leaseholder was required to do that under the terms of the lease but refused point blank. Although Johnston was willing to take on the lease and make the repairs over a five-year period, the owner refused and chose, instead, to pursue the leaseholder through the courts. 'It has been going on for two years. It is now empty and fallen into dilapidation,' she explained, adding that the leaseholder has refused to pay any rent.

With Chelsea Flowers already being advertised and the money from the Trust sitting in the bank, Johnston was forced to rethink her strategy. She took a lease on a property behind the high street with a reasonable rent and Chelsea Flowers opened. Without any passing trade, she was forced to concentrate on credit card business. Johnston applied to the bank for merchant status and became a member of a teleflorists. She advertised in bridal magazines and also joined the London Wedding Agency, which sends out a list of forthcoming weddings and the brides. 'I had never thought about it before because I thought I would be too busy with the high street,' she says. However, the strategy has worked well with wedding business booming, and as the only member of the teleflorists in that area of London, Johnston has also had a lot of telephone orders. Although she would still like to move into the original property, the stress has forced her to switch off and focus on her existing business. 'I was on the phone to the solicitor constantly,' she said, 'It was mentally wearing and I physically felt ill.'

EXPERT OPINION

IT AND PHONE SYSTEMS

BT explains the latest computer and communications technology.

Staying focused

Your IT and phone infrastructure is at the very heart of your business. But getting to grips with the technology and terminology involved can be a time-consuming activity. There are a number of pieces of IT that even the smallest startup should consider:

- **Phone systems** – A telephone system is the piece of technology that directs incoming voice calls to the person being contacted. It is a vital component of any startup's infrastructure, and helps to create a professional image. There is a huge array of possible features and functions, depending on which system you select.

- **PCs/laptops** – The PC is the key building block of any IT infrastructure. However, there are as many different choices of computer as choices of broadband provider. Your supplier should be able to provide advice on the computers that suit your business. Similarly, your supplier should be able to offer you leasing packages, if purchasing outright is not the best option.

- **A server** – If you have more than one computer and they are linked together by a network, you will need a server. Servers store the applications and data that the different users on a network are able to share.

- **Printer/scanner/fax machine/ photocopier** – Some manufacturers provide machines that combine all of these functions. Again, your IT supplier should be able to provide guidance and should also have relationships with the best vendors on the market.

Networking your business

If your business has more than one computer, it makes sense to link them together, or 'network' them. A network plays an important role in helping a startup serve its customers more effectively. For example, by providing all computers on the network with shared access to customer information, any employee who takes a customer phone call is in a position to instantly look up relevant details and provide a professional, efficient response.

- A **local area network** (**LAN**) allows computers to share devices (such as the office printer or broadband connection) and data (for instance, the central customer database).

- A **wireless local area network** (**WLAN**) allows users in the office to access the system without the need to physically plug into it. This can make it easier if you need to add more people to the network and you don't need to run wiring and cabling round the office.

- A **virtual private network** (**VPN**) is software that allows users to connect to the company system, via the internet, when away from the office. Typically, users visit a dedicated website and enter their log in details and password. For staff who spend time away from the office, access to the company network via a VPN can significantly improve productivity.

Building the right team

Being a jack of all trades is a phrase often associated with starting and running a small business. This works so far as being the decision-maker, creative input and tea maker, but what happens when you come up against an area you can't handle – we're not all salespeople, for example. This is the point where you may have to acknowledge that although it's entirely your business, you can't do everything. That's the hard part. The easy (or easier) bit is then building up the expertise you need around you without having to employ leagues of people. Initially you need an extended, partly virtual, team.

The first thing is to identify what skills and experience your company needs to grow and make it a success. Only once you know this can you start to work out who you need to recruit for a successful launch and what your requirements will be in the short and long term. This is something you should have addressed in your business plan (see Chapter 4), along with defining the exact nature of your product or service and its marketplace, and how to recognise the problems of that market, all of which will help you to decide what additional people and skills you may require. Of course, you also need to honestly assess what you can reasonably manage without the expertise of others by relying on your own resources. It's a variation on facing your fears but the whole point is that you don't have to face them on your own, as these are the areas where you need to seek help. It will also show you where your strengths lie.

'It's vital to be strictly honest about your strengths and weaknesses,' agrees **Brial Steel** of Business Link Berkshire and Wiltshire. 'And it should be an ongoing process, continuous improvement comes through continuous monitoring.' Practically speaking, you can learn to market your own product – after all you are the expert on it – and you can run the office and develop new custom. But if for example on top of this you are spending far too much time struggling to balance the books when you don't have a head for figures, it's time to pay someone else to do this. It probably won't be a full-time job, and the time saved will be worth the money.

> **It's vital to be strictly honest about your strengths and weaknesses**

Guidelines

Throughout the recruitment process, you should be fully aware of equal opportunities legislation. This means understanding how discrimination can occur – even unintentionally – during the recruitment process.

Some job advertisements may discourage particular groups from even applying for the vacancy. For example, an advertisement calling for 'vibrant' or 'thrusting' personnel is implicitly ageist as it will deter older candidates who will associate these words with youthfulness. Also, untrained interviewers can form very subjective opinions on the basis of entirely irrelevant criteria – such as background or appearance.

UNLAWFUL DISCRIMINATION

You are not allowed to express a preference in terms of the gender, age or race or colour of the candidate, as this is discrimination.

GENUINE OCCUPATIONAL QUALIFICATION

You are only allowed to state a preference for a man or woman if you can produce a genuine occupational qualification (GOQ) saying why it must be a man or woman. For example, if you need a man for cleaning male toilets.

Ideally, as your company grows, you should monitor the applications received to make sure that they attract applicants from a cross-section of society, with sufficient numbers from diverse groups and sections. Also, the entire selection process should be monitored to ensure that selection occurs on the basis of criteria related to the job requirements – and nothing else.

Recruitment shouldn't just cover immediate vacancies, but should be seen as part of an overall organisational strategy for sourcing personnel

Finding the right people

Get the recruitment process right, and you virtually eliminate the risk of hiring the wrong person for the job. Get the process wrong, and you won't even attract applications from suitable candidates, much less be able to spot them during the selection process. And you will have wasted big money in time and advertising. Recruitment is not just carried out to meet immediate vacancies, but should be seen as part of an overall organisational strategy for sourcing personnel. Once you fill one vacancy, you should be left with a list of candidates who you would consider for the same or other vacancies in the future. This makes the process much easier the next time round.

A recruitment exercise exposes your company to a wide section of the public. These people could be current or potential clients, customers or suppliers. What's more, people talk. If a job applicant has had an unfavourable experience with your company, you can be sure that they will tell others about it. Hence it's vital that the recruitment process creates a positive impression of your company. There are several areas to cover in your mission to find the perfect person to provide the additional help you have decided that you need to launch your business effectively, while ensuring that you go about it in a proper and professional manner.

The job profile

You need to define the role and the person required very accurately in order to attract the right people. It also helps if you to have a clear idea of the kind of person you need and the actual work involved. When listing skill requirements, only mention those actually related to the position. Similarly, when stating prior experience needs, think about how much is strictly necessary for the candidate to do the job well. You may ideally want your new employee to be an office whizz and highly trained in all things, but consider the competencies they actually need for the position offered.

The advertisement

Once you have a profile, you can draw up a recruitment advertisement. This should be clear and brief. You should list the job requirements, the criteria for applicants, the salary package, and the contract length. Also remember to describe your organisation and give the job location. State the application procedure, too. Do people apply in writing, by phone, or fill in an application form?

Where you advertise will depend on the type of position offered. Surveys show that specialist and trade publications work best for managerial and professional posts. Meanwhile, advertisements for skilled workers give best results when placed in the local press. The internet as a recruitment tool is also becoming more and more popular, and can be very cost-effective, so it will pay for you to research the online options available. Some trade magazines, for example, will offer to put your vacancy online as part of the recruitment advertisement package. There is more on where to place your advertisement later in this chapter.

Where to look for staff

> **Check with your local newsagent which paper people buy for jobs in your area and which day is job day – it's usually Thursday**

When you've drawn up the profile of the person you're looking for and written a draft of the advertisement, there are four main routes to making contact. Each has its pros and cons.

LOCAL NEWSPAPER

Everyone looking for a job knows the day the job pages come out. It's the one day that is guaranteed to be a big seller for the local paper as everyone from national to one-man-band companies vie to attract new staff. As such, it isn't the cheapest form of recruitment, but you are guaranteed to get a sizeable response. Most locals told startups.co.uk that smaller companies didn't need to put an advertisement in for more than one week to get a more than adequate choice.

Prices vary from region to region, but the procedure is largely the same. You fax or email through the text of your advert – over the phone there is too much risk of misspelling – then the recruitment classified desk will call you back to discuss options. If you've never placed an advertisement before, don't worry, they will go through with you how big the advertisement should be and how long it should appear to attract a certain response, and then calculate the cost. The simplest advertisements might be charged by lineage, for example £17 per line plus VAT, where each line will fit three or four words. You wouldn't be able to say a great deal or have a company logo, but it would get the message across. But typically, a small advertisement in a local paper will cost in the region of £300. Many local papers are part of a wider syndicate, so you might also be able to get your advertisement in more than one paper.

> **Typically, a small advertisement in a local paper will cost in the region of £300**

For example some local papers have a more business-orientated journal, which can be helpful if you are looking to reach that market. This is again something the classified department will be able to help you with.

- **Pros:** This is possibly the best way to access your region, as the local paper on job day is still the first port of call for many people.
- **Cons:** This is not a very targeted approach, as the paper goes to everyone and unless you make your advert specific, you might have to wade through lots of unsuitable applicants.

JOB CENTRES

The Employment Service has over 1,000 job centres nationwide that can help you find recruits for a whole range of positions and sectors, either locally or nationwide in some cases. It doesn't cost anything to post a vacancy with them and you can benefit from support both before and after the position is filled. Services offered by Jobcentre Plus include advice on recruitment methods and procedures, information about the local labour market such as employment levels, availability of candidates and wage rates, and advice on any difficulties or barriers to filling your vacancies. It is also important to file any other details, such as whether a driving licence will be required. This will just help avoid wasting your and your candidates' time later on.

The details of the job are entered into a computer system that job seekers can either access themselves or through a consultant. If you then agree your expectations with your contact at the job centre, they can let you know when there are enough suitable applicants. You can now create, view and update your jobs yourself through Employer Direct online. You can also email your vacancies at any time.

- **Pros:** You can use the job centre as a base for interviews and the consultants are always on hand to help. It is also free.
- **Cons:** Can be a time consuming process as you are relying on people coming into the job centre to see your advertisements.

Contact

Employer Direct: fax 0845 601 2004; employerdirect vacancies@jobcentre plus.gsi.gov.uk; www. jobcentreplus.gov.uk/ key

ONLINE RECRUITMENT

You don't have to be an online company to think about recruiting online. Often if you place a newspaper advertisement with a local paper, they will have a package to post your advertisement on an affiliated website. But there are also dedicated websites. Monster.co.uk, Stepstone and easyJobs are some of the ones available, where both potential employees and employers can search online. The idea is that you save time by cutting out the middleman, using the website instead. With Monster, for example, you can potentially deal with the whole process online. You log on, post your vacancy and pay for it using your credit card. For a small business, you will probably choose the one-off option, which costs £270 and will post your advertisement for up to 60 days.

- **Pros:** Once you are registered you can control the job adverts yourself, taking them down when you have enough applicants. There is also the added bonus of a team on hand to help you out with any problems. Moreover, you can reach a much wider audience, nationally and possible Europe-wide, without going through agents.
- **Cons:** People are unlikely to see the job accidentally as they might in a newspaper when scanning the adverts. Websites rely on people searching.

Contact

- Gojobsite: tel: 0870 774 8710; www.gojobsite. co.uk
- Monster: tel: 0800 169 5015; www. monster.co.uk
- Stepstone: tel: 020 8762 6700; www.stepstone. co.uk
- easyJobs: www. easyjobs.co.uk

RECRUITMENT AGENCY

There are a lot of recognisable high street recruitment agencies, including Select, Travail, Manpower, Hays and Reed, which can provide you with both part-time and permanent staff. In theory, they all deal with every level of company, from small operations to national businesses. There are also many industry-specific recruitment agencies. With most agencies you can choose how to contact them initially – by phone, email or in person at your local branch. You will then need to provide details of what type of staff you are looking for and the kind of salary you plan to pay. Agency staff will be able to advise you on the current employment rates if you are not sure, or indeed if you are paying wildly over or under the odds. It is also likely that you'll have to undergo some kind of credit check just so the agency knows you can pay the bill.

If you don't have premises, you can hold your interviews at the agency, but they will need to come and view your offices to check they are suitable for the potential employee. It also helps for them to see the culture of your company, the people and environment to help match the applicants. Once you have agreed exactly what the job description is and what the conditions and the salary are, you will have to sign an agreement. This just ensures that the candidate is getting the job they have applied for. But it is important from your point of view that you have the position clearly defined at this stage to avoid difficulties later. This is also important when the agency fee is set. They may take a percentage of the candidate's annual salary, say 20%. However, the amount will vary according to the level the person is coming in at and how hard they were to find.

After you have recruited someone, there will probably be a period during which the fee is refundable – but only a few months. So it is in your interests not only to choose carefully but also to work with the agency to ensure you and your new staff member is happy in the first three months. That way, it will be money well spent not wasted.

- **Pros:** If the agency wants your fee, it is in their interests to find you someone good, therefore you should receive decent support and guidance.
- **Cons:** As part of the process your finances and premises will be investigated and questioned if not up to standard.

Contact

- Hays: www. haysworks.com
- Manpower: www. manpower.co.uk
- Reed: www.reed. co.uk
- Select: www.select. co.uk
- Travail: www. travail.co.uk

(All websites have nearest branch finders)

The response

All applications to job advertisements should be replied to. Remember they could well be or know clients. The sooner the response, the better, as this shows your company is efficient and interacts well with the public. Remember too that all applications – even unsolicited ones – are confidential.

The criteria

Response to your advertisement may be overwhelming, but don't be tempted to introduce random screening methods to save time. For instance, if you decided to eliminate candidates on the basis of geographical proximity to your office, you could easily ditch the application from your ideal employee. Instead, use a checklist of essential criteria, drawing from the person and position specifications you compiled earlier. Screen all applications using criteria relevant to the job specification and nothing else. It's surprisingly easy to let personal prejudice slip in, so it's best to be aware of this possibility at all times.

Stay objective. You could try using a points system to screen applications based on every core skill requirement spotted. This lends a broad and more objective method to the process.

ACTION POINT
MAKE SURE YOU HAVE THE PEOPLE AND THE SKILLS TO LAUNCH SUCCESSFULLY

IDENTIFY THE SKILLS YOUR COMPANY NEEDS TO SUCCEED: Carefully look at the various functions required for the successful running of your business from administration to sales and marketing.

ASSESS WHICH OF THESE YOU AND YOUR EXISTING WORKFORCE CAN REALISTICALLY COVER: If you already have staff on board, honestly assess who can handle the various functions and the skills necessary.

WORK OUT THE SKILLS GAPS: Make a list of the remaining functions to gauge where help is needed.

DECIDE ON HOW MANY PEOPLE YOU'LL NEED TO TAKE ON: Look at the functions and skills needed and assess how many people will be required to plug the gaps and whether they'll be recruited on a freelance, part-time or full-time basis.

KICK OFF THE RECRUITMENT PROCESS: Draw up the necessary job descriptions and decide how to reach the people you need.

CASE STUDY
ALL BAR ONE AND
THE PEOPLE IMPERATIVE

When the Six Continents pub company opened its first All Bar One in 1994, it began a new trend in pubs that appealed a new breed of pub goer, and women in particular. Today the company has more than 50 pubs around the UK, and a key element of this success is down to premises and people. Having come up with the concept, the company turned its attention to bringing it to market. 'The main concern was finding the right sites,' says communications director **Bob Cartwright**. 'We wanted, in particular, sites that were very visible – Leicester Square in London, for example. Having bars in high-profile locations helped establish the brand. Staff were also critical. Hiring the right sort of people is not just about salaries. It is also to do with training, teamwork, flexibility and giving your staff a sense of belonging. We needed staff that could make the customers feel comfortable.'

As well as finding the right premises, staffing is a key area that small businesses can focus on, explains **Nick Shrager**, a member of the National Council of the Institute of Business Advisors. 'It's all about customer retention,' he says. 'If staff make the customers feel welcome, they'll come back – and it's six times easier to sell to an existing customer than to a new one.'

Finding and dealing with suppliers

Many businesses are built around selling goods, and as such are reliant on getting these items at the best possible prices, so that they can make more profit on a sale. This is where suppliers or wholesalers come in. If you've never dealt with these kind of businesses before, you could be in for a bit of a shock. They tend to be quite traditional and it can even be difficult to track down the right one. However, this is a relationship that is worth nurturing, as it is key to the success of your new business.

Finding wholesalers

It's not just large firms that can make use of wholesalers, but how do you manage to find them in the first place? Thumbing through your dog-eared *Yellow Pages* or calling a directory service might yield results, but for the modern small business the lack of wholesaling presence on the internet is a cause of great frustration. Wholesalers tend to stick to traditional tried and tested methods – and this includes attitudes, or a lack of them, towards technology such as the web and email.

Relationships between wholesalers and their customer base are often built up over years of loyal service, so suppliers often rely on word of mouth and local knowledge to attract new clients. You are unlikely to be bombarded by attention-grabbing advertising from wholesalers in comparison with large retailers. 'It can be very hard for people new to trading to find wholesaler contact information and thus it makes it hard to shop around', admits wholesaling specialist **Richard Grady**. 'One of the reasons

! TIPS

DEALING WITH WHOLESALERS

- ! Get to know the wholesalers that you deal with – helps you find out when new products are in stock and get the best deals on price
- ! Don't be afraid to ask one wholesaler to 'price match' another, especially if you are placing a particularly large order
- ! Don't expect huge discounts unless you are buying in huge quantities
- ! Startups are unlikely to get an instant credit account. Pay cash up front for a couple of months before requesting credit.
- ! Don't be intimidated – as most suppliers will be more than happy to help you as much as they possibly can

for this is that very few UK wholesalers have decent websites and even fewer have taken any time to ensure their sites are ranked well in internet search engines. This means that if you are looking for suppliers on the internet, it will take ages and you probably won't have much luck,' he warns.

Luckily, this gap in the market has been belatedly acknowledged with several websites and books that point you in the direction of your nearest wholesalers. However, entrepreneurs will still have to do most of the legwork in researching the quality of wholesale products and getting the best value for money. Helpfully, Grady has compiled his own online resource to accompany his sought-after ebook. Visitors to his website (www.theuktrader.co.uk) can get details on over 700 wholesalers and gain other relevant information. Alternatively, www.thewholesaler.co.uk has a large wholesale directory, with details on products ranging from fireworks to toiletries.

As websites like these may charge you for membership and access, it can be worth sticking to print publications when looking for your wholesalers. Therefore, a quick flick through *The Trader* magazine (monthly at most newsagents) will reveal plenty of wholesale advertisements, as well as a list of contacts.

> if you are looking for suppliers on the internet, it will take ages and you probably won't have much luck

Approaching wholesalers

As long as you have proof of trading, which can be as little as a letterhead or business card, you are entitled to deal with a wholesaler. Suppliers need business just as much as you do, so there's little chance you will be turned away. So be confident when approaching them and focus your concerns on getting a good deal for your business. It is important that you actually visit the wholesaler in person because as mentioned above, wholesalers are quite traditional in their practices, and the chances of getting hold of an email address to contact them are slim.

There is, similarly, a limited amount you can do over the telephone. Your supplier will be happy to send you a list of stock and the relevant prices, but to gain a proper understanding of what you are ploughing your wholesaling budget into, it is vital you have a face-to-face meeting.

However, it is highly advisable to phone ahead before your visit. To save yourself from a wasted journey, it is best to find out in advance if your wholesaler has the goods you require. Stock changes every day at a wholesaler, so lists you receive a week in advance will be out of date by the time you turn up to purchase the items that you need. Many wholesalers also like to assign certain visiting times for customers to look at stock – this is particularly the case with larger and more popular suppliers. Wholesalers with valuable items that require supervised visits will also need you to call ahead. Policies vary according to the supplier, so check out their procedures before you turn up.

The time that you actually visit is up to you, but be aware that the busiest time for a wholesaler will be around midday, when shop owners converge to purchase stock for their stores. If you arrive around 4pm, you will have a less frantic search for your goods, as this is the wholesaler's quietest period. You will also benefit from more attention from the wholesale staff, as they will have fewer customers to deal with. The downside is that stock you have turned up to buy may have already gone, so, again, it is vital that you call ahead to check on what stock is still available. Striking the right balance is important, so don't be put off if it takes a few visits before you get it right.

Spotting a bad wholesaler

> A good wholesaler will take the time to talk to you and listen to your needs

Unfortunately, there is no scientific test you can apply to know if you are going to be sold 300 broken vacuum cleaners that suck in more than one sense of the word. As is common when you are starting up a business, for all the calculations and careful planning, sometimes a good or bad gut instinct can serve you best of all. 'Most people will get a feel for whether they are comfortable with an individual quite quickly and this is often very accurate,' explains Grady. 'I would tend to be happier dealing with a large wholesaler with pleasant premises and a friendly atmosphere, although, that said, I have also traded with some very good suppliers that have operated from very unpleasant lock-up units on rough industrial estates!'

Generally speaking, a good wholesaler will take the time to talk to you and listen to your needs. The more they are prepared to do for you suggests that they are reliable and their stock will not let you down – customer service, after all, is essential to wholesalers who rely heavily on repeated visits from shop owners and small firms. On the other side of the coin, if you turn up to a derelict garage and are confronted by a nervous looking 'wholesaler' who thrusts a box of pickles into your hands before snatching your money and speeding off in his GTi to the sound of wailing police sirens, you should maybe consider looking elsewhere for your supplies in the future. So trust your first impressions. If you are not happy you can always change your wholesaler until you find someone you are comfortable dealing with.

How much should you spend on stock?

Before you set off to visit your wholesaler, you need to work out a budget to suit your business' needs and means. Although the need to budget carefully is essential in almost all aspects of business startups, it is particularly important when it comes to buying stock. Working out how much you need of a certain product and how much money to set aside can be a tricky balance to strike. It is important to work out the demand and profitability of each product before you decide how much to buy. Purchase too few supplies to satisfy customer demand or keep your business running smoothly, and you will suffer financially. On the other hand, if you buy too much unwanted stock, not only will you have a room full of unsold items, you will also be nursing a nasty, not to mention unnecessary, dent in your wallet. It's also wise to keep some money back, because if you don't, you might miss a bargain or neglect other essential areas of your business. Of the two scenarios, over-spending is the least preferable, as you won't be able to correct your order next time if your firm suffers serious financial damage. So, when working out your budget, err on the side of caution.

'How much you buy in one go depends on what you are purchasing the stock for,' says Grady. 'If you have a large high-street outlet, then you

> There is nothing worse than being stuck with a large quantity of stock that you can't sell

are going to need to buy far more stock than an individual trading part-time from home. Most wholesalers have fairly low minimum orders, say from £50 to £300, and this means that traders can buy in small quantities initially. This is recommended so that you can check that you can actually sell the products. There is nothing worse than being stuck with a large quantity of stock that you can't sell, especially if you have invested all of your capital into it.'

Don't forget about VAT

" New traders often forget that the prices displayed by wholesalers don't include VAT "

Unfortunately, we all have to pay VAT and wholesalers are no different, and it is the most common tax you will come across when dealing with your wholesaler. VAT is charged by suppliers of goods and services, and wholesalers certainly fall into the former category. As they are not entitled to any exemptions or a reduced VAT level, wholesalers will charge the standard rate of 17.5% on your purchase. What you must be aware of is the fact that many wholesalers price their goods without VAT, so you may be under the impression that you have a brilliant deal when, in fact, you will have a 17.5% charge slapped on top of it. So the four widescreen televisions you buy for just £1,000 will in fact set you back £1,175.

'From my experience, it's fair to say that many new traders do forget that the prices displayed by wholesalers won't include VAT,' says Grady. 'I know of a couple of people that got very excited at the incredibly low deals on offer and got a shock when they got to the till and found another 17.5% added to the cost.' Although you are obliged to pay the VAT on these, and indeed any other goods, you are entitled to claim the money back if your firm is VAT registered. Input tax (the VAT you pay on raw goods) can be claimed back as part of the legitimate expenses that your business runs up – if you regularly pay more VAT than you collect you can claim this money back on a monthly basis by filling in a return.

To become VAT registered, your firm's turnover must exceed £67,000 a year, although this figure has risen considerably in the last few years. These increases have been aimed at helping new businesses that cannot deal with the burden of filling out continual VAT forms. However, although small firms often grumble about VAT, you can often save money by registering for it and many businesses voluntarily put their name forward even if they are under the threshold. So, if you are VAT registered and you keep in mind the charge when purchasing, you will be able to shape your budget accordingly to ensure that your cash flow is unaffected.

Contact

For the most up-to-date figure on VAT visit: www.hmrc.gov.uk/vat/vat-registering.htm

Are you guaranteed?

There are no specific guarantees that wholesalers use, although the goods you buy will usually have a manufacturer's warranty, which will be passed to you from the supplier once the transaction is made. A wholesaler should be happy to replace faulty stock, although, legally, they are not bound to do so, unlike high street stores. Significantly, the recent regulations that amended the Sale of Goods Act did not cover wholesalers. This means that while shops are now duty-bound to give refunds or exchanges for faulty goods, wholesalers are not. 'The new regulations only cover business-to-consumer transactions, so wholesalers wouldn't be relevant,' says **Martyn Rapley** of the Department for Business, Enterprise and Regulatory Reform. 'However, the main requirements of the Sale of Goods Act, which are continuing, are certainly relevant.'

So it's not all bad news if you have, for example, been sold a hundred solar-powered torches. The original Sale of Goods Act makes it clear that all products sold should be of satisfactory quality and serve the purpose for which they are intended. Most reputable wholesalers offer exchanges or refunds for faulty items, so just because the law now only recognises this right in retailers, this shouldn't damage your chances of getting your money back or getting a decent replacement. However, a word of warning: the new regulations shift the onus of proving the goods were faulty at the time of purchase to the seller – but only in regard to shops. Wholesalers will still be able to demand that you prove the products were inadequate when you first bought them. Also, if you buy untested goods from a clearance warehouse, they will have no warranty at all and you'll run the risk of having a damaged bank balance as well as damaged stock.

Buying online

> **When buying online, make sure you know exactly what you are purchasing**

As befits their traditional image, wholesalers generally prefer to do their trading on the floor of a warehouse rather than in cyberspace. Consequently, there are few UK websites dedicated to wholesaling, and even fewer for individual suppliers themselves. However, this is slowly beginning to change and several websites have been created to allow you to purchase goods online, the most common being sites dedicated to selling pallets of items at knockdown prices. 'When buying online, make sure you know exactly what you are purchasing – read the description thoroughly and study any pictures,' says wholesaling specialist Grady. 'If you are not sure, contact the supplier for additional information. Nothing beats a visit to the supplier so that you can see the products before making a purchase. Also, use a credit card to make your payment, that way you have a right of recourse via the credit card company if things go wrong.'

Buying batches or pallets of goods online from wholesalers is different from buying on Amazon, for example, as you may not be entirely sure what you are being sold due to the varied goods on offer in a single purchase. Make sure you have a detailed list of what is on offer and contact the wholesaler if you have any queries. Although it is wise to exercise caution when purchasing online, you can make big savings as internet sales can often be much cheaper, due to lower overheads, than traditional warehouse buying.

Making a profit

As outlined earlier under 'How much should you spend on stock?', there are several options open to you when it comes to the actual purchase of your stock. On your first visit, however, don't expect wholesalers to offer you a cushy credit account with them, as you probably will have to make some straightforward purchases with them first. This is generally what wholesalers will expect from you. It may be cheaper to set up a credit account, when you've established yourself with suppliers, than get involved in any finance deals with your bank, and it is best to avoid getting into a never-ending circle of loans and deals to fund your stock purchases. 'Wholesalers will expect payment with order unless you have a credit account with them,' says Grady. 'It is not usually appropriate to finance stock purchases with other finance deals or instalments as the purchases would normally be too regular – every couple of weeks or monthly.'

Simple cash payments may be the most beneficial for your business, as many wholesalers give discounts to customers who pay upfront in this way. The method of payment, however, depends greatly on the cash flow situation of your company, and it is important not to risk over-stretching your business by making large cash purchases early on. Try to build up the amount of stock from a low level to begin with, to ensure you can sell all of it on and to save valuable funds for the future.

There are also other simple steps you can take to make a profit on your wholesale stock. Once you have a firm idea of the amount of stock your business can sell on, you can 'price match' wholesalers against each other on large orders. Don't be afraid to ask your supplier to compare prices with someone else for you – wholesalers are generally, contrary to their image, approachable and happy to see your business flourish (as well as keen to keep your custom), and will often knock down their prices to a competitor's level.

Discounts will be roughly in proportion to the amount of money you spend, much like many other trades that offer such incentives to encourage you to place large orders. Therefore, orders under £200 are generally not going to make the earth move for wholesalers in terms of discounts, so to get the best discounts you need to make your purchases on a grander scale. Don't forget, however, that if you buy goods for the sake of a discount and are left with excess stock and a big hole in your budget you could end up in trouble, so make sure you strike the right balance, meeting your customers' needs without buying too much stock.

Don't be frustrated if you don't see instant profits on your wholesale goods. If you continue to stick to an appropriate budget, shop around for value and strike up a good working relationship with your wholesaler, you should start to see results within a few months. Of course, much of this depends on the size and circumstances of your business, but by sticking to this formula you will be on course to meet the potentially large profits that buying wholesale goods provides.

Insuring your business

Making sure your company is protected against as many as possible disasters could ultimately save it and protect all the time and effort you are likely to put in to making it a success. However, finding the right business insurance can be a difficult and complex process. There is a certain amount of jargon associated with the area, which can put off many small firms. As an entrepreneur you might see your insurance as one of those unavoidable costs – you don't much like it but you'll go along with it. However, for many firms it ends up being their life support. You never know if disaster is lurking around the corner, but it is too late to get cover after the incident has happened.

Insurance is also not an area where one size fits all, so don't buy a policy unless you really need to. However, don't fall into the trap of scrimping on costs, as you might find out that you are not covered when the worst happens. Essentially, is important to understand your own risks, know what the insurance market has to offer and to thoroughly read and understand any policy before committing to it.

Why you need insurance

Aside from legal requirements and demands from customers to have a certain level of liability, you might well think that there is little point to your insurance policy. However, there are many examples of businesses going to the wall following a disaster for which they weren't covered. Similarly there are many instances when a company has bounced back after it looked like it had passed the point of no return, all because it was insured to the very hilt.

You might consider the risks that your business faces to be small or even affordable, but if this is the case, then you are probably underestimating them. The chances of your business being hit by a flood or destroyed by a fire might seem low, but disruption to your work can come from many quarters. For example, a crime in your street could lead the police to cordon off the area for a period of time. Despite not being able to trade, you will still have to pay your staff, rent and other costs, and you could lose a very significant amount of business or incur heavy costs while attempting to maintain it. However, all of this could be prevented with a business continuity insurance deal.

As mentioned earlier, some of your clients might ask about your insurance details before they are prepared to do business with you. Public liability is important for many clients, particularly in the public sector. In a business-to-business setting, an insurance policy acts almost like a credential. By having a high level of cover, you are demonstrating that you are a respectable business, which takes health and safety very seriously, and that you fully understand your own responsibilities. So paying for insurance is far from just dead money, but a way of accessing opportunities that you wouldn't otherwise be able to gain.

Essential cover

There is some insurance that you must have, and this is covered below.

LIABILITY INSURANCE

Nearly all businesses need some level of liability insurance, and employer's liability insurance is the most common one. If you are about to take on staff then you should ensure you have this first. Also, if you are thinking of setting up a limited company then it is a legal requirement, as technically the company is the employer. If any member of your staff is taken ill, suffers injury or death and this is deemed to be as a result of their work, then you are potentially liable. Therefore, the law states that you must have cover in order to cope with this eventuality. By law, employers must have at least £5 million of liability, although many policies offer

£10 million. There are just under 400 deaths and nearly 30,000 major injuries at work each year in the UK, therefore you are well advised not to make any savings in this area.

MOTOR INSURANCE

As any driver knows, motor insurance is a legal requirement, but many come unstuck when using vehicles for work-related activities. You might think that your current insurance covers you, but unless your policy includes work use then you are mistaken. The good news is, however, that this isn't usually expensive and some insurers offer it for free.

If you are employing someone who is using their own vehicle for work purposes other than travelling to work, then you have a responsibility to ensure they are fully covered. A work purpose could be as innocent as dropping you off at a meeting – it doesn't matter how minor this seems, they still require business insurance. It is also highly advisable to check with the Driver and Vehicle Licensing Agency (DVLA) that your staff are legally able to drive and take copies of their insurance and MOT documents, as well as their driving licences.

Contact

DVLA www.dvla.gov.uk

PUBLIC LIABILITY

Public liability insurance, though not compulsory, is something only the most cavalier business would cut back on. It covers you for damage against property or persons that you might encounter during your work. Many clients won't deal with you or can't legally work with you unless you have it, so you might consider it to be obligatory.

There are niches you can occupy where price is not the most significant consideration

Pricing

One of the most important decisions to be made when you start a business is the pricing of your products or services. Customers buying standard products that are available from numerous sources will look for the supplier with the cheapest prices. This makes it difficult, if not impossible, for the small firm to compete with major suppliers who have the advantage of bulk purchasing or mass production. Fortunately, there are niches you can occupy where price is not the most significant consideration, being outweighed in the eyes of the customer by quality, service or uniqueness.

'Small companies often make the mistake of charging very low prices because they feel they must compete on a price-only basis,' warns marketing consultant **Annmarie Hanlon**. 'But there will always be a large company that can afford to drop its prices to squeeze the small company out. Instead, you should compete on product or service quality. A small company can give an attention to detail which is difficult for a big company dealing with 20,000 customers to achieve.'

> You should compete on product or service quality. A small company can give an attention to detail which is difficult for a big company

Pricing confidence

Having spent five years as a director of the Prince's Youth Business Trust, Hanlon speaks from the experience of being midwife at the birth of numerous businesses. 'There is less confidence in a cheap service than in a more expensive one,' she says. 'Hairdressing is a good example, where there is an idea that if you are paying your hairdresser more you are getting a better hair-do. I know a hairdresser in the Midlands who charges more than anyone else in the area. Customers receive a welcoming neck and shoulder massage on arrival and are given a hot towel to wipe their hands. With these added attentions, a premium price is perceived as appropriate.'

Location and environment

Hanlon points out that location and environment are also important. 'If an establishment in a back street and with no reception area charged the same prices as a lush Mayfair location, its customers would feel they were being ripped off. It's all about ensuring the price is appropriate for the service.'

This is illustrated by what she calls 'the salmon sandwich issue'. She explains: 'If you buy a salmon sandwich from your local sandwich shop to take away in a paper bag you are happy with a price of £1. If you go to a well-known department store, the sandwich is nicely packaged and you have a perception that the quality is better, so £1.50 might be acceptable. Then there might be a premium product with finest Scottish smoked salmon and delicious trimmings. For that you might well accept a price of £2.10 because you think it is right for what is being offered. But if the same £2.10 sandwich was being sold for 45p you would wonder what was wrong with it.'

Offer a specialised service

In the retail sector, specialisation can sidestep price competition. Offer a wide selection in a narrow field. Observe what is lacking in an area and not encompassed by the big chains. It's a matter of finding a demand in your area that's not catered for, where your customers will feel they are getting value for money as opposed to cut prices. Family convenience stores that buy from middlemen – wholesalers and cash and carries – cannot match the prices of supermarkets, which buy in vast quantities direct from manufacturers. But their strength can be their location. They normally serve a localised market, such as a housing estate, or they may be situated on a route used by people going to and from work. Open for long hours, they are handy for people calling in for newspapers, confectionery or snack foods, or an 'emergency' purchase such as milk or sugar, aspirin or cigarettes – items that do not justify a trip to the supermarket. And people who call in for just one item often make impulse purchases of others. It's a case of convenience outweighing cost.

Ultimately, when you launch your business, to maximise your profits you will need to think creatively and strategically about your pricing structure to make sure, if possible, that you can charge the maximum by offering a premium product or service that is niche to your area. If there are larger companies offering a similar service, this will be a must.

> **"To maximise your profits, you will need to think creatively about your pricing structure"**

TELLING THE WORLD

WHAT'S IN THIS CHAPTER

■ With everything falling into place, from the completion of your business plan and working on the practicalities of where you'll be based to considering the kind of people you may need to employ, it's time to properly formulate and implement your pre-launch marketing strategy – basically tell the world about your company and why they should buy from you. This will ensure you're perfectly placed to get your business off to a flyer. So it's important that you have an understanding of what marketing is all about and the options open to you. Read on for find out about the best approach to take…

What is marketing?

Marketing is the means by which your business identifies, anticipates and then satisfies customer demand. If carried out effectively it will not only ensure that your business is seen and heard, but will also give it the flexibility to adapt to fluctuating customer demands and a changing business environment. Companies that really succeed are those where the owner has a vision for the firm and is dedicated to seeing it through. A marketing plan will help achieve focus and establish the vision. Marketing will help you understand who your potential customers are, place and price the product compared with the competition and also position the company in the marketplace. It will also help identify future opportunities for self-promotion.

Although there are established guidelines to follow, marketing can be a difficult skill to develop. But in terms of successful impact on the future commercial effectiveness of the business, it is worth cultivating. It can offer improved returns and profitability and a greater understanding of realistic business development opportunities. There are no hard and fast rules for timetables for your marketing. Ultimately, it is up to you to set your own. However, as general rule of thumb you need to ask what would the business like to achieve three years from now compared with where it would be if you didn't employ a marketing strategy.

With respect to how to set your marketing budget, there are several possible approaches, none of which can claim to be the right way. They include using a percentage of sales, the same spend as last year (which is unlikely to be relevant to a startup), a similar spend to key competitors, and the dubious 'what we can afford'. Of course, in the end it will come down to what you can afford, but initially you need to plan your strategy to find out how much marketing you think is necessary, identify the essentials and go from there. Also, as you see later in this chapter, there are some good marketing methods that don't cost much at all.

> **Businesses that really succeed are those where the owner has a vision for the firm and is dedicated to seeing it through**

Sonja Garsvo, former public relations chief at Apple Computers and now a personal business adviser at Business Link London City Partners, recommends factoring the marketing budget into your business plan from the bottom up. 'If you can't afford a marketing budget, you have to ask yourself how viable your product is,' she says. One of the major problems for startups when considering marketing is quantifying in advance the expected result for a given spend. But consider Microsoft. While your ambitions may be more modest than those of Bill Gates, his company's domination of the software industry is a testament to the power of successful marketing. Gates targeted potential competitors, undercutting rival Apple Computers, while launching a sustained marketing blitz to become one of the richest men in the world, with PCs dominating the home computer market. Industry observers attribute Microsoft's success as much to its marketing prowess as Apple's lack of it. Of course, in recent years, Apple has carved itself a lucrative niche in the technology sector thanks not only to wonderfully innovative and stylish designs, but also because of – yes, you guessed it – excellent marketing. What's more, Microsoft is now a major shareholder in the company.

Sales versus marketing

Don't confuse sales with marketing. It is a common enough mistake for any small business to lump sales together with marketing under the perception that the two disciplines are different heads of the same beast. This is because tactics can overlap. However, they are not the same. The mission of sales is to increase turnover through a number of tricks, such as margin reductions, discounts, two for the price of one, special offers and so on. The mission of marketing is to identify the market, build the company and promote the product.

Marketing that attempts to embrace the two areas is a complex, expensive and resource-intensive activity. In the long run it is far more productive to have a dedicated marketing manager or assign the task to a marketing team.

Building a marketing plan

Any marketing plan should include the four Ps:

- Product
- Pricing
- Position
- Promotion

Building a marketing plan also means drawing up a blueprint for effective marketing. It can also be a useful way of ironing out differences between colleagues about where the business is heading and creating a common goal.

> **A marketing plan should be a statement of intent – where you are, where you want to go and how you are going to get there**

Product and pricing

The key to product and pricing is research. The more thorough your marketing plan is, the better. If your business is going to operate within a specific locality, will the market support it? For example, if you plan to open a restaurant, how many already exist, what type of service do they offer and what are their prices like? How do they position themselves – greasy spoon, haute cuisine or take away? Will the locality support another restaurant, or is the area already saturated? Check out rivals' prices, too, and position your product accordingly.

You need to check whether once you have started your business and want to introduce new products or expand into other markets, the prospects for growth are viable. Perhaps there is a niche for the product/ service or the competitors have the market sewn up. Think about how you will sell the service – directly, mail order or via an agency, and the distribution method you will use, where your office will be located and whether you will need to supply after-sales service.

Position

Positioning means creating an identity for your business. You want to stand out from the crowd and be distinctive, so you need to develop a brand identity that is instantly recognisable. This will build a platform from which to launch your product. A business name is important and should reflect the value of the product or the service. See Chapter 6 for more on this subject. To create the brand identity, find a good local designer who can come up with letterheads, signage design, business cards and packaging. Designers can also be found in the business section of your local library.

Design is one those curious trades that everyone thinks they can do themselves. There is an element of truth in this, but professional designers can create a unique identity and appearance for your business. A good local designer need not be expensive and is likely to be a small business itself, sympathetic to your needs and ambitions. However, graphic design is not fine art and you need to make sure that your logo and brand identity reflects the visions and values of your company. This means you need to give the designer a clear brief about your company and what you want it to achieve, including the market you are targeting, as this should all influence the design they come up with. In fact, if a designer doesn't ask for details about the values of your company, your market and your competition – and perhaps examples of logos and branding you admire – then think twice about commissioning them. Ultimately, they should be producing a look and feel for your company that is significantly different to your rivals, appealing to your target audience and also right for your business.

All of these considerations have to be factored into a marketing plan and will form the foundation on which the fourth P – considered to be the classic marketing tool – promotion, is built.

> **You need to give the designer a clear brief about your company and what you want it to achieve**

Promotion

Customer targeting is the first and most important step in planning any kind of promotional activity. **Jeff Holden** of the Chartered Institute of

Marketing recommends asking the following questions to provide a clearly defined target audience:

- What kind of people buy or will buy your product?
- What do your best customers tend to have in common?
- Can you reach all of your customers through the same communication channels?
- Do customers fall into different groups?
- Are there different buying circumstances, for example, planned, impulse or special occasion?

By answering these questions, you will discover who your customers are. The next step is finding effective channels to communicate your message. These fall into three categories: media advertising (above-the-line), non-media communications (below-the-line) and public relations. Media advertising consists of television, radio, the press, cinema, outdoor and transport. Non-media consists of sales literature, direct marketing, sponsorship, sales promotion and point of sale. Public relations involves a range of activities that attempt to generate a positive attitude towards your company or products.

Getting your message heard

There are three key points to remember when advertising: reach, frequency and impact. Reach means getting through to the right audience, in the right circumstances and at the right time: 'Who wants to know about investment products when they are cleaning the kitchen floor and don't have the money to invest?' asks Holden. So successful reach is about selecting the right media and scheduling advertisements for appropriate times. Frequency is about giving the audience a reasonable chance for the message to sink in amid the hubbub of everyday life, while impact pretty much speaks for itself. Your message must have impact to cut a

A message must have impact to cut a swathe through the myriad of distractions that confront consumers every day

swathe through the myriad of distractions that confront consumers every day, and it must be presented at the most appropriate time.

Media advertising

The three major aims of above-the-line promotion are to inform, remind and persuade your customers about your products, services and the company itself.

The measure of advertising cost is the amount of business that you can generate per pound spent on advertising. Cinema advertising can be ideal for a local restaurant bringing in late evening diners. A recruitment agency can benefit by advertising on panels on local transport and can reach thousands of people in the right categories every day. Many small businesses are finding that local radio can also be a cost-effective medium. However, Business Link business advisor Sonja Garsvo warns against the scattergun approach. 'Shout as loud as everybody else and get attention but be focused about it, don't advertise for the sake of it; think about who you want to reach and the best way of reaching them,' she says.

Non-media communications

Non-media communication takes a number of forms and its methods are within the reach of every startup business. Sales literature is a familiar tool, ranging from a glossy company brochure to the single-sheet product flier dropped through the letterbox, stuck behind the windscreen wipers of a car or direct mailed. It should be designed with a specific target audience in mind and should convey what the product's key features and benefits are. Direct marketing can be the most effective means of communication, and it embraces all forms of promotion where the buyer is required to respond directly to the advertiser rather than through a retailer or dealer. It includes selling off the page as well as direct mail and telephone sales. Don't forget *Yellow Pages*, and you may want to consider online information services, such as Scoot.

It's also worth seriously considering setting up a website for your company. Getting someone to design and programme a basic one shouldn't be that expensive, and, anyway, keeping it simple is the best strategy as overly complex websites can actually deter visitors. You could also consider creating one yourself, as there are lots of software packages around that can guide you through the process. However, if you are going to set up a website, make sure you consider how you will let customers know that you are on the internet.

One of the clear advantages of below-the-line marketing over media advertising is that responses can be measured. However, it is worth noting that a 2%–3% return rate is considered the average, 5% is very good and 0% means something is seriously amiss. Sales promotion and point of sales can be used to offer something extra and build in loyalty, such as buy three curries and get one free during the following week. This also

CASE STUDY
DOSH SOFTWARE AND THE DIRECT APPROACH

Dosh Software was set up by accountant **Jonathan van der Borgh** to develop new accounting packages for small firms. van der Borgh was keen to get a retail presence, but the company was fighting for space on the shelves at stores, such as PC World. He quickly realised that direct marketing would be a quicker and easier way to establish the brand. As a new company, explains general manager **Tony Trevillion**, Dosh has to cut the cloth finely and any expenses have to be justified. That is why direct marketing had so much appeal. Dosh could mail to discrete groups, targeting the recipients and honing in on their customer base of accountants and bookkeepers.

One of its first promotions was through an accountancy publication. Dosh placed an advertisement in the magazine, which is distributed to 70,000 readers. In addition, it refined that list and placed a further 10,000 trial copies of its software on the cover of the publication, but only to be received by smaller accountancy firms. The results of each campaign were tracked and within just one or two weeks, the company knew how successful each mailing would be. The mailings were then followed up by telephone calls, both to customers who responded as well as those who did not.

has the added advantage of blocking out the competition. Offers such as these can be made at the point of sale or via mail drops, and are often a useful means of giving a startup business a leg up.

Sponsorship can also be an effective tool. Is there a local nursery or community project that needs some equipment in your area? You can provide it and in return work out a deal in which your company gets some promotion. If the cause is worthy it can generate positive word of mouth approval, too, as long as you are not seen to be shouting too loudly about the sponsorship and your generous donation, as this is often viewed cynically and considered opportunism.

Public relations

PR is generally a cheap form of communication

PR takes a number of forms, with its purest form viewed as the means by which a company can communicate honestly and accurately with its public. It includes media releases, product launches and premises openings. To do it effectively, there are simple guidelines to follow. Send a press release to the local paper, or hold a launch event and target the appropriate trade journals. To find out the relevant titles, consult the business section in your local library. Check out the media directories *Pimms* and *PR Newswire*, as both list trade journals, then call the title and find out which journalist covers your area.

Keep press releases simple. Journalists are bombarded with hundreds of press releases every week and have tight deadlines to meet. If your press release is too long, there is a very good chance it will end up in the bin before the third paragraph is reached. Do not make any grandiose claims, as these are usually seen through very quickly. Simply explain concisely and clearly who, what, where and when. Invite the reporter along to an opening, but make sure it doesn't clash with press days because no one will turn up.

Try and build a relationship – you may have other information that a reporter could turn into a story and in return you may get a free plug. Remember that the editorial content in newspapers and magazines carries a lot more weight with readers than the advertising. So make the time and effort to send out regular press releases, try to identify individual journalists to cultivate relationships with, offer your services to publications as an expert commentator, propose that you'll write a free series of useful (and short) articles or sponsor newsworthy local events. Letters to the editor can also be a surprisingly powerful marketing tool, although its effectiveness may take time to develop. If you have a local market, you probably read the same local newspaper as your target audience does – and both of you are likely to read the letters page, as it is often the most popular part of a newspaper. Don't write in unless you have something constructive to say, but you can make sure that you have by reacting to news items, commenting on new government policies and legislation, and any local issues (traffic and the environment are good candidates for a business' viewpoint). Your letter can apply a spin that reflects your business' concerns, and always ensure your business' name is part of your signature.

! TIPS

SUCCESSFUL MARKETING STRATEGY

For successful marketing, bear these simple rules in mind:

! Start by setting clear objectives for where you want your business to be, in say, three years

! Define your target market and identify your audience

! Decide on the brand and the values you want to transmit, which will be the platform for your business

! Plan your promotion strategy

! Set a budget

! Devise a schedule

! Decide how the strategy will be measured, such through increased sales, direct responses, coverage received in local press, etc

! Implement the programme according to the schedule

! Monitor and evaluate the results, so you can assess effectiveness and make more informed future marketing decisions

KIRSTY'S STORY
WE DECIDED TO DO THE EARLY PR OURSELVES

While the website and creative brand were being developed and then refined, **Kirsty McGregor** started concentrating on marketing her business Entertainthekids.com, designed to inspire parents. Deciding PR was key, she chose a specialist agency from a selection of four. 'We had quite a few ideas for them, but we really didn't get the supportive response we were hoping for from our chosen agency. In the end we decided we should just try to do this early PR work ourselves. After all we had the ideas and the enthusiasm, and we would do as much as we could with virtually no budget. So this is what we did and the results we achieved:

- 'Approaching celebrities (via their agents) with children for an endorsement. *Result:* Kym Marsh provided us with a quote.
- Approaching the monthly parenting magazines for a chance to show them our idea with a view to building a relationship with them in readiness for our launch. *Result:* We met two magazines whose editors were willing to review the site and have made personal contacts with several others.
- Asking my son's nursery, and begging our old primary school to allow us to carry out some market research on their parents. *Result:* 320 questionnaires distributed, nearly 20% returned, all very positive and they proved we have priced the product accurately.
- Writing a blog and getting it published by a business magazine. *Result:* You're reading the results which first appeared on the startups website.
- Entering the inaugural *Manchester Evening News* Venture Award for young (!) up and coming entrepreneurs, making it into the final three and getting great coverage in the newspaper.'

Low-cost marketing strategy

A good business marketing strategy doesn't have to cost that much. At its simplest, a marketing strategy is all about improving your chances of making sales – usually by making more potential purchasers aware of your products or services, or by making them aware of its desirable qualities (perhaps including its price). In any case it makes sense to optimise your budget. Given the choice between big-bang and little-but-often, good business marketing is less about getting big bangs and more about producing smaller amounts very regularly.

The impact of your marketing will also be improved greatly if you can use multiple channels. Prospects in particular are more likely to become buyers if they read about your business in their newspaper, see your advertisements, find your website, enter your competition, take home a brochure, hear you speak at a seminar, and learn what a great company you are from a third party. So you should spread your activity. You should also maintain the momentum, as business marketing is a long-term activity.

You don't, however, need to spend big, as most of the ideas in your marketing strategy are likely to involve moderate costs. But it will require quite a lot of time and effort from you on a regular basis. Read on to discover some of the most cost-effective marketing techniques. The key is to choose the ones that best support your marketing plan, and mix them in with more expensive options to help keep your costs down. Most (but not all) take advantage of the fact that you have a computer and an internet connection.

> " Good business marketing is less about getting big bangs and more about producing smaller amounts very regularly "

Build a mailing list

Collecting the names is the hard part, so give your prospects a reason for them to provide you with their name and address – competitions, an emailed newsletter, the promise of advance information and discounts, maybe even a loyalty card. Work at keeping your list accurate and up to date. Try to get hold of email addresses as well as (or even in preference to) postal contact details. Email is cheaper and more versatile than postage, and it can be integrated more efficiently with other aspects of your marketing, notably your website. If your database of names has been gathered in the normal course of business, you might not have to register under the Data Protection Act. This is a complex area, however, and you should check the situation with the Information Commissioner.

Contact

Information
Commissioner:
www.information
commissioner.gov.uk
....

Once you have your list, use it. Concentrate on customers more than prospects as they will be more valuable to you, both for repeat business and because they'll act as a reference. Looking after your customers so that you retain their custom is actually cheaper than attracting new ones. So be personal. Remember birthdays and anniversaries. Say 'thank you' when they buy (if only by email). Offer them the chance to comment and criticise. Give them special offers not available to anyone else. Make sure they know that your Christmas 'thank you' gift is going to a select few, and that they're in this group.

Ask them to check out new products or services, because they will appreciate being treated as special, and the risk is lower because they're more likely to buy. Look at their past purchase history if possible, and tailor special promotions to them. Find out whether they prefer you to use their first names or a more formal mode of address, and make sure all your mailings and other communications use the appropriate salutation.

Use discount vouchers

A good way to bump up sales volume is to offer discount vouchers, but they can also send a message about your business. It could be customer care (distribute them to favoured clients only), but coupons work better as a value-for-money flag. Distribute them in print advertising ('cut here'), by direct mail, by hand (on the street corner, if appropriate, or at trade shows), and even by email or via the web ('quote this reference to get your discount'). You can also include 'next purchase' coupons with customer orders. Due to the fact the selling point is usually price, you can afford the coupon to be a fairly cheap production in terms of design and print.

Distribute postcards

Postcards are also cheap and easy to produce, especially if you use colour on one side only. They can be mailed to prospects, stacked in help-yourself dispensers, and you can use them for a variety of marketing messages, such as 'see our new product', 'gasp at our new prices' or 'look at our short-term cut-price promotion', and 'enter the competition or the free prize draw (and get two entries if you give us a friend's name and address)'. A reply-paid licence makes it easy for someone to return the card, and these are simple and economical to set up with the Post Office.

Run competitions and giveaways

People love competitions, even if someone else wins. They are an excellent way to garner mailing list names, while sending branding messages, as the kind of contest your run implies the kind of company you are. Contests can also make for good PR, especially if there's a fun element that will attract media coverage. Of course, you can also simply give them something free, as people like to get gifts, even if they have to pay a premium price for a more expensive item to qualify for the freebie. This could be a free makeup purse with purchases, wine and fruit in your room if you book the weekend break, a CD of business tips with every seminar booking, or a pizza with every DVD film rented.

> **The aim is to boost sales and to tell the world that you're a generous, value-conscious supplier**

The aim here is both to boost sales and to tell the world that you're a generous, value-conscious supplier. It also improves your competitive sell, since it becomes more difficult to compare like with like.

Start a loyalty programme and a club

The customer gets a good deal from a loyalty scheme and you get a keen customer (and their contact details). A simple approach is to give customers a card that is marked after each purchase and results in a free or reduced-price offering after a specified number of regular-priced purchases. Easier to operate is a loyalty card scheme where regular customers get a discount on purchases on presentation of the card.

You can extend the programme into a full-blown club, sending out newsletters, launching exclusive special offers (great for shifting slow-moving stock), discounts on related products or services (it's generally easy to find other suppliers willing to give your club members a 10%–20% discount in return for capturing the buyer's details for their own database) and seminars and other get-togethers.

Work on your elevator pitch

Every entrepreneur should prepare a short presentation that sums up the great things about their venture. As mentioned earlier in this guide this 20–30-second piece is called an elevator pitch, as you could potentially deliver it while ascending a building in an elevator before the lift stops at your floor. Work on this so that you can recite it in your sleep, but not seem as though you're delivering a canned presentation.

When people say: 'So, what do you do?' the question they're really asking is: 'How do you make money', but actually saying that is regarded as impolite. So your elevator pitch should answer the unspoken question, but in such a way that identifies the problems you solve or the benefits you can offer, and implies that your business is very successful because it's so good at those problems and benefits.

Make a fun screensaver

Contact

Xara Screenmaker 3D: www.xara. com/products/ screenmaker3d/

Try Xara Screenmaker 3D and give the screensaver away to customers, prospects or anyone who visits your website. All those PCs suddenly become advertising billboards for your business. Screenmaker is recommended because it's cheap, very easy to use and good fun. It also produces pretty good screensavers from your text and/or images (logos, photographs and drawings).

Make a mini CD

Instead of handing out a parcel of brochures and your business card, give your prospects and customers all they need on a single disc. And it doesn't have to be a conventional CD-Rom, as you can get neat half-size mini-discs, and 'business card' CDs, which are rectangular but still fit into a standard CD drive. Both have enough storage space to fit at least 30MB of content, which will most likely be enough for your whole website and/or lots of product information.

Work on your website

Search engine marketing has become a specialisation that commands fairly high prices and cannot guarantee success. Search engine 'optimisation' involves tweaking your website so that it's more likely to appear early on in the list of results when someone enters a relevant keyword, but that's as far as it goes. In fact, most websites (especially business-to-business) get a minority of visitors from search engines and directories. Rather than spending time and money on a programme of promoting to them and buying keywords, you might be better to concentrate on your own mailing list and make sure that any other marketing materials reference your website – sign-written vans, business cards, promotional flyers, Christmas cards, promotional gifts and so on. In any case, there's quite a lot that you (or your webmaster) can do without calling in the expensive pros (see box).

Work on your references

Marketing should focus on benefits rather than features, meaning what you can do for your customer rather than how you do it, so use case studies and testimonials to prove your point. Ideally you need real clients. You can use a photograph and direct quotes to prove they exist. However, a startup could get by with some hypothetical situations, but make it clear that these are not real. Customer stories are good business-to-business website material, and you can use clickable links for specifications and other non-chatty material to prevent the reader being bombarded with statistics or technicalities. You can also produce them as single-sheet case studies and include them in brochures, but make sure they're both relevant and up to date.

Keep up with your email

People who use email expect a speedy response, and providing one is a simple marketing technique that supports lots of good messages:

Maximising internet marketing

- Use META tags for keywords, title and description. All these should emphasise three or four key concepts using words that you also repeat in the text and the headings on the page.
- Make sure you're listed in all the relevant free directories. The operative word is 'relevant', so don't submit your website to every free directory, or you'll be bombarded with junk mail and solicitations to buy further services. Once you've identified the best ones, you might think it's worth taking the inevitable offer of paid-for fast-tracking to get your listing in there sooner.
- Most visitors go to commercial websites for information, not for entertainment. Good web design starts with easy, obvious navigation and relevant, easy-to-use content, so avoid jarring colours and idiosyncratic typefaces, over-elaborate grammar and any humour unless it's been thoroughly tested. Include 'click for more information' rather than over-long pages scrolling down to infinity.
- Refresh your website regularly. Give the punters a reason for returning, with frequently updated information and tips they will find useful that relates to your business, new products, downloadable freebies and competitions. Redesign it thoroughly once a year, and tell everyone on your mailing list about all major updates (and most minor ones too). You could even send out a regular e-alert about what's new on your site, but avoid doing this to frequently as it could prove annoying.
- Choose the right names for your website. That's right, more than one name, with the separate domains all redirecting visitors to your main website. Many businesses will have a slogan or catchphrase, many will be known by contractions, abbreviations or initials, and most are prone to at least some misspelling. Get domain names for as many of the possibilities as you can, because registration is so cheap right now that you might as well cover all the bases (see Chapter 6 for more details about this).
- For each name, set up a separate webpage that almost immediately takes your visitor to your main website. With judicious use of the right keywords in the web page's test and its HTML META tags, this will greatly improve your chances of appearing on Google and other search engines when someone enters the relevant search-for term. Why? Because Google gives a lot of weight to 'site popularity', the number of webpages that link to yours. The more links to your website, the higher you'll be in the results list.

we're alert, responsive, aware of customer concerns, professional, up to date and so on. If you can't reply to incoming email within an hour or so, use an automated system to provide an instant response of some kind. This could be a simple: 'Thanks, we'll get back to you as soon as possible'. But if you've organised your email addresses correctly, a more targeted response should be possible, meaning that incoming mail addressed to products@yourcompany.co.uk could elicit an automated response that includes a PDF document containing product details or an appropriate website link. You can do quite a lot with Microsoft Outlook rules, or check out some of the autoresponder packages on offer.

Always use email signatures

A couple of lines at the bottom of a message identifying you and your company is a simple way for sending out your contact details. Make sure every email carries your 'signature' (including replies to incoming messages) and that everyone in your organisation uses the same signature format. It shouldn't be too long, but should give two or three alternative ways to contact you and your company, your website address and include a marketing message of some kind, such as 'Sale now on' or 'Winner of the Best Company Prize 2007'.

Do email marketing

This is among the simplest and least expensive marketing options. An email doesn't carry the materials and overhead costs of a paper mailshot, and you (probably) don't need the expensive and risky element of visual design. You know almost immediately whether the address is 'live' – still active, or spelled correctly – and you can ask for a read receipt to indicate whether your target has received the message. What's more, you stand a good chance of getting an immediate response, since the easiest time to click on 'reply' or a link to a webpage is while you're actually reading the mail.

This doesn't mean that all email marketing is inherently good, however. For a start it is indelibly associated with spam – unwanted and unrequested junk mail. Make sure that the people on your list actually

> " An email doesn't carry the materials and overhead costs of a paper mailshot, and you (probably) don't need the expensive and risky element of visual design "

want (and preferably are expecting) the material you're sending them. There are laws about this now, though they are depressingly feeble. The 'From' and 'Subject' lines are crucial in email marketing. The recipient must recognise the sender – company name or brand are good options if your own name will mean nothing. And the Subject is what will persuade them to read on, so put real effort into finding the right words. People don't read emails, they skim them. You still need good copywriting in an e-newsletter or a sales letter, but if possible you should also include clickable links or buttons for instant access to key online areas.

You can send a test mailing to a subset of your mailing list using two different subject lines. When you track the response, you can see which subject worked best and use that for your main mailing. The same holds true for other marketing methods such as banner advertisements and paid search campaigns. You can start with a low investment, track your returns, and make changes before deciding whether to invest more or try a different tactic. Internet marketing is useful to marketers on a budget because it is flexible, trackable, and offers vast reach for little investment.

Finally, always include an 'Unsubscribe' option in your message, but you may as well make sure that people know what they're missing when they do unsubscribe. Clicking the Unsubscribe button should take them to a web page, which asks them to confirm their decision and to identify what they specifically want to remove. They might not want to unsubscribe from everything and may want your occasional product updates, but not the regular newsletter.

Contact

PUSH: tel:
0845 310 9969;
www.pushgroup.
co.uk

....

ACTION POINT
KEEPING HOLD OF YOUR CUSTOMERS

Looking after customers is far more important than attracting new ones, according to **Alastair Campbell**, managing director of The Ideal Marketing Company. 'It is far more cost effective to target your resources towards holding onto a customer you already have than to spend a fortune trawling the country to attract a new one,' he says. 'After all, it costs seven times more to attract a new customer than to maintain an existing one. 'A whopping 75% leave because of "perceived indifference", he continues. 'That means that they stop doing business with you because they feel that you aren't interested in them; that you don't make them feel special anymore. So while you may think you are treating your customers well, most of them probably think otherwise and could be quickly tempted away by a competitor.'

Perhaps you really are going out of your way to serve your customer, but they just don't realise it. Well perception is reality, so if 75% are leaving because of perceived indifference, here are Campbell's five easy-to-implement ways on how to change their reality:

CAPTURE THEIR DETAILS AND KEEP IN TOUCH WITH THEM At least once a month write to them about a special offer, special product preview, clearance sale, new product line, open evening or whatever. This lets them know that you are thinking about them and looking for new ways to serve them.

ASK THEM HOW YOU ARE DOING Conduct a customer satisfaction survey on an annual or regular basis depending on your customer base. You can even offer an incentive if they complete the form.

CONDUCT REGULAR CUSTOMER FORUMS This allows you to tell your best customers more about what you are up to and to find out from your customers what they like about your service and products. It can also be a useful opportunity for customers to meet your staff (especially background staff) and of course other customers. If you're feeling brave, let them talk about you while you are out of the room for an hour and then listen to their feedback on what they like and don't like about your company.

DEVELOP MORE THAN ONE CONTACT POINT If a buyer leaves or your contact leaves, the relationship between your two organisations disappears overnight, but if you have more than one point of contact, the relationship is far stronger and can withstand the odd member of staff moving on. When a carefully planned company pairing system really works (as it does with Northern Foods and Marks & Spencer) your two organisations become so closely intertwined that no other company will get a look in.

BE HONEST Own up to mistakes, and don't pretend to be something that you're not. You can't build a long-term relationship based on mistrust. A customer would prefer you to hold your hands up to making a mistake rather than trying to shift the blame where it doesn't belong.

REMEMBER Most companies spend their hard-earned marketing and sales effort attempting to attract elusive new customers when they probably have most of the business they will ever need sitting on their database.

CASE STUDY
ATTIK AND THE ART OF TAKING RISKS

Attik is a brand business creating advertisements and design-led identities for many of the world's most successful companies. Formed in 1986 by two 19-year-olds, a £1,000 business grant from The Prince's Trust, some practical advice and a mentor, **James Sommerville** and **Simon Needham** opened their first office in Sommerville's grandmother's attic, hence the name. Needham also cites self-promotion and a 'no holds barred' approach to selling themselves 'in the early days' as a crucial factor.

'We tried PR companies to see if they suited our needs and shared our vision, but it didn't work so we took on an internal PR person who understood our way of thinking and working. When we first started we also had quite aggressive marketing campaigns, such as going around the streets and sticking flyers on walls and buildings, and we'd also do this to recruit people – something no one was doing at the time. We've even got a 6m by 4m poster on the wall next to our Sydney office. We didn't ask, we just put it there.'

This may not be an everyday method to establish brand recognition but it ties in neatly with Needham's fearlessly opportunist nature. 'Taking risks is all part of the game,' he says. 'You can be comfortable and run a business with 10 people and not aspire to grow any further, but you can also be prepared to take a gamble, although you should always have a plan in place in case it doesn't work.' To increase brand recognition as well as revenue, Needham created a separate concept entitled *Noise* seven years ago. Billed as a design bible, *Noise* is an annual publication containing the creative thoughts of all five Attik studios and sells thousands of copies each year.

'The industry needed something more ballsy instead of a standard brochure,' Needham explains. 'We gave it away to begin with, but when people actually came to us and asked if they could buy it, we stood back and let them'.

EXPERT OPINION

WORKING ON YOUR FIRST WEBSITE

BT on establishing your online presence.

A professional online presence is no longer just a 'nice-to-have' for businesses, it's a prerequisite – no matter what size your company is or the sector you operate in. For small businesses, in particular, an online presence, when done properly, opens up a world of possibilities and opportunities, including creating a new sales channel, reaching new customers, providing cost-effective marketing and a platform to network with other businesses.

Starting out

A cost-effective approach can be to start with a website that you develop yourself. This is easier than you might think, doesn't necessarily require specialist skills and can be done with tools that are available off the shelf, or as part of a broadband package from your internet service provider (ISP). The latter provides an extremely simple route to marketing and selling online, with template-based software that requires no technical skills or training. BT Business offers a fully functional website and domain name for only £5 per month, which uses drag-and-drop tools that make getting started quick and simple.

As you grow online

The next option is to use a service where you supply the words and photography to the designers and they use a series of pre-defined designs and pages to produce the website. This is great if you want to add functionality and a more professional feel to the website. Another option is to use a web consultation and optimisation service, which will look at your website in detail and tell you areas where it could be improved in order to help drive traffic and sales.

A website tailored to your business

The most flexible option is to have a bespoke website built just for you. This offers you the ability to choose the entire look and feel of the site and add in advanced functionality to meet your needs. As well as the initial build cost, you should always consider the potential ongoing costs of having a bespoke website as updates and changes are inherently more expensive.

Social networking

Social networking sites are very popular amongst consumers as a way to get online, share information and make new contacts. However, they can also be used in exactly the same way by small businesses: as a first foray online, giving visitors information about your products and services, and as a way to attract new business.

There are now social networking sites, such as BT Tradespace, that have been specifically designed for small businesses, and allow you to take advantage of the latest web-based technologies to help build an online presence

Tradespaces are free and quick to set up, even for those without any technical knowledge. Users simply fill in the details and upload images and logos and choose the community that they'd like to belong to, for example, 'business services' or 'weddings'.

Each BT Tradespace includes a blog, photos, podcasts, contact information and maps. You can also choose to add extra services like Click-to-Call functionality or multiple communities for a low monthly fee.

In addition to creating an online presence, Tradespacers can also use the service as a marketplace to sell goods to consumers and other businesses using the PayPal element of the service to process payments for goods and services securely.

EXPERT OPINION

Importance of good web design

Web consultants Ker-ching on user-friendly websites. Every website should be built with its purpose in mind. How well a website fulfils its purpose is influenced by several factors considered here.

Speed of site loading

Firstly, does it load quickly? Remember that many potential visitors may not have the same connection speed available to others. If, for instance, a web user is forced to wait several minutes for a large graphic to load, they will very likely move on to another site. These visual effects, though important in boosting visual appeal, must be used judiciously. There are numerous fast loading visual alternatives, such skinny horizontal graphics rather than the ones that occupy a lot of vertical space. There

are places on the internet to check the website load time.

Importance of keywords

A website must deliver what it promises. It is essential that the keywords of a website be justified. When a visitor to a site expects to be greeted with something and is finds that the website's content is very different, annoyance and breakdown of trust naturally follows. Not a great way to start.

Display contact information

If misunderstandings do occur or questions arise, the user will want to know how to contact the company that the website belongs to. By displaying contact information and location, not only is the visitor assured that the site actually belongs to the company, but the people who prefer email or postal mail, etc are also catered for.

Concise and direct language

The text on the website should also appeal to the visitor. Yes, the language used on a website is a powerful tool. The use of 'you' and 'your' frequently adds a sense of personalisation to the delivery of the message to the customer. They will know that their needs are a priority. Also, the purpose of the website should always be reflected in the words used. Concise, direct language will help the user to focus on what is on offer rather than become confused by irrelevance.

Keep it fresh!

Because of the vastness of and ease with which users browse the internet, the freshness of a website cannot be underestimated. An updated site will help ensure that a returning visitor does not become bored and escapes to a more appealing exciting page.

User involvement

Finally, the integration of some form of user interaction into a website is also a key factor in its success since this is a great medium by which users can contact the owner of the website. Indeed, emails, filling out forms and various methods of user feedback will keep visitors only a few clicks away and they will be encouraged by your great service.

For more information on this subject or to speak to an expert contact Ker-ching on 01273 467602 or visit www.ker-chingmedia.com.

OPEN FOR BUSINESS

WHAT'S IN THIS CHAPTER

■ So the time has finally arrived. After months of preparation including researching the viability of your proposed business, finding the appropriate name, putting together your business plan and implementing your pre-launch marketing campaign, it's full steam ahead and time to open your new company for business. You'll be feeling a mixture of trepidation and euphoria, and will have to prepare yourself for a few months of heavy work to get your business off the ground. Key to your early success will be setting up effective processes for invoicing, and the vitally important payment collection, not to mention setting yourself a realistic salary. Read on to find out how to approach these essential tasks…

Paying yourself

Few people start their own business solely for the purpose of becoming extremely wealthy, and even fewer actually succeed in achieving this. So right from the off, it's essential to consider how much you should be paying yourself.

When starting up you are likely to want to plough everything you can into making sure you give your business every chance of succeeding, but aside from the issues of needing to keep enough back for running costs and marketing, etc, you need to be able to live. At the other extreme, don't think that now you are in business you really should have that executive Mercedes. The first 12 months, or however long it is until you think you'll be in profit, will be an incredibly difficult period, and it is fair to say that there are more people who scrimp by than make a bucketload of cash straightaway.

Essentially, you need to be realistic. It's more than likely that you have given up the comfort and security of a regular salary and you can't be expected to suddenly survive without any income at all. You are also likely to have financial commitments that you will still need to meet, in addition to the new ones you'll be taking on by starting a business, so it's important to make sure you take enough to support sensible living costs. If you don't, you'll only be tempted to borrow more or build up another debt on a credit card – something that will inadvertently place more pressure on your business. Starting a business is also one of the most stressful things you can ever do. Failing to ensure you have enough money to relax when you are away from it will only increase the strain, and again, will prove detrimental to your business.

So how much should you pay yourself? This will be dependent on the sector you are going into and is probably the best place to start looking for answers. Talk to others in the trade or to people with similar sized-businesses and ask how much they were able to pay themselves at first, and what they can afford now. You should be aiming to pay yourself the same as the person in shop next door, not the same as the managing

> " You need to consider, right from the very start, how much you need to live on and what you can afford to pay yourself "

director of Vodafone. If they are not willing to tell you, try contacting trade associations, who should be able to help.

Once you have got some idea of what others in the sector are earning, try to fit a similar figure into your financial estimates and see if it's viable. If it isn't, then it could be there's a problem with your business plan as a whole, and it is something you will need to address before you take the plunge. The key is to plan ahead. You need to consider, right from the very start, how much you need to live on and what you can afford to pay yourself. If you don't, then you will soon be tapping into resources you hadn't accounted for and immediately putting your business on the back foot.

Remember, be realistic. Don't be afraid to treat yourself every now and then, but don't go overboard. You will need every penny of your startup funds and profits to put back into the business to help it grow. But don't under calculate what you can live on either. Be honest about what you need to 'get by' and incorporate that into your costs and your business plan.

Making a sale

> **Closing the sale is not simply a matter of asking for an order, and establishing terms of delivery and payment**

Some people seem like they were born to sell, while for many the thought brings them out in a cold sweat. But if you want to make your business a success, then you need to sell what you do – at least until you have the resources to build up a sales team. And although you may not consider yourself a salesperson, if you can launch a new business, you'll probably also be able to sell your product or service. In fact, when you speak to your bank, and potential recruits and suppliers, you're essentially selling your business to them to get them to work with you.

From clothes shops and online retailers to cafés, bars and restaurants, a lot of businesses don't need salespeople in the classic sense, with sales driven more by marketing, such as ads in the local press, calls to action on websites, direct mail flyer drops, etc. But for many more businesses, salespeople are a key aspect of generating income and driving profit.

In many cases, simply having the best product or service is not enough. You still need a marketing strategy to raise awareness, and once you've launched, you'll need a sales plan alongside it to build up a list of key prospects and sell directly to them. In fact, this is where any sales effort should start – drawing up a list of potential customers. This should consist of people you think should buy from you. Initially, buying in a database of contacts that fit your criteria from one of the many list brokers can be a good way to start.

With the list in place, you need to create a sales story or pitch before you start making contact. You launched a business on the basis that people would want to buy what you offer, so re-visit those reasons. Write down brief points about what you offer, how it can benefit your potential customers and what sets you apart from your competition. Hone the points down to three or four and devise the best way to build them into an engaging story.

Having drawn up the first draft of your pitch, try it out on friends or colleagues who know a little about your sector and canvass their opinions. Tell them to be honest, and ask them to suggest improvements, which you can consider taking into account to make your sales story more effective.

Making contact

Now it's time to start approaching your prospects. Cold calling can be effective, but it isn't for everyone. In such cases, it can be useful to send through an introductory email, which you can then follow up, giving you a reason to make contact and also providing a softer opening question: 'Did you receive my recent email about…'

One problem to overcome is getting through to the right person. If the list you've bought is all it's cracked up to be, this shouldn't be a problem, so it's important to ensure the contacts are bang up to date. However, there is often someone referred to as a 'gatekeeper' standing between you and your contact. This could be a receptionist or PA who

CASE STUDY
POWERCHEX AND THE COLD CALL

The service **Alexandra Kelly's** business offers could be used by many types of company, but strategically thinking about the best sector to sell to, and not being afraid to cold call laid the platform for future success.

Kelly founded her employment-screening firm Powerchex after being made redundant and spotting a gap in the market. Powerchex screens the histories of new recruits to the finance sector, validating everything from credit and police records to employment references. Kelly's team offers a guaranteed five-day turnaround – a promise that impressed the 2007 Startups Awards judges enough to name Powerchex the Service Business of the Year.

When starting up, once she had the IT infrastructure in place, it was time to get some customers on the books. But Kelly wasn't willing to offer her services to any old client, she was determined to specialise in helping financial companies, an area that she thought would want her service more than most. And selling her services to the right contacts in the right market has worked wonders.

'It was hard to turn down people that approached us from outside the financial sector,' she explains. 'When you don't have any clients, turning down money isn't easy, but it paid off in the end. We're now asked to bid for contracts as a result of how specialised we are.'

Kelly already had a lot of contacts in the very industry she was pitching to from her previous job, but found that, for her business, cold calling was still more effective than networking for getting the first client on board.

'Even people that were willing to meet for lunch and chat didn't want to sign up,' she says. 'Yet, some of those same companies became clients through us cold calling junior members of their team.'

has been instructed not to put salespeople through. This means the less you sound like a classic salesperson the better, so clearly introduce yourself and where you're from, and be polite and friendly, perhaps saying you have only a few questions and won't take up much of your target's time. Don't open the conversation by asking them how they are and not telling them who you are, as this is standard – and highly unproductive – cold-calling fare. Ultimately, if you befriend the gatekeeper, you're more likely to get through after a few calls.

Remember that the point of these initial calls is not necessarily to make a sale, but to nurture a key contact that you can arrange to visit to guide them further towards a sale. Although it depends on your product or service, few businesspeople will agree a sale without at least one face-to-face meeting.

Once you have a meeting arranged, you then need to work on a short, engaging presentation that adds key points to your initial phone conversations. Try to keep this to no longer than 20 minutes – even shorter if possible – and then be prepared to field questions. PowerPoint presentations are effective, but a little old hat these days, so if you can use more engaging graphics projected, say, from your laptop, you may make more of an impact. And remember to say that you will need a few minutes to set up, and find out if they have a plain white wall or projector screen you could use.

Presenting well

As we all know, first impressions count, so when you meet a potential customer for the first time it's important to come across well. Good preparation will help build your confidence and calm your nerves, and always begin by taking a deep breath and smiling, as this will help to relax both you and your audience.

During the presentation speak slowly and calmly, making regular eye contact, as this engenders a feeling of trust and helps you maintain their attention. You should also come over as enthusiastic and passionate, as this can be infectious, but don't overdo it. Also, pay attention to the mood of your audience all the time, and adjust your presentation accordingly.

Always begin by taking a deep breath and smiling, as this will help to relax both you and your audience

For example, if they start fidgeting or looking bored, move on swiftly if you have more key points to make and wrap up as quickly as you can.

Once you've finished and you've invited questions, try to answer confidently and knowledgably, but also don't be scared to say you don't know the answer to a particular query, as this is better than bluffing your way through, and won't come back to haunt you later. You can always research the answer and get back to them.

Before you leave, make sure you close the meeting effectively. Ask them for their opinions and if they are going to buy. If they say yes, or are undecided, find out what the next steps are, what additional information they need and what factors they will be basing their final decision on. This will help you at the next meeting, if necessary.

Of course, rejection is just as, if not more, possible than clinching a sale, so be prepared for it and take it on the chin. Have the presence of mind to ask your audience the reasons for them not wanting to buy from you, as this can be key information in the development of your offer, and will mean you'll get something productive from the meeting. Also ask your audience if they would mind if you contact them in six months or a year's time to review the situation.

Once you've got your first few sales under your belt you will start to build up a network of customers, and further sales should be a little easier. For one, you could well have some good testimonials to back up your pitch.

> **Shaking hands is simply the first in a series of steps to ensure the deal goes through smoothly**

It is easy to think that once you have closed a sale, you can relax. Far from it. Often, shaking hands is simply the first in a series of steps to ensure the deal goes through smoothly. Remember to enter the sales negotiation armed with information. If the value or risk of the business transaction is high, it's wise to get as much financial information about the client as possible, to minimise the level of risk to the business and protect against bad debt. Closing the sale is not simply a matter of asking for an order, and establishing terms of delivery and payment. You should also restate your credit terms to the buyer and present them with your credit application form (see the section on 'The basics about credit' later in the chapter), while establishing a named contact responsible for payment.

CASE STUDY
LUXTECH AND THE WISE MOVES

The quickest route to sales isn't always picking up the phone and talking to someone directly. In **Russell Lux's** case, the environment in which he set up his IT support services company Luxtech was ripe for networking, and he exploited this to the full.

Starting up in the spare room of Lux's London flat, Luxtech was founded in January 2001 and raised its first invoice in July 2002. Embellished with £2,000 of funding, which came from Lux's savings, the business was initially simply equipped with a computer with broadband connection.

Lux initially gained clients through word of mouth. He targeted solicitors and accounts as they are client-based businesses and could recommend his services on to others.

'I built up a good reputation,' he recalls. 'London is a huge market to attack, but I had to do business through an introduction. It was very difficult to walk in off the street and introduce yourself.'

The increasing number of clients saw the business naturally outgrow the flat, prompting Luxtech to relocate to a small serviced office. It turned out to be a smart move, which saw a sharp increase in clients. This was because Lux used his networking skills to win the business of 22 other startup companies who also used the serviced offices within the first six months.

It's a trick he repeated when moving to larger serviced offices in Camden, north London. Luxtech took on 42 extra clients – every business in the building.

'We moved into serviced offices because we didn't have any infrastructure costs – we didn't have to pay for desks, chairs or telephone systems,' Lux explains. 'We found the place through the internet and made lots of business contacts while there.

'It was great for them because we were on their doorstep – they had IT support literally down the corridor. It was like a large corporate – you had an IT department, a finance department and a marketing department there.'

The importance of getting paid

Half of all new businesses fail during the first two years. All too often the cause of failure is not the quality of the product or service, the effort and talents of the people, or the sales and marketing. It is quite simply down to financial failure – running out of money – which leads to closure, if not bankruptcy. In many cases, this failure could have been avoided by simple but effective planning from the outset. In too many new businesses, well-qualified people enthusiastically develop their goods or services, but pay insufficient attention to cash flow. Late payment erodes profits and stifles growth. A sale is not really made until it has been paid for, so the discipline of ensuring prompt payment, called credit control or credit management, has to be a priority if a business is to succeed.

Granting credit to a customer involves the risk of non-payment and so should only be done after checking and assessing that risk. A bad debt means that a company could have to make sales five – or even 10 – times the value of that bad debt just to recoup the loss. Research shows that the longer a trade debt remains unpaid, the greater the risk that it will never be paid. For many companies, their receivables – the money owed to them by their customers – are their largest assets. Figures from BACS – the banks' automated clearing system – show that growth businesses have a combined overdraft of £4 billion. Reducing the amount owed by debtors cuts the overdraft and frees up capital to be used to finance the business, and reduces the stress of running the business.

Credit and creditors

❝ Late payment erodes profits and stifles growth ❞

Making sure you are paid should start even before you have made your first sale in the form of some basic training. Your local chamber of commerce should have courses in basic credit control, including such topics as how to collect a debt over the phone. These are open to non-members. Meanwhile, the government-sponsored Better Payment

CONTROLLING CASH FLOW

Matthew Holmes, MD of Liquid Accounts offers advice on keeping the money coming in.

When you are starting out in business it's very easy to get carried away with the novelty and excitement of it all, and forget about the more mundane stuff such as admin and accounting. However, most new businesses fail in the first three years (around half by year two and three-quarters by year three) because they're not in control of their cash flow. So it's incredibly important to get some systems in place right from the beginning (ideally using some software, even if it's just a spreadsheet). It's easier to do it *now* while you've still got the time, and can get into a habit, regularly setting some time aside to get your finances up to date, and review what they're telling you. (Are your sales going up and down? Are you making enough money to cover your costs?) Liquid Accounts regularly gets clients coming who only realise they've got a problem when they've got their first VAT or tax return to do, or their business adviser cannot help them until they've got some up-to-date figures. Here then are Liquid Accounts' top five tips for getting it right:

- **Make sure you bill as soon as possible:** It may sound obvious, but as soon as you've done the work, send the invoice! Don't be afraid to be prompt – you're only asking for money that's owed to you, and they're not going to pay you unless you ask for it. If your payment terms are 30 days (see below), and you wait another two weeks before you raise an invoice, you are only going to get your money after 44 days at the earliest.

- **Set payment terms and stick to them:** If you decide to put on your invoices when you will like the bill to be paid (normally 'on receipt', 7, 14 or 30 days), known as payment terms, don't be afraid to make a quick call *on the first day that the invoice is overdue* to ask when you can expect payment. If someone is a habitually bad payer (or you need to improve your cash flow), don't be afraid to shorten your payment terms, or use your rights to charge interest (under the Late Payment of Commercial Debts (Interest) Act 1998). Big companies in particular can be particularly bad payers, and so don't be afraid to use these rights

– that's why they exist. Remember, you need the money more than they do!

- **Have a debt collection system in place:** To make sure that all the above happens you need to have good accounting software that flags up for you when people haven't paid and someone keeping an eye on things and doing the chasing. Early on, this is probably going to be down to you, but as you grow you may consider having someone do this for you, such as a professional debt collection agency.

- **Consider using sales order processing and purchase order processing:** On a basic level, this can mean anything from making sure that you get a signed letter of confirmation for *everything* you sell and *everything* you buy, through to issuing a full contract for each piece of work you do. Whichever route you take, it will make it easier for you to chase a debt or dispute a bill if a problem arises, and even without a full contract in place, it will be easier for you pursue a legal course of action. And you will be more likely to get a result (if they've signed for it, they can't say that they

didn't want it!). Big companies will automatically have these processes in place, so don't put yourself, as the little guy, at a disadvantage. Any good accounting software should have sales order processing and purchase order processing as an option, and so it should only mean an extra five minutes' work – think of it as an insurance policy. Your accountant, lawyer or debt collection agency should be able to advise you on what you need.

- **Consider changing to cash accounting:** Liquid Accounts' top tip is that if you are VAT registered, consider changing to cash accounting. This means that you only pay the VAT on your invoices once you've received the money, and it will really help if you don't know exactly when you are going to get paid. Obviously you would need to take advice from your accountant and check the rules of cash accounting before switching, but the good news is that you don't have to notify HMRC of the change. Again, any good accounting package should have cash accounting built in as an option.

Practice Group (BPPG) was formed to reduce late payment of commercial debt and publishes advice on the subject. From the outset, establish procedures for credit applications by customers:

- Produce a credit application form: specialist books or advisers will show you how
- Make credit terms very clear
- Ensure that all staff are aware of your credit policy
- Make payment terms a condition of sale
- Make sure that every buyer signs, agreeing to your credit terms.

Then, to help ensure you receive prompt payment:

- Design a clear invoice, which will always states agreed payment terms
- Send out invoices promptly and keep paperwork up to date
- Establish a timetable for chasing debts, starting with the first request for payment: the invoice.

Payment should never be an afterthought. Establishing it as a priority means you can then consider granting customers credit where appropriate. But this should be calculated risk, never be a gamble. You must know who you are dealing with, and this should be part of the preparation before a sale.

It is important to establish a potential customer's credentials. Obviously if your sales are low value/high volume, this will not be practical, but many companies have a small number of major customers, the effective management of whom is crucial to success. In these cases, a visit to a potential customer's premises will usually tell you a lot. The annual report of companies is also useful, although the information could be out of date. For particularly high-value or high-risk orders, obtain a credit report from a credit reference agency. Such reports cost between £3 and £25, depending on the level of information.

For very small orders, buying a credit report may be uneconomic and you may wish to take the risk yourself, but for significant orders, it's well worth the expense. Bank and trade references should always answer specific questions, such as: can I grant £500 credit, or what proportion

Contact

Better Payment Practice Group www.payontime. co.uk

of this firm's payments to you are overdue? However, they should not be solely relied upon. If you have a new customer, confirm their address to avoid fraud, and find out how long they've been trading. If they are on a short lease, they could disappear with the goods. Also confirm that they have the cash to pay. There's no need to check their profit and loss account yourself, because a credit reference company will do it for you – and they will suggest a credit limit and a credit rating. For potentially high-value orders, take a credit report prior to negotiation, to avoid wasted effort. Credit costs and knowing the risks in advance helps in pricing. Remember, credit control is a continuous process. Always monitor your debtors as their circumstances may change.

Decide on a credit limit. A credit reference agency may recommend one or do it yourself, deciding whether a firm is a high risk – a late payer, for example with adverse information like a county court judgements against them or dubious individuals involved – or low risk, with a good payment record and strong credit references. If you decide to grant credit, set up an account and write to the customer confirming this. Always have delivery of goods confirmed through a delivery note and follow up with a phone call, confirming that goods were delivered satisfactorily. Then invoice immediately, restating credit terms, and quoting an order number if appropriate.

Credit control is a continuous process

! TIPS

ASSESSING CUSTOMER RISK

If your sales are high value and low volume make sure that potential customers can pay, by:

! Confirming their address
! Establishing how long they've been trading
! Visiting their premises
! Consulting their annual report
! Running a credit check through a credit reference agency

Collecting payment

When payment is due, don't be afraid to ask. After all, it's your money, and if you have done the job right, you are entitled to be paid. Any disputes or complaints that delay payment must be addressed immediately. Some customers will pay promptly while others are habitual late payers. You will need to establish a timetable for chasing debtors (see the box for an example) and to keep receivables under control. The suggested procedures should be supplemented with phone calls – one of the most effective methods of chasing debts – faxes, emails and visits.

Some customers will pay promptly while others are habitual late payers

'We're very much involved in advising small-to-medium-sized firms in ways to tighten procedures and collect debts,' says **Trevor Phillips** of consultancy Credit Professionals. 'Debt collection requires pleasant persistence. It's a selling job. Companies have to persuade customers that they have to be paid. Once a debt is more than 60 days overdue, a company has probably exhausted all its own internal resources for collecting the debts, therefore, it is necessary to intervene with a third party.'

Many debt collection agencies have relationships with credit reference agencies giving them leverage to collect. Of course, there is a cost, typically between 1% and 5% of the sum, depending on circumstances. Under the Late Payment of Commercial Debts (Interest) Act 1998, a company can charge interest to its debtors on late payments. Many collectors have solicitors associated with them and can handle litigation if it is necessary to sue for a debt. It shouldn't be seen as a sign of weakness to pass on a debt to a collection agency. Simply view it as an extension of your business. A new business should be equally as professional as a large one in pursuing outstanding debts.

Whether you have a manual accounts system or a computerised one, it is important to prioritise debts, chasing the largest first. It is crucial to establish strong relationships with major customers to ensure prompt payment. Remember, the longer a debt is outstanding, the less likely it is to be paid.

Timetable for debt chasing

Here's a sample schedule for chasing money you're owed:

- The sale: send out invoice
- 21 days: send statement reminding payment due after 30 days
- 30 days: if not paid, send reminder statement, restating terms and pointing out payment is overdue
- 45 days: send reminder, restating payment is overdue
- 50 days: stop supplies until paid
- 60 days: send final reminder
- 90 days: assign debt to collection agency

Late payment and how to avoid it

> **Future growth always depends on cash flow**

Some businesses choose not to undertake their own credit control, but have someone else do all or part of it for them by outsourcing. Other techniques worth considering are credit insurance, factoring, retention of title or payment in advance. 'There are a range of ways in which third-party outsourcers are being used,' says **Colin Thomas** of Graydon UK, a credit referencing agency. 'If you have limited resources, you can bring in an outsourcing company that can provide some immediate level of expertise. Future growth always depends on cash flow,' he continues. 'Outsourcers can cover the entire order-to-cash cycle. You can choose whether your outsource partner operates in your name or in their own name. In the cash collections field, you may prefer them to operate in your name at the receivables stage and then in their own name for accounts that become overdue.'

Credit insurance

Credit insurers, such as Euler Trade Indemnity, will insure against the risk of bad debt. Insurance companies can be contacted through the Association of British Insurers.

Factoring

Factoring is a popular choice for new businesses because it helps avoid cash flow problems. Both factoring and invoice discounting involve the small business borrowing against sales as a means of sustaining cash flow. Invoice discounting involves a company loaning you a large percentage of the money for each invoice as soon as it is raised, which is then repaid plus a commission fee when payment is received from your customer within a specified time period. Under factoring the company will also chase the debt for you, for a larger commission payment. The key difference between the two is that in invoice discounting you continue to chase the payments yourself and the service is usually undisclosed to customers. There are two types of factoring: recourse factoring, which excludes bad debt protection, and non-recourse factoring, which includes it. In the latter case, if a credit-approved customer fails to pay an undisputed debt, the factor will credit you with the amount of the debt.

Contact

- Association of British Insurers
- Euler Trade Indemnity

Retention of title

A sale is only really made when it is paid for. Retention of title, keeping ownership of goods until they are paid for, however, has only limited application. It cannot be used where you are supplying a service, such as cleaning or architecture, or where the goods supplied are then made into something else, as in flour in a bakery.

Payment in advance

Credit is a privilege, not a right, and in some circumstances it may be appropriate to ask for full or part payment in advance – for example, when making a large order, which would extend the supplier's financial resources, or if a customer is deemed uncreditworthy. In other instances, credit terms could be reduced to, say, one week, instead of the normal 30 days.

Credit is a privilege, not a right

Private limited companies and their subsidiaries are obliged to publish the time taken to pay suppliers in their annual report and the Federation

Contact

- Better Payment Practice Group: www.payontime. co.uk
- The Institute of Credit Management: www.icm.org.uk
- The Asset Based Finance Association: www. abfa.org.uk
- The Federation of Small Businesses: www.fsb.org.uk
- Companies House: www. companieshouse. gov.uk

of Small Businesses produces annual league tables of companies' payment records, while credit reference agencies focus on recent payment trends. Adverse information, such as county court judgments or previous insolvencies involving directors, clearly indicate high risk. This information is available from official sources such as the Registry Trust or the Insolvency Service for a fee, but is also included in credit reports. Basic information can be obtained from Companies House, but, again, a credit report includes this information. Good credit management should aid, not inhibit, the sales effort. The key is obtaining good information and setting up effective procedures. Making the effort at the beginning can save much wailing and gnashing of teeth later on.

Dealing with debtors

A new customer can equal more profits to your firm, but it could also spell disaster if they turn out not to be what they originally seemed. It may sound obvious, but it's vital to be sure of customer's identity to help avoid the heartache of receiving a 'gone-away' notice in response to your invoice. Start by getting complete and correct contact details for every customer via a proper account opening form. This must include the correct address and telephone details, which should be checked against alternative sources, such as the *Yellow Pages*. In the case of a limited company, request the full limited name and registration number, and for a proprietorship and partnerships, ensure that you take private address details and telephone numbers. The Better Payment Practice Group has a sample account opening form on its website (www.payontime.co.uk/ collect/credit_app_pre.html). Using a credit reference agency to check the credit viability of new and existing customers will often reveal any address anomalies, which can then be confirmed directly with your customer.

Once you have established the new relationship, maintaining regular contact means you quickly become aware if a debtor relocates. Do not just issue invoices and wait for payment. Contact customers by phone to enquire politely whether your invoices have been received, and in doing so, you can verify that the address and telephone details you have remain accurate. Ask delivery staff to alert you to anything suspicious about the way goods or services are delivered, such as if the customer insists on collecting the goods, without adequate verification of their trading addresses.

Tracing a debtor

If a letter is returned via Royal Mail marked 'Addressee not known' or 'No longer at this address', never assume this is actually the case. Many practised debtors simply return a letter as 'gone away' to give themselves more time. Start by taking the following steps:

- Check your own information to see if you have made any errors on the original details. If you identify an error, reissue your invoice immediately using the correct details.
- Dial telephone numbers and re-check via a directory enquiry facility to ensure that you have the correct number.
- Try a recorded delivery letter, as this may be accepted and thus confirm occupancy.

If the debtor appears to be no longer trading from the premises you have details for, then consider the following:

- Contact the debtor's local Royal Mail sorting office as they may have forwarding addresses, or may confirm that the subject is still at the original address.
- If you operate in the vicinity, use your delivery drivers or staff to seek information from the address or from its neighbours. However, you must have due regard to the Data Protection Act 1998. In particular, do not divulge any information about a debt to non-interested parties. You should say that you are seeking general information on a 'private matter', asking if there a forwarding address that they know of.
- If you know any other suppliers that your customer uses, contact them to enquire if they have been notified of their change of address.
- For businesses rather than individuals, use the *Yellow Pages* for the area of enquiry to identify and telephone businesses/newsagents in the

locality who may well know the business or have useful information on the business' status. Again you must have due regard to the Data Protection Act when making such enquiries.

- Look at the status or credit reference report you may have obtained when opening the account as this may give you alternative addresses. In the case of a limited company, you are entitled to contact the directors, particularly the company secretary, who has an obligation to inform any interested party of the status of the limited company.

You can contact these individuals at their home address or an address lodged with Companies House, but you cannot make them individually liable for any debt. A polite question should help you establish whether, for example, the company has entered liquidation, or a Creditors Voluntary Arrangement. If this is the case, you may need to seek professional advice about your rights as an unsecured creditor to a limited company. If these efforts fail then you could seek the help of a professional collection/tracing company who may quote costs, usually from £50 to £60.

Handling debt collection and your debtors professionally and effectively can help protect your company against a bad payment that could send the business under.

Contact

Credit Services
Association:
www.csa-uk.com

> **You are likely to spend more on T&E than advertising**

Travel and expenses

Few people actually know how much they spend each year on travel and expenses and most would have to take valuable time researching to get the answer, and they should. Travel and entertainment – or T&E as commerce likes to call it – amounts to the third largest controllable corporate cost, just behind salaries and data processing. You are also likely to spend more on T&E than advertising. So it's even more concerning that so few companies can actually put an annual total on such a vital part of their operation. As a startup, this is your opportunity to redress the balance and keep a close track of T&E from the start. Small businesses are hardly likely to rival a major corporation in terms of T&E spend, but it could still be a leakage in your profits and is something you need to keep under control.

Every business, no matter how small, will benefit from a formal travel policy and improved T&E management. With any travel policy, the balance is between the benefit of the travellers and the cost saving for the company. And this isn't simply a cost issue. Time out of the office has to be managed efficiently. No one can afford to miss too many important calls and it may be difficult to hand over to anyone else to 'hold the fort' while you are away. Then, of course, these days there is concern over a company's environmental impact, of which travel can play a major part, particularly with respect to air travel.

Whether you work for yourself or run a company employing several people, travel expenses will need to be minimised wherever possible, and there are a number of easy steps that you can take to help control your costs.

Don't just take the most obvious route

A business can save almost a third by sending an executive via Paris to Los Angeles instead of flying direct from London. If you operate away from London and would be paying for a connecting flight, say from Aberdeen or Manchester, it may well benefit you to skip London and go direct to Paris.

Think about downgrading

When arranging business flights, ask yourself if business class is really necessary. Of course, for many startups 'slumming it in the back' may well be the only affordable way to go – but it can make better business sense anyway. Equally, using secondary airports or 'no-frills' airlines can cut costs significantly. For example, a return flight to Geneva, from London Gatwick, is six times cheaper with a low-cost carrier.

Look out for loyalty schemes

If you will be travelling to see the same client several times a year, there may well be an opportunity to negotiate a better rate. It is also important to remember that a travel policy is more than just about the flights. Using the same hotel chain on a regular basis can also cut costs with a negotiated rate. And for individual travellers, who happen to be with the company too, loyalty schemes are worth using. Free points towards flights and hotel bills all help the bottom line.

Get in the professionals

You could use a company, such as American Express, which will help you to implement and follow a travel policy, organising travel for you and negotiating better rates on your behalf.

Bookkeeping

HMRC has teams of advisers on hand to help out should you run into difficulties

One of the most daunting things about giving up full-time employment to start your own business is the prospect of looking after the company accounts. For an ex-employee who is used to having his or her tax and National Insurance contributions (NICs) deducted at source via PAYE (pay as you earn), the prospect of dealing with the vast, looming shadow that is the Inland Revenue can be quite daunting.

It's tempting to say that there's no need to worry and that the entire bookkeeping process is child's play, but that wouldn't be strictly true. If it were, accountants wouldn't be paid so well. But HM Revenue & Customs (HMRC) is not – perhaps contrary to popular belief – a bullying, authoritarian organisation. On the contrary, its aim is to help businesses manage their accounts as effectively as possible. To this end it publishes regular newsletters and leaflets giving tips and guidance on bookkeeping, and has teams of advisers on hand to help out over the phone should you run into difficulties.

Before you even launch your own business, talk to your local HMRC offices. Call them, make an appointment, explain the details of your business plan and ask them exactly what you need to do. They will provide you with advice, relevant leaflets and a selection of forms – such as VAT registration – which you should complete before beginning trading. This is vitally important. If you start off with all the necessary information, it will make the bookkeeping process much easier. It also helps to have a contact within the local offices whom you can call should you run into any difficulties.

Sole traders

If you are setting up as a sole trader rather than as a company with employees, then your bookkeeping work can be kept to a minimum. There's the added advantage that sole traders pay less tax than any other class of working people, although you have to be careful that you don't fall foul of the IR35 regulation. This rule, which quite simply states that if you look like an employee, you are an employee, was introduced to prevent contractors working on site for single clients for long periods of time, effectively acting as employees, but invoicing as sole traders or single-employee limited companies.

As a sole trader, you have to keep track of monthly income and expenditure, which means holding on to all invoices and receipts. You will also have to talk to HMRC about NICs – the easiest way to handle these is by setting up a direct debit, and the amounts involved are quite small. You could manage your accounts by hand, but it's easier to do it using a computer. A spreadsheet will suffice, containing columns for income, expenditure and VAT (if you are VAT registered). This means keeping track of all invoices (along with the dates they were issued and paid) and all receipts for work-related transactions, including any ground rent, telephone bills, heating and electricity costs and so on. If you work from home, some of your household expenditure may be tax deductible. This is all the information you will need to fill in the tax return form each year. You can then either attempt to calculate the amount of tax owed

> "You can manage your accounts by hand, but it's easier to do it using a computer"

yourself or send the form to HMRC and let it do it for you. It's actually all quite easy and shouldn't take more than a couple of hours each month.

Partnerships and limited companies

Things get a little more complex once you start employing people, because you will have to look after their salaries as well as the general company accounts. You will have to manage the deduction of their tax at source, payment of employer and employee NICs, plus any pension schemes, bonus arrangements and non-salary expenses. The process is far quicker and simpler than it ever was thanks to bookkeeping software packages, which also let you plot graphs of profit and loss or income and expenditure, track overdue payments (both incoming and outgoing) and the more advanced tools can even automate the submission of the relevant forms to HMRC. Options available include QuickBooks Mind Your Own Business (MYOB), Sage Instant Accounting/Payroll and Liquid Accounts (online accounting software), which can all be used for companies of up to 20 employees – and don't be put off by the relatively low cost of these packages. Most of these packages are powerful accounting tools that can double as business assessment and stock control systems, giving you a real feel for which areas of your business are doing well and which are failing. For the sake of convenience, it's best to ask your accountant which software package he or she prefers to use and then buy that one for internal use.

When it comes to doing your company accounts, you will be better off finding a good accountant. Note that they won't do the donkey work of everyday data input for you, unless you are prepared to pay extra – a lot extra. What they will do is take the figures you have provided for the year and plug those into various forms to tell you the amount of money you have to pay for each class of tax. Aim to go for a chartered accountant and preferably choose on the basis of a friend or colleague's recommendation. A good accountant should make recommendations as to where you can save money, in addition to completing the relevant forms and dispensing advice as needed throughout the year. See the section on accountants later in this chapter for more details.

VAT considerations

For companies, and sole traders for that matter, with annual turnovers exceeding a certain amount (currently £67,000), quarterly VAT returns must be completed and sent to HMRC along with any payment due.

The VAT form is very simple – just a single page – and usually works in the company's favour. This is because, although you must pay VAT on any income generated, you can claim back VAT paid on some goods and services, such as office supplies, vehicle servicing, fuel and so on. So the extra accounting is definitely worth it and even companies with turnovers less than the VAT limit can still register voluntarily. Not all products and services attract the standard 17.5% VAT rate, so request your local HMRC office for its introductory video that explains the basics of VAT accounting. If that's not enough, you can also enrol on a brief course, again run by HMRC, which will go into greater detail.

Try to keep track of changes to tax regulations. This means listening to the entire budget speech! Your accountant should do this for you, but it doesn't hurt to know about VAT limits, along with changes in basic tax rates and company car regulations yourself. Above all, tempting as it may seem, don't ever attempt to 'cook the books'. Penalties for tax evasion are high. It's not worth the sleepless nights and feelings of guilt just to shave a few pounds off your tax bill, and there's always the chance that you will be found out, especially if you are audited.

The percentage of companies audited each year by HMRC is quite small, but the organisation has effective ways of tracking suspicious returns. The auditing process is thorough and time-consuming, since all receipts and invoices must be checked against the returns and shown to the investigating accountant. Also, the Statute of Limitations is biased in the auditors' favour, so you may have to dig out paperwork going back many years. This means that you may want to take out auditing insurance with your accountant. The work involved during an audit is considerable – allow for three days at the very least – and could become very expensive if you pay your accountant by the hour.

> **Above all, tempting as it may seem, don't ever attempt to 'cook the books'**

Contact

For the most -up-to-date VAT registration information HMRC: www.hmrc.gov.uk/vat/vat-registering.htm.

....

ACTION POINT
KEEPING ON TOP OF TAX
AND ACCOUNTS

In your first year of operation it will seem as though there's an endless array of forms to be completed and taxes to be paid, whereas in fact there aren't really so many. Although your accountant will guide you through the process, it pays to understand the tax and accounting demands on your business, and if you bear in mind the following basics, you won't go far wrong.

During the tax year you must:

- Deduct the correct amount of PAYE from your employees' pay
- Work out the amount of National Insurance Contributions (NICs) that you and your employees have to pay
- Keep a record of your employees' pay and PAYE and NICs due
- Make monthly or quarterly payments of the total PAYE and NICs due to the Accounts Office
- Manage VAT return completion and payment on a quarterly basis

At the end of the tax year you must:

- Send a Return (form P35) and an End of Year Summary (form P14) showing details of each employee's total pay and the PAYE and NICs due, to your HMRC office
- Send details to the Inland Revenue office about expenses you have paid to employees or benefits you have provided (forms P11D and P9D)
- Give each employee (who has paid PAYE or NICs and is still working for you at the end of the tax year) a certificate showing their pay, PAYE and NICs details (form P60)
- Give each employee a copy of the information you have given your HMRC office about their expenses payments and benefits provided (duplicate of form P11D)

At the end of your company's accounting year you must:

- Send a formal return for your company's accounts to your HMRC office
- You should receive copies of the *Employer's Bulletin* from HMRC along with the Employer's Annual Pack. Request the copies if you haven't received them within a month or so of starting your business, as these provide useful tips on the above duties, plus contacts and advice for business owners

Ultimately, you should remember that you are expected to account for every single business-related penny spent – this includes invoices for trade magazines and newspapers, for example. Although there may be some discretionary leeway, you are expected to show each month's transactions in sufficient detail that your profit and loss, income and expenditure – and therefore tax – can be clearly calculated.

Why you need an accountant

You might think that a startup or small business isn't big enough to warrant an accountant, but unless you are an expert in tax and finance – in short an accountant yourself – this simply isn't the case. An accountant can provide your business with a great deal of essential support. If you are just starting a business, your accountant will take the form of another business adviser. They can give advice on your business plan and the tax issues of registering your company. Some accountants offer bookkeeping services, but if they don't or if you wish to handle this yourself, you can get help with setting up manual or computerised bookkeeping systems. And most importantly, you need an accountant to assist on things such as whether it is necessary to register for VAT or PAYE and the procedures involved. You can also ask them for help with budgeting and forecasting cash flow, as well as credit control and general financial advice. They can also offer you up-to-date information on any general or legal enquiries.

> **An accountant can provide your business with a great deal of essential support**

An accountant isn't just there to help you manage your money. They can also advise you on the best way to arrange additional finance without putting your business at risk. Once you have the finance in place, there needs to be some control to ensure the growth of your business is handled in the right way. Many of your concerns will be financial – adequate working capital, good stock control, invoicing and so on – and an experienced accountant's advice can prove invaluable in such matters. Furthermore, can you honestly say that you are on top of all the essential taxation issues? Well, that's also an accountant's job – taxation is a large business expense and an accountant can effectively minimise these costs.

Finding an accountant

A simple internet search will throw up lots of accountants in your area. There are many ways to track down the right accountant for your new business, one of the best of which is through recommendation. Simply ask friends and contacts if they would recommend their various accountants. Also ask businesses around you if they use someone locally. Your solicitor and bank manager will be working with accountants all the time, and they will probably have a good idea of the firms most suited to your type of business, making them also a good source of recommendation. Equally, your local Business Link or Enterprise Agency will be able to help you in your search.

Make sure you ask people what they use their accountant for, as you might not need the same kinds of services. You should also quiz them on what would they recommend about them, their weak points, and if they are always on hand when needed. Most importantly, it is advisable to choose someone who is a member of one of the main professional accounting bodies. There is no legislation to stop anyone setting up as an accountant, so asking for member accountants in your area will ensure you are getting someone fully qualified.

Qualities to look for in an accountant

You need to make sure that the accountant you choose for your company is at least familiar with your business sector. It will be less help to you hiring someone who's used to dealing with manufacturing companies if yours is in the leisure industry, as they won't be as familiar with specific legislation. Also, look at the size of the firm. As you are a startup, look for a small to medium-sized business accountant as they will probably specialise more in small business work, charge less than a larger firm and give more direct access to more experienced partners.

The accountant needs to be able to get into your business and show an interest in it

Make arrangements to visit several firms in person to meet the people you will be working with and to make comparisons. 'A lot comes down to personal chemistry,' maintains **Paul Watts**, corporate finance partner at HLB Kidsons. 'The accountant needs to be able to get into your business and show an interest in it, as well as just doing your accounts, if they are to advise you properly.' You are likely to be working closely with your accountant, so if you don't get on at a basic level, your professional relationship may be more difficult than it needs to be. It's good to ask if you can speak to other clients, in the same way that you would ask for references, and this will be a real test of the calibre of the firm. If they are confident that their service has impressed, they shouldn't have a problem referring you to a few people. Equally, a good accountant should want to make an appointment to come and see your business. 'It's important to go out and see clients,' says Watts. 'You can't fully understand a business until you have been taken round it.' And allow each accountant to pitch to you, as it isn't just about what you want, but also what they are prepared to offer.

So you have followed all the rules and carefully chosen your accountant, but this is the first time you have had one, so how do you know if they are doing a good job, and what do you do if you think they are not? To gauge their performance, look at what you are getting from them. At a basic level, are your accounts and tax returns prepared on time? Are you being billed as agreed and are your phone calls and letters answered? On top of this, take note of the advice they've given you. Have they come up with ideas you wouldn't otherwise have thought of? And if not, is that because you haven't liked the ideas, or because there haven't been any?

It is possible just to say to an accountant that you no longer want to work with them – you can effectively 'sack' the firm. But don't rush into doing this at the slightest hitch, as it's important to build a relationship with your accountant, which is difficult if you are changing every six months. Problems can often be ironed out, so keep careful track of the service and speak to your accountant if you need to. But, ultimately, remember that you are not paying for poor service.

Agreeing terms

Your accountant should be a good investment

When you are considering taking on an accountant, it's important to establish who your contact will be at the firm and who you can speak to in their the absence. This, along with the services they are offering you and the fees they will charge, should form part of the engagement letter. Like the contract, this should be signed by both of you, and will form the basis of your working relationship. As such, it is important to get as much information on it as possible. If the accountant is to handle your tax, your accounts and your payroll, it should say so.

This is also the point where you talk about money. Traditionally, accountants charge by the hour with more for a partner than for a junior member of staff. However, many firms are prepared to be flexible with regards to payment, and you might negotiate a fixed one-off fee for a full audit, for example, or pay monthly rather than all at once at the end of the year. The latter should be popular with both parties as it ensures regular payment when the money is available. However, going for the firm that charges the least can sometimes be a false economy, according to Watts. 'Don't always go for the cheapest firm, look for one that adds value,' he advises. 'For example, how much does the hourly fee vary for a partner and other staff and will photocopying and phone time be included in the cost or be extra?' Most importantly, don't be afraid to question anything on the engagement letter or to ask for something to be added. As with most contracts, it is in both your interests. In exchange for an hourly fee, you should get someone who saves you money, prevents you sitting up late with accounts that won't balance and who can provide general business sense. All the more reason to choose carefully.

EXPERT OPINION

THE BENEFITS OF GOOD BOOKKEEPING

John Hewitt of Company Builder explains why keeping your books up to date is worth the effort.

Bookkeeping is one aspect of business that many people dislike with a vengeance. Personally, I cannot understand that because we love bookkeeping! However, over the years, I have continually bumped up against people who have the following 'points of pain' with bookkeeping:

- **Keeping up to date:** What a bore it is. There is never enough time to do everything my growing business needs without worrying about the books! All I need to know is who owes me money. *Can you relate to these comments?*

- **Meeting deadlines:** I am so confused by all the deadlines I have to meet, I have no idea which ones are legally binding and which ones are not. *Are you confused by deadlines?*

- **Current information:** I wish my books were up to date – I might be able to see why I never have any money – but how do I get them done? *Do you know how your business is doing every month cash flow and profits-wise?*

- **Visits and inspections:** I have just had a letter from the VAT office – they are coming next week to do a full inspection – what do I do? The Tax Office said as I have no records they will build up my income from what I spend – how much do I put down? *Not had an inspection yet – you will – sooner or later!*

- **Defence against HMRC assessments:** I have just been through a tax enquiry and they reckon I owe a massive amount of tax and now I face bankruptcy because I have no records to fight the additions the *Tax Office have estimated. Tax enquiries are the way the government polices the self-assessment regime:*

- **Free time:** I used to be good with my books but as the business grew I just could not keep all the plates spinning. *I value my free time too – but bookkeeping cannot be ignored.*

- **Complications:** When the business was small the books were easy – but as it grew things became more complicated and so I leave it to the accountant at the end of the year. *How do you choose a bookkeeping method that is right for you?*

- **Helpful spouses:** My wife knows a bookkeeper and told me she would pass everything over to them – but now I cannot contact them and they have all our stuff. *Your books are the most valuable part of your business – protect them.*
- **Bookkeepers:** I really want some help with my books – but where do I find a bookkeeper? How will I know if they make a mess of the job – I don't understand what they are doing. *A good bookkeeper is an invaluable asset to any business.*
- **Misconceptions:** My bookkeeper keeps hassling me for receipts – why does she need them – I never did! My tax bills will rocket if I use a bookkeeper and all the sales are declared. *Do you know any others?*

The trouble is, most business people just do not realise how valuable an excellent set of records is to them. Or how their books are the cornerstone of their defence when subjected to an in-depth tax or VAT investigation. They hold:

- The key to how profitable your current activities are
- How important each of your customers are with their order size and frequency of buying
- How much money you have tied up with your customers who have not paid yet
- How much money you are committed to paying your suppliers
- All contact details of everyone you deal with
- The indications of how each of your employees are performing
- The exact amount due in respect of VAT can be seen building day by day – so no nasty shocks at the end of the quarter
- Instant reports of profits/stock levels/ cash flow/debtors/creditors etc, available at the touch of a button

Records will help you get the maximum money if you sell your business, because everything the buyer needs is clear and accessible. An excellent set of records is also your best defence against an in-depth tax or VAT investigation. For more information on this subject or to speak to an expert contact Company Builder on 0800 7710268 or visit our website (www.companybuilder.co.uk).

REVIEW AND IMPROVE

WHAT'S IN THIS CHAPTER

- Once you've got your business up and running, it's vital to maintain the momentum and look for ways to improve the way you work continually. Thinking strategically while managing your company day to day will be a challenge, but there are several ways you can achieve this ranging from managing your time effectively and keeping yourself and your team motivated, to reviewing and boosting performance through training. The key is to put measures and policies in place that drive you to constantly review, improve and generally work smarter. Doing this means you'll not only boost the performance of your company, but also steal a march on your rivals. Read on to find out some of the key areas to address…

Time management

It's not just owners of small businesses who claim that 24 hours are just not enough in a day, but do they seem to complain about it more than most? It is certainly a frequent cry from the small business community where many owners are the managing director, accountant, PR and coffee maker. It almost seems obligatory that, when starting out, you will be at your desk late into the night, early in the mornings and throughout the weekend. Can you operate in this way for long at an effective level? The European Union (EU) obviously thinks not, as its many rules on working hours suggest that the evidence shows that people do not work effectively at such a pace, and it is unfair to expect your staff to do this. So why do owners and managers do it themselves?

Without doubt, new businesses owners want to be efficient, and one way of keeping costs down is to take on as much of the workload as possible. And if, during the regular nine-to-five working day, you are handling customers or clients, then it is more than likely that the administration will follow in the evenings or at weekends. The increasingly global nature of business, particularly for anyone running a website as part of their business, for example, also means that working hours are extending – a work phone call at 9pm or even 4am is not unusual for

How many working hours?

A recent Bank of Scotland survey found that entrepreneurs work on average a 50-hour week compared with the EU norm of just 35 hours work a week. For those businesses growing at over 10% a year the average working week is 52.3 hours. The survey reported that overall, Britain's 1.4 million small businesses are collectively putting in a staggering 31.2 million extra 'working weeks' each year. Seven in 10 (71%) small business owners claimed to feel stressed by running and managing their business, compared with only half (54%) in the previous year.

website owners. But the key to making it all work is time management. **Imogen Daniels**, an adviser at the Chartered Institute of Personnel and Development (CIPD), believes 'time management can make an enormous amount of difference to small businesses'. However, she also believes that you have to find the right solution to suit your business and your personality. Managing your time more effectively can be as simple as being more organised, such as keeping your desk tidier and having a more efficient filing system, or a good software package. However, if you're the kind of person who hates tidying, there's no point forcing yourself to keep everything on your desk neat, as you'll simply resent it and soon stop making the effort. There will be another solution that suits you better, such as placing key documents in a certain place on your desk. As long as the important stuff is in one place, it doesn't matter if your desk is cluttered.

You're likely to have gone into business because you have a particular skill or want to do something you enjoy under your own supervision. Getting bogged down in all the administration and other chores that come with running your own company can be frustrating, prevent you from enjoying what you do and could result in you ultimately losing interest in the business, which could prove disastrous. What's more, you won't be dedicating enough time to what you do best, which is running your company. And if you are stacking up the hours so you can fit it all in, you'll be far from your best most of the time. So for the sake of your health, sanity and business, it is worth applying a few time management techniques to reduce time spent on administration and free up time to dedicate on the work you're better at and enjoy more. In the end, it's your business that will benefit.

> **You should never lie to customers, avoid revealing that that you have no other work. Simply say that you can fit them in**

Work rate

Any self-employed person, and certainly any new business, will agree that it is practically impossible to turn down work. Even if you are manically busy, it is very difficult saying 'No' because of the fear that all existing work will dry up and that you will be left with nothing. Unfortunately, although understandable, this approach has been responsible for bringing down many a good company. That's because, although business may be booming, individuals and companies that overstretch themselves are in serious danger of missing deadlines along with the faith of their clients – which means business won't be booming for long. However good the work, it is of little use when the deadline has passed. Clients are also quick to point out this failing to others and may recommend you, but with the words of warning: 'Good, but a hopeless timekeeper'.

The key is to be honest with yourself and your customers, and make sure that the people who are employed to carry out the key work that delivers your products and services – one of whom will be you – are doing just that, rather than taking on less productive roles that don't make the most of their skills. This will have the impact of maximising your work rate, allowing you to get through as much of it as possible, and so turn down less.

Ultimately, if you aren't confident that you can deliver good-quality work within the required timescale, don't take it on, for the reasons outlined earlier. So always be clear on your existing workload when talking to customers. Clearly, you want to avoid losing business at all costs, but sometimes being honest and saying you need a little more time doesn't necessarily mean the work will go elsewhere. A customer may decide to be more flexible and give you the time you need to do the work properly – and will appreciate your honesty and commitment to only delivering the best possible product or service.

> If you aren't confident that you can deliver good-quality work within the required timescale, don't take it on

Photographer **Jonathan Pollock** has built up a team of freelance assistants, whom he calls on at busy times. This frees him up to concentrate directly on his primary function, photography, and allows him to take on as much work as possible, without cutting corners. They help with building sets and also staff the telephones when he is at work. 'You don't want to miss a call from your next potential client because you are too busy to answer the phone,' he advises. In terms of balancing work and personal life, which is essential to prevent you from becoming jaded and maintaining your work rate and hunger for the business, he advises that everyone books a holiday well in advance and sticks to the dates. This will give you plenty of time to book in any necessary cover for when you're away or plan work around your break. He also suggests' 'Never tell anyone that you have no other work. Of course, as well as busy times, you also need to prepare for quieter periods, which using freelance help is ideal for as you simply won't employ them at this time.' Pollock's tip during leaner times is: 'Although you should never lie to customers, avoid revealing that that you have no other work. Simply say that you can fit them in.'

Be prepared

Another common failing among inexperienced business people is that they underestimate the time a job will take and consequently undercharge. It is easy to think that a job will be cracked in a day or two, but it is much better to add on extra time to cover any changes that a client might request. Some people are afraid of charging for that seemingly unnecessary day in case they lose the work to someone else, but experience does prove that clients will be prepared to pay a little more for the confidence of knowing that a job will be done properly.

Often clients will ask: 'How much will you charge?' at a very early stage of negotiation. One tip is to throw the question back and ask what size budget they have and, if appropriate, how long they expect the job to take. Imply that you are flexible. You do not want to lose the work in a haggle over fees, but also stress that you want a decent rate for the decent job that they will get. Try to gain as much information as possible about what is required before naming your fee and timescale. Questions that may have seemed unnecessary at the outset can save a lot of embarrassment and heartache down the line.

The second of the MORI/British Gas Time surveys mentioned earlier showed that small business owner-managers are setting aside more time to plan. Commenting on the findings, a British Gas spokesman says he believes businesses were dedicating more time to planning because owner-managers were 'working smarter'. Owner-managers were seeking more external advice and keeping a careful watch on spending as two ways of managing their time more efficiently. Forward planning was allowing them to allocate the right time to jobs, employ the relevant number of staff to achieve deadlines and giving them time to chase up new contracts.

Keeping on track

Staying on top of your working schedule is hugely important, particularly with a newly launched company, as you won't have slotted into any kind of routine or work pattern, and taking your eye off the ball can demolish your reputation before it's even built. It is all too easy to forget to send an invoice as one job is completed and you dive headlong towards the next deadline. Losing control of the cash flow in that way is bad enough, but worse still, a disorganised manager could completely lose sight of a whole commission. Time management consultant **Gerard Hargreaves** is a great believer in lists. When working with British Gas on its biannual Time survey of small and medium-sized companies, he suggested making lists as a top tip because it helps organise the tasks in your head and helps prioritise the tasks ahead. Keep the diary up to date, make sure that conversations with clients are logged and that agreed actions are noted somewhere prominent, so that those actions do actually go forward.

Keeping lists and being aware of what is needed next does help to reduce the stress

Pollock has a page-a-day diary for just this purpose. 'It was one of the first things that I did when launching on my own,' he says. 'It sounds a little silly, but it is so crucial.' Each day is split into hours so Pollock can log meetings in the correct order and it has space for him to include priority tasks. He keep this diary up to date all the time, filling it in as he speaks to clients. 'I keep lists of props that are needed and tasks to be done, and I tick them off as they are completed so that, at a glance, I know what still has to be worked on,' he explains.

The Chartered Institute of Personnel and Development's **Imogen Daniels** is also a great believer in lists, claiming they organise events in your own mind, regardless of whether you actually keep the list beside you through the working day. She also finds that 'people gain a great deal of satisfaction from achieving listed goals and being able to tick things off'. Again, the answer lies in finding the solution that suits your character – some people prefer loads of Post-it notes stuck around their computer and office, while others prefer accessing a complex diary on their computer. 'There is an enormous amount of fire-fighting that goes on in small businesses,' says Daniels. 'Keeping lists and being aware of what is needed next does help to reduce the stress.'

Delegation

> **Learn to let go and trust others to take on some of the burden**

One of the biggest challenges facing entrepreneurs is delegating tasks effectively. When it is your own business, it is very hard to let go, but delegation is a sign of sound management. Even early on in the life of your business, it is pretty difficult to do everything and there comes a point when the cost of employing someone else to help is less than the cost of work lost because you can't cope. Chartered surveyor **Simon Smith** has first-hand experience of this. After setting out on his own, he quickly found plenty of demand, and a recent merger with another business has meant extreme pressure on his time. Instead of being out and about winning business and handling the tricky side of the operation, he found himself bogged down in administration and routine jobs that were taking up disproportionate amounts of his day. With a wife and three young children at home, he also found it hard to justify spending weekends at the office. 'I knew I needed someone to help out, but there has to be a balancing act between cost and help,' he says.

In his sector, Smith knew there was a history of recent graduates receiving low salaries and a consequent backlash of students unwilling to enter the profession. After months of seeking out the right person, he appointed a recent graduate who will spend the next two years working towards full qualification. Smith knows he will have to give time to the new recruit to ensure he is in the best possible condition to pass his exams – and also give him the right sort of work to meet industry criteria. But the benefits will be that he has time to return to his core business and concentrate on doing what he does best.

Of course, in many cases there is not need to actually take someone on, but simply to delegate the work to someone already within the business. And this shouldn't just be done for the more menial tasks. Passing on responsibility to staff can be a great motivator and often people rise to the challenge if given the chance. As long as you monitor the situation carefully and build in review processes, little damage to your business is likely to be done. 'Often owner-managers have a strong emotional attachment to their business and it will have affected them in a lot of ways, from financial to family,' says Daniels, 'but they do have to learn to let go and trust others to take on some of the burden.'

CASE STUDY
ATTIK AND THE FIVE PATHS TO SUCCESS

Attik is in the brand business, creating advertisements and design-led identities for many of the world's most successful companies. Today, the company is a complete 'brand communications group', designing and implementing creative design solutions for a host of large companies, such as BT and Infogrames. Attik has grown to such a level that it has five offices in three different countries, including the UK (London and Huddersfield), Australia (Sydney) and the USA (San Francisco and New York). But even though the company is one of the most recognised in its field, co-founder **Simon Needham** believes that the same principles apply today as to when it was a small business with only a few employees. Here are his five roads to success:

- When you take risks, prepare yourself for some losses by always having a back-up plan in place just in case
- In the initial stages of starting and running your business, never let your thoughts get past the first year of trading
- Get yourself known. If someone's already heard of you they'll come knocking on your door.
- There are times when things aren't going to go as well as you'd like but stick with what you've got and you'll get through it
- Grow reluctantly and only when you need to and use freelancers (no fixed overheads/costs) wherever possible

Self-motivation

The key to the continued success of your new enterprise is maintaining the levels of motivation that drove you to launch the business in the first place. Motivation is more important than a business plan, or funding, or even business skills, according to entrepreneur **Leonard Tondel**, director of the Home Business Alliance. He believes that self-motivation is something you either have or haven't got. Successful businesspeople have it, while frustrated employees don't.

However, as time goes on, entrepreneurs can suffer from a drop in self-motivation. This can be brought on by anything from too much success (if there is such a thing!), which can cut the drive to succeed, and delegation, which can result in a reduced sense of control, to failure and excessive stress, which can sap motivation. The key to avoiding this, and therefore maximising your potential, is to understand what motivates you. Ask any self-employed person what drives them, and the

! TIPS

STAYING MOTIVATED

- ! Find a mentor to help you steer your self-motivation in the direction of success
- ! Set yourself realistic targets, and draw up a checklist
- ! Think positively by congratulating yourself on all the things you have achieved
- ! Visualise success by thinking in terms of what you will achieve rather than the obstacles in your way
- ! Make time for family and friends as strong relationships can help support your success
- ! Recognise that breaks are beneficial
- ! Look after your health – if it breaks down, so does your business success
- ! If you work from home, separate your working time from your leisure time
- ! Identify what really motivates you – money, independence or a fresh challenge – then pursue that goal
- ! Take a step back to gain a broader perspective

answer is likely to be simple: 'Money'. But owner-managers who think purely financial factors keep them motivated may be fooling themselves. 'Enthusiasm that's purely profit-based wears, thin very quickly,' advises Tondel. 'So if you are going to start a business, make it something you will enjoy doing.'

Experts believe that the real source of motivation is likely to be rather more complex. Being your own boss comes top of the list for most small businesses, followed closely by flexibility and flexible hours, according to research by **Andrew Oswald**, Professor of Economics at Warwick University. Money comes a poor third for most self-employed people, including those who believe they are driven by the clatter of pound coins and the rustle of large cheques. A whopping 49% of the thousands of self-employed people he has studied call themselves very satisfied, compared with 29% of employees, and yet the popular view that self-employed people are happier to take risks is unfounded, Oswald argues. 'Their gambling behaviour is no different from the rest of the population,' he says.

The motivational picture for small businesses is less clear cut, according to **Cary Cooper**, Professor of Organisational Psychology at the University of Manchester Institute of Science and Technology (UMIST) and a director of business psychology at Robertson Cooper consultants. 'People who start their own businesses have typically worked in a larger organisation and enjoy the amount of control and autonomy that self-employment gives them, when they see the direct rewards for their labour,' he says. But although that autonomy may make most self-employed people happier than the average wage slave, Cooper's studies of top business people have shown that the desire to prove themselves is often what drives them. 'Money is not the big motivator,' he says. 'Many top entrepreneurs have had unhappy experiences in childhood, and are motivated by something negative. They want to go on and prove they can succeed, and are driven by control and power.' While those negative experiences may drive many to set up their own businesses in the first place, motivation grows with the enterprise, argues Cooper. 'As the business expands and they employ people, it's like an extended family with everyone depending on your success,' he explains. 'The drive

> " 49% of the thousands of self-employed people he has studied call themselves very satisfied, compared with 29% of employees "

that keeps you going then comes from your feelings of responsibility to everyone who depends on you.'

Although small business owners' lives have become more stressful, with increasing red tape and too little time to finish too many tasks, most would never contemplate working for anyone else, according to research by Abbey National Business Banking and the Federation of Small Businesses. Running a business now means longer working hours, less free time and a negative effect on family life, but the attraction of being your own boss still outweighs going back working for someone else. Once the business is up and running, stress can undermine self-motivation unless you find some way to control it or channel it. Set yourself targets, recommends independent business adviser **David Street**, former director of the Institute of Business Advisers, and dig out that business plan, too. 'Small businesses tend to use business plans only when they're trying to raise money,' he says, 'but they can also help you set realistic performance targets.' At the Royal Bank of Scotland, Head of Business Banking **Jason Oakley** agrees, saying: 'Your business plan should be the life and soul of your business and the key to targets you set.'

Formulating realistic goals for you and your team means you're more likely to achieve them, which will feed motivation all round. Gradual delegation of the jobs you don't enjoy or excel at will also boost your self-motivation, enable you to play to your strengths and boost the performance of your business.

Enhancing performance

> **You need to analyse the quantity and quality of what you do in the day**

In the early days of a business you need to put the hours in to make it work, but you also need to analyse the quantity and quality of what you do in the day. You are likely to be highly motivated – which will drive you to work very hard when you start out – and if you're not you should seriously consider why you've launched your own business. However, racking up the hours alone doesn't mean you're performing to your maximum.

If you are working long hours, make sure the effort you are putting in is as effective as possible, and that you are not wasting your time. So look at how you are spending your time during the day, and work out just how much of it is actually being spent productively. Then think of ways that you may be able to do certain tasks more effectively. For example, if you are spending a long time doing an essential, but rather repetitive or highly intense activity, there will be a maximum period when you'll be at your most productive before you become jaded and distracted and your performance levels starts to fall off. Try to recognise when this occurs and recharge your batteries by taking a short break and then switching to another task, returning to the original work with more vim and vigour later on.

A great way to monitor the time you're spending on each task is by completing a time sheet for yourself. This is simply a sheet of paper (or you can do it on a spreadsheet on your computer) divided into the days of the week under which you write the times between which you have been working on a particular job, and the nature of that work, building up a list throughout the day. Many companies use time sheets not only to ensure their people are spending their time productively and to keep on top of which projects they have been working on, but also to assess the time – and therefore cost – spent in terms of man hours on certain jobs, to inform decision-making and assist customer costings.

'In the early days of a business you need to put the hours in to make it work, but you also need to analyse the quantity and quality of what you do in the day,' says **David Broad**, management consultant at M2R. Broad also recommends networking as a great way to gain the necessary insight to improve your performance levels. 'Managers in larger companies have to motivate their staff, while in very small businesses often the owner just has to motivate themselves,' he points out. 'Going on a course or networking helps you to find a group of people who are all speaking your language, and can help enormously.' Networking can help to direct your motivation towards properly defined goals, and generate more business too.

'Keep in touch with other businesses and find out how they've managed to keep things fresh and meet their targets,' counsels Oakley. 'Exchanging views can inspire new ideas that apply to your business and may be proven winners.'

Personal development

> **It might be hard to envisage needing a career pattern when you are your own boss...**

It can be hard to get up in the morning when you are your own boss – late night drinking, a wakeful young child and extreme tiredness can all contribute. Motivation is one of the essentials for anyone working for themselves, but there is far more to it than simply gearing yourself up to start the day, and it isn't enough to keep your career on the straight and narrow. It is equally important to establish a career path that you work towards maintaining. It might be hard to envisage needing a career pattern when you are your own boss, but in reality, personal development is still important, and the same also goes for your staff – an employee who receives training will see that they are moving forward by gaining key skills, feeling valued and satisfied in their position, making them far less likely to leave than an untrained member of staff.

Move on up

Once you are your own boss, it is too easy to believe that all you need do is simply keep working–but that will not be enough, as anyone who has survived a recession can tell you. Standing still in career terms is never an option, no matter how small your business. Take the example of a copy typist. There was plenty of work in the past on old style typewriters, but those who weren't able to become computer literate would have quickly found themselves, quite literally, redundant.

If you worked for a large company, chances are that you would have been offered training as required, with follow-up opportunities where necessary. Your employers might have even been prepared to give you time off for outside course work or even contributed towards the cost of independent training. Although your business may be no more than a one-man band, you can still adopt the same strategies for yourself. The only difference is that you will have to be more organised than if you were part of a large organisation. As a small business, attending a block release course will mean that no one is back at your desk, keeping the business going. The financial and practical implications need to be carefully thought out, too, but there is still no reason why you shouldn't better yourself.

Personal development can help your business in several unexpected ways. Not only will you be better able to carry out the related task, but it may also help motivate you through a rough business period or provide fresh ideas if the business becomes stale. Another valid reason for making sure you keep up to date with career developments is that you never know when you might take a job with another company, either because you have sold your business or you have been asked to join at board level. Hopefully, your own business will be so successful that others will want you on their board as a non-executive director.

By ensuring that you keep up to date with developments in the sector and by being seen as an industry leader, you have a chance of winning those lucrative positions. Alternatively, many owner-managers sell their business on after the first flush of success. If you manage this, you may well want to start afresh and need to have developed your skills along the way.

Legal requirements

For most business owners, personal development is all about becoming better at the job and gaining confidence in their own ability to handle various situations, but there is also an increasing need for gaining knowledge about the latest statutory requirements. The government has placed a lot of emphasis on the need for improved quality at all levels of business. Its new laws on corporate manslaughter (where individuals can now be prosecuted for the deaths of employees and members of

> **Many industries are experiencing calls for better quality and greater responsibility towards the consumer**

the public in their charge) are just one example of where individuals are being forced to take responsibility. **Mark Redfern**, a director of training at Searchlight Solutions, has seen increased demand for senior management training to keep abreast with the new legislation. 'People are having to become very well versed on the legal side and keep up to date with current and forthcoming legislation, such as the Companies Act, the Data Protection Act and the Human Rights Act,' Redfern reports. He adds that Searchlight tries to address problems before they arise, so that trainees are in the best position to manage their businesses correctly.

As an owner-manager of a small operation, courses as mentioned above may be hard to justify, but there are external options too. Professional director **Martin Pedler** has strong views on the need for better quality directors and believes the recent legislation on corporate manslaughter in particular will give a wake-up call to the nation's bosses. 'I think people have a fear factor about what they are taking on,' he says. 'It will not be long before the first corporate manslaughter case is taken against an individual rather than a company. It will set the cat among the pigeons.' Pedler adds that ignorance will be no defence for directors who haven't kept a close eye on what is happening within their businesses, and it could land them in jail. He believes that the first custodial sentence meted out will launch a surge in demand for greater training among directors. The same rules will apply to owner-managers and will put great pressure on all bosses to adhere strictly to health and safety regulations. If companies and directors can show they have tried to maintain proper standards, the courts will have no grounds for conviction, but cutting corners or non-compliance in any way will open the door.

Corporate manslaughter rules are not the only area that has been tightened up in terms of director responsibility. Many industries are experiencing calls for better quality and greater responsibility towards the consumer. The insurance industry, for example, has established its own self-governing watchdog, but in 2007 the government announced plans for the whole sector to come under the rule of the Financial Services Authority. One of the expected consequences is that industry pundits believe greater numbers will have to hold recognisable qualifications. Experience alone will not be enough to convince regulators that you are fit to run the business – you will need qualifications too. Insurance is not alone in this type of development, and it's something that could stop you operating your own business in the future.

Staff training

Developing the skills of your workforce through training boosts morale and helps provide a better service to customers. They, in turn, are happier and more likely to return, swelling profits, which then benefits the business and encourages higher salaries. This is very much a win–win situation, and should encourage new business owners to view training less as a drain on resources or an annoyance that takes up employees' valuable time, but more as a very useful investment.

In addition, it can help solve a growing problem for many small businesses: how to attract and retain the right people. With unemployment levels lower than they have been for years, finding people with the right skills is becoming increasingly difficult, while recruiting is proving to be more and more expensive and time consuming. So when you do track down the perfect candidate, you need to do all you can to keep them. Having a training programme or 'people development' strategy in place can help to both attract and keep key members of staff, giving your company a positive profile in the recruitment marketplace.

Bosses, too, can also benefit from career development and training as touched on earlier. Completing a course will provide a boost in self-confidence and renewed interest in developing the business. A better-trained boss will be more motivated, and this is reflected throughout the business, whatever its size. The director of development at the Institute of Directors (IoD), **John Weston**, calls it a virtuous circle. 'Better directors run better businesses and as a consequence you create wealth and employment,' he says. One of the IoD's prime missions is to improve professional standards across the UK, and Weston believes that by starting at the top, the professionalism will filter right through the business. The IoD offers a series of courses designed to cover most aspects of running

> **Having a training programme or 'people development' strategy in place can help to both attract and keep key members of staff**

a business, which are available to members. They are designed for like-minded people and many who have been through an IoD course say that the most valuable part was not the formal course work, but learning about other directors' experiences.

Choosing training courses

Contact

For more details
of the IoD courses,
contact:
Institute of Directors:
www.iod.com

There are two ways to go when choosing courses: you can follow the structure of your chosen career or develop across a spectrum of skills. The options have led to the development of an IoD chartered director qualification, because, as Weston points out: 'Most directors have followed vertical career ladders, but our membership comes from a horizontal level of achievement and we needed a qualification that would appeal to that.' In other words, when you have become an accountant, lawyer, etc, you have a career structure that takes you up to the boardroom level, but once there you may well need the skills of a completely different career.

To follow your chosen career you need to make specific decisions about what to learn. Most fields have relevant industry qualifications and there will be a well-trodden route – one that you are likely to have done or have followed before you decided to go solo. Learning a new set of skills is likely to be more of a challenge. For example, it is easy enough to employ an accountant, but it might also pay dividends if you understand the basics of it as well. The UK has a raft of colleges offering full and part-time courses and you can find out more by searching the internet. Bear in mind that different rules of entry (and payment) apply for mature students, and take into account your current workload before committing to a course – one or two evenings at college a week may not be feasible.

Another very good source of courses are local councils. Many run a variety, specifically designed for part-timers. These are often evening classes that require a little, but not too much, homework between sessions. These could vary from a basic accountancy course to learning a new language – or a completely unrelated skill, such as upholstery, which could provide another source of income should the tough times arrive.

However, if you are looking for a more academically inclined qualification, then check out your local university, although part-time courses are usually limited. The other alternative that most take is the Open University, as it allows you to work at a distance and at your own speed.

MBAS

If you want to learn more managerial skills, something like a Masters in Business Administration (MBA) might provide the solution. An MBA often takes several years to complete, but can be combined with a full-time job. Students complete course work in a series of block releases. An MBA is usually divided into 12 modules, comprising eight compulsory sections and four optional ones in which a student might choose to specialise in a work-related subject.

Nottingham University has a variety of MBA courses. Centre director **Chris O'Brien** says that most students are in full-time work, although some choose to concentrate on the course – and there are attractive bursaries to help them afford the tuition. Most students are in their 30s, although there are both younger and older exceptions. O'Brien stresses that the aim of the course is to give a framework from which students can help run businesses. 'They have an understanding of business, which allows them to move businesses forward in a changing environment,' he says.

Contact

For nationwide information on MBAs:
Association of MBAs:
www.mbaworld.com

ONLINE TRAINING

The time spent getting to and from a course and the inflexible times of lectures is often the reason that more business owners and managers don't take up training or education. This is where online training comes in, where you can work over the internet from any location, starting and stopping lectures when you choose, and it is becoming more attractive, particularly when the cost of getting online is as little as £12 a month.

Companies such as E-Learnity work closely with an employer to provide the necessary training package for its staff. Others such as REDTRAY also offer courses on an individual basis. The downside is most of the courses are technology based, but this is beginning to change.

Contact

E-Learnity: www.
elearnity.com
REDTRAY: www.
redtray.co.uk

....

Another criticism is the lack of one-to-one help, but a lot of online courses now offer telephone support, while tools such as Microsoft NetMeeting help course members share questions. The Open University is just one academic institution to make use of the internet as a way of reaching students.

ACTION POINT
KEY WAYS TO IMPROVE YOUR BUSINESS

You may think that once you have started up your business that a lot of the hard work is over, but successful entrepreneurs are the ones who continually try to improve or expand their enterprise. Sitting on the sidelines twiddling your thumbs while competitors make progress could prove to be disastrous for your venture. To help, startups.co.uk has summarised 10 ways help you get ahead.

TAKE ON EXPERIENCED STAFF: Since October 2006 it has been illegal to discriminate against workers on the grounds of age, so incorporate this change into your thinking when recruiting. Older staff offer maturity and experience that could provide the keys to the success for your business. Don't believe that old dogs cannot learn new tricks and remember that they might have a thing or two to show you.

TRAIN UP: Skills shortages are a big problem in UK workplaces. To help combat the problem, the government has extended Employer Training Pilots across England, following a successful trial period. The scheme allows you to train low-skilled staff towards a vocational qualification, with the associated costs met by the government. Getting involved should see your skills levels rise… and consequently your profits. Visit www.dcsf.gov.uk/rsgateway/DB/RRP/u014276/index. shtml for more information.

EXPANSION THROUGH RECRUITMENT: Perhaps you could update your business plan if you are doing well and take on a few extra staff. If demand is great enough and you can budget carefully, new workers could drive your business onwards and upwards.

EXPAND YOUR OFFER: How about branching into other areas? If there is a niche market being ignored in your local area and your business is doing well, why not exploit it? Do some market research on demand and how any potential expansion would fare, but be careful not to over-stretch yourself. However, a targeted, well thought-out expansion into a closely related field could prove to be very profitable.

DON'T JUST BANK ON BANKS: Research has shown that the majority of small firms go to their high-street bank whenever they need new finance, despite the fact that many are unhappy with the level of service and the charges that banks impose. If you are looking for more capital, why not consider other options, such as venture capitalists, business angels, or, if you are struggling to make ends meet, factoring? Although not all kinds of businesses can gain such help, it is well worth a try if you need a cash injection.

GO PUBLIC: The government has announced that red tape on securing public sector contracts will be cut and that work will be awarded on a regional, not national, basis. Both measures are good news for small firms, who can now compete against a reduced field at a fraction of the cost for government contracts. From pavement maintenance to IT work, there is around £13 billion worth of contracts out there…

GET YOUR MESSAGE ACROSS: If you have spent the last year relying on local newspaper adverts or the *Yellow Pages*, it may be worth widening your options slightly to help boost your business. Cinema advertising often proves effective, as do panels on the side of buses. Or you may want to put together a radio advertisement to reach out to local customers. If you come up with a targeted, attention-grabbing campaign at a reasonable cost, you should be able to boost takings significantly. See Chapter 8 for a thorough discussion on marketing.

GET SUPPLIED: Getting quality, affordable stock is essential in making your business profitable. If you feel that you aren't getting the best deal from your wholesaler, do something about it. Most are happy to negotiate over prices, and good wholesalers reward loyalty by offering money off or extra products to repeat customers. If yours don't, find another one. Do some research on suppliers in your local area, and if all of them don't offer good value, then look further afield, as the savings you make could be critical.

GET PAID ON TIME: Late payment has been seen by many businesses as acceptable practice for many years, putting small firms in debt that they can ill afford. With tardy payers being one of the biggest obstacles to profits and expansion, it's important that you act to get what's owed to you. The government has introduced legislation recently to tackle the problem, allowing firms to take clients to court for compensation. If all your chasing proves fruitless, consider using these laws. See Chapter 9 for more details on tackling late payments.

KEEP THE CASH FLOWING: Debt is not necessarily a bad thing for small firms attempting to grow. However, it's essential that you keep up with repayments or your whole business could be at risk. Make sure you operate a well-organised cash flow system. Try to negotiate repayments so that you can pay in instalments when it suits you best, try to use a business debit or credit card to cut down on paperwork, make sure your records are well looked after, and ensure that you are aware of all outstanding debts. See Chapter 9 for more details on tackling debtors.

CASE STUDY
DOSH SOFTWARE AND THE GOLDEN CONTACT LIST

Dosh Software was set up by accountant **Jonathan van der Borgh** to develop new accounting packages for small firms. By constantly reviewing and updating the details it holds on former and existing customers it has developed a strong direct marketing database which is proving a great source of business, while helping the company deliver excellent service levels. 'If you buy a cold list, you will be lucky to get a return of half a per cent,' explains general manager **Tony Trevillion**. 'It is always easier to sell to someone that you have sold to before.' This has meant an investment in database technology to help Dosh keep up-to-date and accurate listings, but it has been money well spent. No opportunity is lost and Dosh uses every invoice mailing to existing customers to make full use of the postal charges. As well as an invoice, customers could receive additional information about the company or questionnaires regarding customer service, all within the weight limit allowed for second class mail.

'The nice thing about direct marketing, as an accountant, is that you can measure the success. You know all the costs – the creative outlay, the mail, the time involved and the envelopes,' says van der Borgh.

Over to you...

Well done and congratulations. If you've read this far you must be serious about setting up your own business, but now it's up to you. You've taken the journey through this guide from idea to launch, and now it's time for you to put all the theory into practice – and perhaps flick back through these pages along the way to make sure you're on the right track.

You should now be under no illusions of the task ahead, and have a much better idea of what starting up involves. You'll also have read plenty of examples of those who've gone before, and how they've overcome obstacles and faced challenges along the way, finally achieving what they set out to do – running their own company on their own terms.

Remember, no one has launched their own business without making mistakes along the way. This is all part of the process, and it's how you deal with these situations and learn from them so you avoid them in the future that matters. As for the challenges, you're bound to face plenty, but approach them in the right way and they'll make you even more determined to succeed.

This should be an enjoyable, liberating and ultimately exhilarating experience. And hopefully you'll be making the web pages of startups. co.uk in the not-too-distant future as one of our entrepreneurial success stories.

Good luck!

ALSO BY CRIMSON PUBLISHING...

STARTING YOUR OWN BUSINESS
THE GOOD, THE BAD AND THE UNEXPECTED

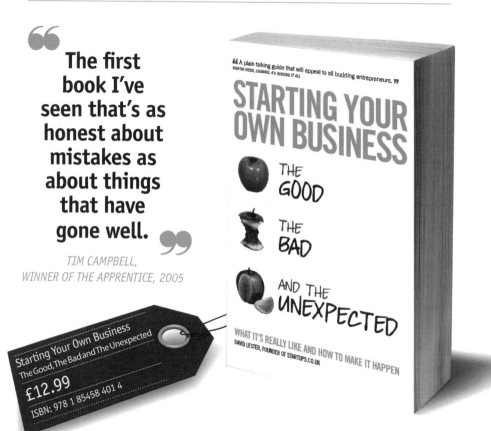

"
The first book I've seen that's as honest about mistakes as about things that have gone well.
"

TIM CAMPBELL,
WINNER OF THE APPRENTICE, 2005

Starting Your Own Business
The Good, The Bad and The Unexpected
£12.99
ISBN: 978 1 85458 401 4

Takes you behind the scenes to what it's really like to start a business, revealing the challenges, hurdles and excitements along the way.

Jam-packed with practical advice and real life examples, this book is written by David Lester, a serial entrepreneur who started his first business aged 22 and sold it for millions before he was 30.

This guide will prove invaluable to anyone who is thinking of starting their own business.

Order online today at **www.crimsonpublishing.co.uk**

ALSO BY CRIMSON PUBLISHING...

STARTING YOUR OWN BUSINESS
THE STARTUPS GUIDES

- **All you need to know to open your own successful restaurant or shop**

- **No-nonsense advice from small-business experts**

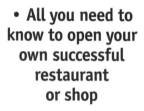

Starting Your Own Restaurant
£14.99
ISBN: 978 1 85458 436 6

Starting Your Own Shop
£14.99
ISBN: 978 1 85458 435 9

These are the first titles in the new Starting Your Own... series from startups.co.uk, the business experts. The books take you step-by-step through the startup process, giving you all the information you need to make sure your business has every chance of succeeding. All the writers are experts in the small-business sector, and have interviewed some of the top entrepreneurs in specific markets to give practical and inspirational advice.

Order online today at **www.crimsonpublishing.co.uk**

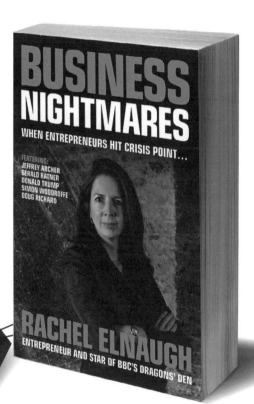